Autobiography of a Navy Mustang (November 20, 1952 to September 1981)

by

Ed Hudson

DORRANCE PUBLISHING CO., INC.
PITTSBURGH, PENNSYLVANIA 15222

Dorrance Publishing Co., Inc.
701 Smithfield Street
Pittsburgh, PA 15222
Visit our website at *www.dorrancebookstore.com*

ISBN: 978-1-4349-2965-5
eISBN: 978-1-4349-2317-2

Table of Contents

INTRODUCTION

I write this memoir in hopes of preserving a portion of my naval history that may be passed down to my grandchildren and their children. It is my intent to tell of events that happened during my time while serving in the United States Navy from 20 November 1952 to 30 September 1981. During those years, I served both as an enlisted man and as an officer. I am what is known as a "Mustang," a term that is used to define one who came up through the ranks from enlisted to officer. I enlisted in the navy and after serving as enlisted status for eleven years, ten months, and ten days I was commissioned as an officer, Navy Ensign. I spent the next seventeen years as an officer. I retired from the navy on 30 September 1981, after having served a total of twenty-eight years, ten months, and ten days

It is my desire to tell of the places I've been, the people I've met, and things that happened during that time. Many of the people with whom I served, I can no longer remember their names, but I can remember their presence at certain duty stations or at certain events. Some of the events are not necessarily related to the military. Some of the people continued to appear at different times and places. It was always good to see shipmates, no matter where or when. A lot of the happenings occurred while I was in a liberty status. I hope this will be entertaining as well as informative. I will strive to take you through boot camp in San Diego, California, and the other schools I attended, as well as all the various duty station assignments, from the shores of the Mainland United States and Hawaii, to the shores Bermuda, Okinawa, the Philippines, and Vietnam, citing the promotions I received along the way. During my years of service I went from the lowest to the highest of the enlisted pay grades (E1 to E9) and from 01 to 05 of the officer pay grades.

I strive to put this writing into chronological order. However, in some instances, I can remember certain events happening at certain duty stations during that tour, but not necessarily in order of their occurrence. Therefore, some of the events may have occurred before or after the description of another event, but always, they did happen during that particular time that I was stationed at that particular duty station.

INDUCTION AND BOOT CAMP
20 November 1952 to 03 March 1953

At the time when I turned eighteen years old, 26 September 1950, everyone had to register with the Selective Service Board on their eighteenth birthday. I registered with Selective Service Board #22 at 207-1/2 E. Virginia St., McKinney, Texas. My Selective Service number was 41-22-32-223. The draft into the army was in effect. If a man was not going to school or enrolled in a college, he was subject to be drafted. I was still in high school, so I didn't worry about the draft. After graduating from high school in May 1952, I went to work in Dallas, first for the Murray Gin Company and later for the City of Dallas, Water Department, Meter Division. However, I now did have to worry about the draft somewhat. During that time, I was sometimes dating Diann Henley, who lived at 4500-1/2 Junius Street, but most of the time I was dating Lila Faye who lived in Pleasant Grove. In fact, I thought I was really in love with Lila Faye and had let her wear my class ring from high school.

In September 1952, I did become concerned about the draft, knowing that when I reached my twentieth birthday, I would most likely receive my draft notice to be inducted into the army. Man! I did not want to go into the army! On Saturday, 20 September 1952, I went to the Navy Recruiting Office on Pacific Ave. in downtown Dallas to sign up to go into the navy. I had talked my friend, Cloyse Bell, into going down and signing up with me. We arrived at the recruiter's office about ten o'clock on a Saturday morning to find the recruiters very receptive of us. They were friendly and eager to talk to us. One recruiter took me into an office and another took Cloyse into a different one. The recruiter asked me all sorts of questions concerning my education, background, work experience, and my reason for wanting to join the navy. A friend of ours, Rufus Potete, was in the navy reserves stationed at the Naval

Air Station in Dallas. He told me to apply for a naval aviation rating and to ask to be assigned to a multi-engine aircraft squadron. During this interview with the recruiter, I told him that I wanted to be an aircraft electrician.

I was given a series of exams to take before being considered for induction. After completing the tests, I was told to wait while they were graded and a decision made as to my acceptance. Later, I was told that my test scores had placed me in category two of four categories, and that I was not needed at the time. I was told to go home and wait; they would call me when I was needed. With the Korean War in progress at the time, I just knew that I would be inducted immediately, but I wasn't. I wanted to know what I should do if I received my draft notice. I was told that when that day came, I should call the recruiting office for instructions.

When I came out of the office, Cloyse was sitting in the lobby waiting for me. I asked him how he did on the test and he said that he didn't take the test. He said that he had changed his mind about going into the navy. I had already committed myself and was somewhat disappointed that Cloyse had changed his mind and was not going with me.

I continued to work for the water department for about two weeks and quit, deciding to spend time at home while waiting to be called. After about a week I ran out of money and had to go back to work. I went to work at the Austin Brothers' Steel Company until I received my draft notice. I received the notice by mail on 18 November 1952, with a reporting date of 22 November. I called the Navy Recruiting Office on the nineteenth and was told to report on the twentieth.

I went to work at the steel company and told them what had happened and that I had enlisted in the navy to keep from being drafted. I guess you could call me a "Draft Dodger." I was informed that they were considering me for a pay raise. Too late, I had already committed myself to the US Navy.

I reported to the recruiting office as directed on 20 November to get my physical and to complete my induction. Everyone being inducted into the armed force—whether army, navy, air force, or marines—was run through the same medical center for their physical exam. There were people from all over Texas, Oklahoma, New Mexico, Arkansas, and Louisiana being examined that day along with me. We were all stripped to our underwear and paraded from one examination room to another. I was poked, prodded, and fondled in places and areas that I didn't even know I had. I had my eyes examined, my teeth examined, my testicles squeezed, and a finger poked up my anus. That was a shocker to me. Finally at about eleven o'clock the physical was completed and we were told that we could get dressed and wait in an area until the result of the exam was announced. I was informed that I had passed the physical and then I was sworn into the United States Navy with a designator as High School Airman Recruit (HSAR). It seems that I was the only HSAR in the group. I received my first request; I was assigned to naval aviation. There was no backing out now and I would be boarding a train bound for San Diego, California. I was permitted to go home and pack a few clothes and told to report to the train station at 1700 hours, (5:00 P.M. civilian time). I was in the navy now and on military time, and my base pay, I believe, was a whopping fifty-two dollars per month. Men in the military at that time did not pay into the Social Security System, but my service number was 451 41 02.

My sister Alice and my brother-in-law Harvey took me to the train depot to see me off on my departure to San Diego. There was a mean-looking guy there barking orders to all of us recruits, trying to get us assigned our berthing quarters. I was put in a Pullman car with three other men, one named Blanchard from Gatesville, Texas, and two men from Oklahoma named Seaton and Suggs. We became good friends and spent most of the trip together playing cards or going to the club car. None of us had much money to spare, so we had to make our own entertainment. In fact, money was so scarce that a penny was worth having. Blanchard and I teamed up in an illegal action of matching pennies in a brother-in-law scam. It was called "Odd Man Wins," in which one of us would have heads and the other had tails. When we thought the third man was onto our scheme, we would let him win by us both having the same side of the coin. We didn't take a lot of money this way, but enough that we could get a soda now and then. We were not of age to get a beer. Blanchard and I continued this act until someone noticed what we were doing and told us that it was illegal. We stopped because we didn't want to have a record before we got to boot camp.

This was the first time I had ever been on a train, except for the interurban that ran through Anna, and then I had only ridden south to Dallas for about fifty miles and north to Sherman for twenty miles. The train took us through country that I had never seen before. In fact, until this trip I had never been out of the state of Texas. I really enjoyed seeing all the countryside, especially the mountains and river valleys. I tried to stay on the outside landing of the last car so I could better see the countryside as it went by, but in Colorado it got too cold up in the mountains. I had to stay inside. After two days and three nights, we arrived in San Diego. We were transported from the train depot to the Naval Training Center by bus.

The time of arrival at boot camp was about five in the morning. We were fed breakfast and then marched into a room and given a series of exams. We were all tired and may have been told, but I don't remember, that scores of these exams would play a major role in determining our assignments of jobs and the field of our navy career. My scores on the exams were GCT 53, ARI 58, MECH 64, and CLER 51. The monitors kept telling us not to worry about how we do on the score, just finish the exam. Had I known how important these scores were and how they would affect my career, I would have tried harder for a higher score. Anyway, after the tests were completed, we were taken into the barber shop where our heads were stripped of our hair. Some of the men really got upset because all of their pretty curls were gone. From the barber shop, we were taken to a place and issued some dungarees, a duffle bag, and bedding. At that time in naval history, we had to carry our own mattress covers and blankets from base to base. It made for a lot of extra baggage. We would receive our complete clothing allowance at a later time. We had to change clothes immediately and pack all of our civilian clothes to be shipped home. From there we were assigned to various departments in the area and given certain jobs. My job, would you believe, was to help all the other new arrivals in packing their civilian clothes to send home. Of course, I packed mine first.

About mid-afternoon we were formed into a small company headed by a man named Schoolcraft. He was a Boiler Tender First Class Petty Officer (BT1). He was a small, scruffy man with a very loud voice. We could hear him scream out orders from half a mile away. We were not assigned a company number at that time because there weren't enough men. We were placed in a barracks for the night where we stayed until Schoolcraft told us to go some other place. We had to march wherever we went, even to the chow hall and back to the barracks. I said, "MARCH!" Man! We didn't know how to march. Schoolcraft was yelling all the time, "GET IN STEP, LEFT, RIGHT, LEFT, RIGHT; CAN'T YOU MEAT HEADS KEEP IN STEP?" I can still hear him, even today, yelling, "HUDSON! Get in Step!" Our names were stenciled on our rear end just above the left back pocket in which we could not put anything. The next day we were marched to the clothing store, called small stores, and issued our complete clothing allowance, along with a sea bag in which to keep them. To our disbelief, all the clothes would not fit into the sea bag. Then we went to an area where we made stencils with our name and service number and were taught how and where to mark our clothes. It was a crime to be caught wearing any other person's clothing. We were also issued a hank of string called "clothes stops" that had metal rings on it. These metal rings could be slid up and down the string so that short pieces could be cut to use for tying things of various sizes. Then we were shown how to fold and roll our clothes and using the clothes stops, tie them so they would remain that way. We learned that with our clothes folded and rolled properly, they would all fit into the sea bag. By the time we got all this done, we learned that there were now enough men to form a company.

Our company number was Recruit Company 906 with four platoons of thirty men each. I was in the second platoon second squad. Finally, we were marched to the infirmary and given a lot of shots. I think we were vaccinated for everything. My arms felt like they were going to fall off my shoulders. From there, we went to the armory and were issued the dumbest thing yet, an M-16 rifle that had the firing pin removed. It could not be fired, but we had to treat it as though it was in perfect operating condition. We had to carry that thing wherever we went. We were raked over the coals if we even thought about abusing that so-called rifle. But, instead of referring to it as a rifle, it was called our "piece."

BT1 Schoolcraft decided to appoint a Recruit Company Commander (RCC) and an assistant. I was happy that he didn't call my name as a prospect. He had various men step out of ranks and march the company around the parade field. The first four or five men could not give proper commands during marching drills. Finally, he selected a man named Bartels as the RCC and Endicot as the assistant. Both men were good Joes.

The next day after the shots, we were loaded onto a bus and taken to Camp Elliot somewhere out in the desert east of San Diego. It was a hell hole as far as we were concerned. It had a barbed wire fence around it, as though we were prisoners. They told us the fence was to keep people out, not to keep us in. It was hot in the day and very cold at night. This is where we were to complete four weeks of our basic training, which consisted mostly of marching day and night. There were some indoctrination courses in fire-fighting, naval history, military justice (UCMJ) (Uniform Code of Military Justice), shipboard procedure aboard the "USS Never Sail," and a few hours on the rifle range learning to fire a real working M-16.

There were men called "Master at Arms" (MAA) positioned everywhere. We had to have a "walking chit" to go anywhere alone. The Master at Arms is like a police force. They are there to keep the men in line and to report any infraction of the rules. No one wanted to encounter the MAA. The walking chit was needed even to go to see the doctor or any other place. It had to be signed and dated with the time by someone in authority when the mission was completed in order to return to the company area.

Washing our clothes was a daily chore. Each day the clothes rack was inspected by someone and a report submitted to the company commander with the names of the individual recruits that had discrepancies. Each piece of clothing had to be hung a certain way and each recruit was required to have clothes hanging on the rack. The underwear was hung inside in and facing a certain direction. The outer garments were hung inside out and facing the same direction as the underwear. If the garment had buttons, all the buttons had to be buttoned. Each man was issued two mattress covers. There was a special rack, set aside, on which to hang these covers. They had to be hung inside out with the open end facing a specific direction. Thinking back, there had to be a lot of man-hours wasted on those inspections each day. There was a special scrub rack and scrub brush called a kayak brush. It was about eight to ten inches long and three inches wide with very stiff bristles. Sometimes a hazing, called a "kayak party," would occur in the camp. An individual who was causing problems for the rest of the company by not complying with the rules would be subjected to a kayak party by some of the members of the company, especially if the whole company was punished for that individual's actions or lack of action. In the wee hour of the night, that individual would be man-handled, taken into the shower, and scrubbed with that brush.

There was one man named McNew from Minnesota that seldom took a shower. He was also a sound sleeper. I was glad that I didn't sleep near him. Those who did were continuously doing something to him. As far as I know, they didn't give him a kayak party, but some things just as bad. They would pick him up, mattress and all, carry him into the shower stall and place him over the drain, then turn all the shower heads on. He would wake up when the water reached his body. But, of course, his mattress would be soaking wet by this time. Sometimes, if it was cold, they would carry him outside and lay him on top of the mattress cover rack. The top of the rack was about four feet off the ground. It's a wonder he didn't injure himself when he woke up from being cold and trying to get off the rack. Of course, these acts were illegal and anyone caught performing such acts would be subject to disciplinary actions.

I mentioned that we marched most of the time, but we did other things, too. We had inspections daily and drilled with those useless rifles. We did the sixteen-count manual of arms until we thought our arms would drop off our shoulders. The sixteen-count manual of arms consisted of the changing to sixteen different positions of the rifle in a certain series within a specified time. If a man got out of sequence, his rifle would get tangled with the rifles of the men next to him. It took awhile for us to be able to complete that sequence while in ranks. We could do fine alone out of ranks, but someone would always mess up in ranks. One day a man named Denier was just having a bad day. He was so uncoordinated that Schoolcraft jumped all over him. It made Denier mad and he wanted to fight back. Denier was bigger than Schoolcraft. Schoolcraft said he was ready to go into the boiler room and remove his uniform jumper and take Denier to task. We knew what the outcome would be. We had to hold Denier so he would not get into the fight and get a court-martial for hitting a superior. We also took those rifles to the rifle range and pretended to shoot at targets. The instructors were trying to get us used to sighting them in before letting us use the real thing.

We were not allowed much in the way of entertainment. There were no movies, no radios, and definitely no TVs to watch. Late into the third week, we were allowed to go to a place called the "Ship's Store" and allowed to buy a few items of a personal nature and candy, if we had the money, which I didn't. From that time on, we could go to the telephone exchange in the evening and make phone calls home. The exchange had several operators and phone booths. Also, there was a desk to place your request and to pay for the calls when completed. The operators were all women, which were beautiful to our eyes since we had not seen any for more than three weeks. Sometimes I would go there to watch them and just to get away from the barracks routine, even though I didn't intend to make a call or even have any money to make a call. I considered that entertainment.

About 19 December, the companies ahead of my company were allowed Christmas leave to go home over the holidays; we weren't. Also, the time stopped as far as advancement in training toward completion of boot camp. Yes, we still drilled every day or were given various details to perform, but the time didn't count. However, we had completed our stay at Camp Elliot and moved to the Naval Training Center in San Diego. Because of this Christmas leave period, my boot training was extended from eleven weeks to thirteen weeks. After the leave period, our company was assigned "Service Week" performing mostly mess detail. That consisted of a week in the galley serving the chow at every meal and cleaning up the mess after everyone had been fed. I served food sometimes and washed food trays and dinnerware at other times. Our day usually started at three in the morning and finished around ten at night. There was not much rowdiness from our company that week. We were always too tired for any mischief. The time of year was January and very cold in Southern California. That was another reason not to cause minor disturbances about the barracks.

After our service week was over, we started back on our regular recruit training. We marched and drilled and paraded for the inspector. I signed up and was selected as a member of a whale-boat crew. I was an oarsman. There were eleven of us; ten oarsmen and a coxswain. The coxswain steered the boat and told the oarsmen when and how to row. There were six whale-boat crews that competed in a race each Saturday morning for company points. In order to compete in the Saturday race, each crew had to qualify the Friday evening before. The top six fastest qualifying times were chosen for the race. On our first try at qualifying, we set an all-time new qualifying time record. It made Schoolcraft so elated that he made a big wager that we would win first place in our very first race. The next day we came in last place. Schoolcraft was so mad at us that he made us march the rest of the day. His wife had made a cake for us to eat after the race and he brought sodas for us, but because we had come in last, he wouldn't give us a bite of cake or a drink.

We were not allowed to go on liberty, meaning go off base, until our last two weeks.

Schoolcraft told us that he had better not hear of any of us getting a tattoo while in town. My friend, W. S. Person, with whom I grew up, had an uncle who had many tattoos. We both had said that we wanted one. He had gone into the navy a year before I did and he came home with lots of tattoos. So, sure enough I got one on my first liberty, just to stay up with my friend. It hurt a lot more than I expected. I did not let Schoolcraft know about my tattoo, but I have regretted the decision to get one ever since.

It was also at this time the company was allowed to have a radio. The radio could be used at certain times only and was to be turned off at TAPS. There was an electrical outlet behind my bunk. It was one of the very few within the dorm. I would sneak the radio to my bed after TAPS and place it under my pillow. Keeping the volume low, I would listen to it and fall asleep. One night, I caught a would-be thief. The man was going behind the bunks feeling in the pockets of all the trousers he could find. He tripped over the electric cord plugged into the wall. There had been several items reported missing each day for about a week. I told him that if he would give everything back he had taken, that I wouldn't report him. Of course, I would get in trouble also for having the radio under my pillow. The next morning, all the reported lost items were lying on a table in the center of the dorm. No one ever knew who had put them there.

Finally came the day of graduation from boot camp. We were all a very happy bunch of men. I had been promoted to Airman Apprentice (AA) on 16 March 1953, and issued orders to report to Aviation Indoctrination Program (AN-P) School at Norman, Oklahoma. Man! That was just about two hundred miles from home. I was now an Airman Apprentice with two green stripes on my sleeve. There were several of us with orders to Norman, but most of the other men had orders to various units throughout the fleet. I was given a fourteen-day leave to go home and then report to Norman, Oklahoma.

Mom and Dad and my sister Lillie had moved to a dairy farm just north of McKinney. I knew about where the place was located, but not exactly. After leaving the boot camp base, I made my way to the Greyhound Bus Station to catch a bus home. If you haven't ridden a bus across the country, you can't begin to know what it's like. Especially in 1953, there were no interstate highways. It took two full days and three nights to make the trip from San Diego, California to Dallas, Texas. I think I boarded the bus about 3:00 P.M. I arrived in Dallas about 7:00 A.M. three days later. Then, I had to catch another bus to McKinney. I got off the bus about a quarter mile from where Mom and Dad lived and walked to their house. It sure was good to be home after my time in boot camp.

The following are pictures taken at boot camp. One of them is Seaton from Oklahoma and the other I don't remember the name.

High School Airman Recruits Hudson and Seaton
Camp Elliot

Camp Mayham

Navy Training Center (NTC) San Diego, California, January 1953

AN-P SCHOOL, NATECHTRACEN NORMAN, OKLAHOMA

22 March 1953 to 15 May 1953

My leave period was getting near the end, so it was time to catch the bus and head for Norman, Oklahoma. I had never been there before, but trusted the bus company to get me there safely. I arrived on 22 March 1953, and was enrolled in class number 12 to start training on 23 March for eight weeks in an introductory course of Naval Aviation. I was assigned to the lower dorm in a four-dorm barracks with seventy-nine other men. The discipline was not as strict here as it was in boot camp. Everything seemed so relaxed. There were not near as many MAAs about the base. A person could walk to the mess hall, and we didn't have to march everywhere we went. We could even go to the movie at night, if we wanted. But, one had to have a liberty card to go off base.

McNew from my boot camp company was there, also. I hadn't known that he had orders to AN-P School. We became casual friends, since neither of us knew anyone else there at the time. I had not been one of his tormentors in boot camp, so he felt that he could trust me, but he was not in my dorm either. There were some other men from my boot camp company in AN-P School, but I don't remember their names.

We were given lectures in each field of aircraft maintenance that the navy had to offer. I had wanted to enter the aviation electrician field from the beginning of my entry in the navy. I didn't know that the scores of those first exams I had taken that very first day when I arrived in San Diego would be the determining factor of eligibility into that field. It required a combination of GCT and ARI scores of 105. Mine were GCT 53 and ARI 58, for a total of 111. I made it by just six points above the requirement. Because of that score of 111, I was not eligible to apply for many other fields. After each indoctrination lecture, we would be told of the eligibility requirements and then we would know the fields that we could request. Just because we wanted and requested a particular field, didn't mean we would get to pursue it. In some fields, we were even given some hands-on experience. We tried our hand at reciprocating engine repair, fabricating sheet metal patches for structural repair, and working on radios and electronic gear. The aircraft that we were allowed to get around were World War II vintage, such as F6F attack, F4U fighter, and TBM bombers. They tried to teach us aircraft recognition and Morse code. I could never get the hang of either of those tasks.

From the time of reporting to AN-P School I was placed in a four-section duty status, meaning that every fourth night I had some sort of night duty to perform. Usually my duty was guard duty walking a beat called a post, usually two to four hours long. The midnight to two and two to four were two-hour watches. One afternoon I looked on the watch bill to see which post I was assigned. If it was my duty day, I had a post watch assigned, I just didn't know the time or place. Sure enough, there was C. E. Hudson on a post from midnight to two in the morning. Lo and behold! There was my name on another post for the same time frame. There was no way I could be in two places at the same time. If I went to one post, I would be U. A. (unauthorized absent) from the other. The best thing for me to do was go to the duty office and let the Chief of the Watch know about the mix-up. While I was talking to the Chief, another person was talking to the Duty Officer about the same thing. That's when I met Cecil E. Hudson from Tennessee. The Duty Officer made the decision as to which watch each would stand. I don't remember the watch that Cecil drew, but mine was away out in the boonies. It was supposed to be an aircraft parking ramp, but there were no aircraft.

Upon arrival at Norman, I started an allotment of twenty-five dollars a month to be sent to Mom and Dad to help them with their finances and daily living expense. Although I was only making sixty-six dollars a month, I could get by with very little as long as I ate all my meals in the chow hall. Later, Cecil told me that there had been a mix-up in his pay. The disbursing office was trying to take an allotment from his pay for which I had applied. The disbursing office knew something was wrong because the service numbers were different. We went to the disbursing office and got it straightened out.

If we didn't have duty on the weekend, we were allowed to go on liberty. I went home on three of those weekends, hitchhiking all the way to McKinney, Texas. On one of those weekends, I invited McNew to go home with me. We double dated. I fixed him up on a date with Diann and I went with Lila Faye.

One time I decided to go see my Uncle Marvin and Aunt Nanny, who lived in Chickasha, Oklahoma. I had not seen them in years, and they were so happy to have me as their guest for the weekend. I saw several of my cousins. Orville was driving a truck delivering milk. I went with him Saturday morning. Billy and Bobby were still at home, and V. Dub lived close-by. They wanted me to come another weekend, but I didn't. Other weekends when I didn't have enough money to go anywhere, I stayed in barracks on base and studied.

I, like most other men of my age group, was always trying to prove myself in one way or another. I soon learned that there were people who could do things of which I was incapable. Some things I'm glad that I wasn't able to do. One man in the dorm named Holt, could place his hands on the arms of a chair, then lift his feet off the floor and twist his body up over his head, and raise his entire body and legs to extend straight up toward the ceiling. It amazed me to the point where I would try to duplicate this feat. I nearly broke my wrist trying, but could never accomplish it. Another man must have been an alcoholic. I went with him to the club one night, even though I was under age, and tried to keep up with him in drinking beer. In Oklahoma at that time, the beer was called three-two beer. I think the alcohol content was 3.2 percent. I nearly passed out and he had to help me get back to the barracks. That night taught me two things. One is that I couldn't drink much beer without getting sick, and two is that I didn't want to learn how to drink beer. I did not go to the club anymore while stationed there. Then there was this other character from Tennessee, I don't remember his name. He would run at his locker with his head down and ram the locker with full force. He said that it didn't hurt, but we could not understand his purpose. It could be to gain attention for a recommendation for discharge. There are just as many weird people in service as there are elsewhere.

Norman, Oklahoma, is in what is called "tornado alley." There were several storms that came through while I was there. On each occasion, we were herded into huge concrete warehouses for shelter to wait out a possible tornado. I never saw one during any of the storms, but I can remember peering out into the black sky praying that there wouldn't be any. Years later, after seeing some of the damage they can cause, I am glad that there weren't any.

Each week we filled out a dream sheet stating which career field we wanted to pursue. I always wrote AE for Aviation Aircraft Electrician in all three choices. Toward the end of the course, we would be interviewed by someone to determine the field which we were qualified to choose. The last time the instructor told me that I had to state three different fields, so I also chose AT for Aviation Electronics Technician and AO for Aviation Ordnance. He finally told me that I would be sent to Aircraft Electrician ("A") School in Jacksonville, Florida. That made my day.

I graduated from AN-P School on 15 May 1953, with a class standing of 122 in a class of 324 and a final mark of 84.02. That placed me in the above-average group. Several of the people who were in my class were loaded on a plane and flown to Jacksonville, Florida, the day after graduation. It was a navy R4D, a two-engine plane with a small tail wheel used to carry cargo or passengers. This was my first airplane ride. It was kind of spooky, yet fun. Here again, I enjoyed seeing the countryside as we flew over it.

Airman Apprentice C. E. Hudson, March 1953
At Home on Leave

AE ("A") SCHOOL, NATECTRACEN, JACKSONVILLE, FLORIDA

15 May 1953 to 8 October 1953

I arrived at Naval Air Station (NAS), Jacksonville, Florida, on 15 May 1953 for enrollment into the Aircraft Electrician (AE) "A" School. However, I had a week of indoctrination and waiting for a class to be formed before enrollment. This place was even a little more relaxed than that in AN-P School, but we still had some restrictions and we still had to march from the barracks to school and back. We even marched to the chow hall at lunchtime. I was again assigned berthing in a barracks with four, eighty-man dorms with bunk beds, two high, and lockers in which to keep our belongings. I had a top bunk. Tables were in the center for studying purposes. There was a head (bathroom) for each dorm, which had multiple sinks in one area and one shower stall with multiple shower heads. Modesty was out of the question. There were individual commode stalls with doors. Reveille was held at 0530 hours each morning except on Saturday and Sunday. Unless we were in the duty section, we could sleep in on those days.

Finally, enough men were aboard to form a class. I was enrolled in class 53-21 on 25 May for a nineteen-week course in aircraft electricity. The class leader was Airman Bluish from New Jersey. To the rest of the class he was the "Old Salt." He had already been out in the fleet of the navy and had returned for schooling. The rest of us were fresh out of boot camp, except for the AN-P School. Bluish knew the ropes, so to speak. He knew his way around, so we thought. Again, we were assigned to four-section duty. Each dorm was assigned one section. I don't remember which section our dorm had, but I do know that we had watches to stand on our duty nights. Lo and behold! There was McNew! It seems that he was going to follow me wherever I went. I hadn't known that he had been accepted to AE School.

The school was to teach us the basics of the electrical systems in naval aircraft. We were to be taught basic electrical theory of resistors, capacitors, coils, transformers, motors, and generators. The first few weeks went by pretty smoothly. There were math classes and the teaching of simple basic magnetism theory and the composition of conductor and insulation materials. As the time progressed, the subjects became harder and harder, requiring more and more time of study. We were taught how to read schematics of electrical circuits and recognize the various symbols that represented resistors, capacitors, motors, lights, and switches, etc.

One day we were given the task of wiring a circuit involving the operation of an aircraft landing light. The switch had two positions. One position of the switch would extend the lighting mechanism and illuminate the lamp, and the other position would turn off the lamp and retract the mechanism. The circuit was so simple that I just knew that it would be a piece of cake. Not only did the circuit have to work properly, all the wiring had to be routed correctly, clamped, and spot tied in a neat and orderly manner. When the inspector examined my handiwork, he commented that the job was completed in a very neat and orderly fashion, but there was one major discrepancy. The switch had been hooked up in reverse positions. The retract position extended the light and vice versa. In other words, I had flunked the assignment. That was a very worthwhile lesson I had learned. The most important thing was to pay attention to the details. In fact, by failing, I probably learned more than had I passed. I never failed another assignment while in school.

Getting paid during that time in naval history was something I'll never forget. The navy did not give checks. We had to fill out a pay chit and stand in line to receive our pay in cash. The cashier was located in the mess hall and the line was formed outside. It didn't matter the weather, rain or shine, I was paid every two weeks. A pay list citing the amount of each person's pay was posted on the bulletin board outside the mess hall. We had to fall in line in alphabetical order. One day I noticed another C. E. Hudson on the list. The man was Carl E. The only time we saw each other was in the pay line. I never learned where he was from. He was way ahead of me in school. About halfway through school, he was no longer in line. I guess that he had graduated and left for his next duty station. This was the second C. E. Hudson I had met during my first year of service.

One day in July, we were formed in ranks for a special award. None of us had been anywhere or done anything to merit an award that we could think of. Everyone in the military was awarded the National Defense Service Medal. The award was for serving in the Armed Forces during a time of conflict. The Korean War was in progress at that time. We called it the battle of the Gedunk, for the fights that had occurred at the snack bars and clubs. Now I had one little ribbon to wear on my work uniform and a medal for my dress uniform.

About the eighth or ninth week, McNew informed me that he had flunked the last exam and was being set back a class. It meant that we were no longer in the same company or building. From that time on, I only saw him a few times. It seemed that he had lost interest and was no longer trying. He was later dropped from school and I never heard of him again.

I guess you could call me a loner. Although I had friends, I seldom went with anybody to the snack bars, clubs, or on liberty. We were not allowed to wear civilian clothes on base. In order to go on liberty we had to be in uniform, go to the Chief of the Watch for inspection and pick up our liberty card. If we didn't pass inspection or our name was not on the authorized liberty roll, we didn't get a liberty card. There were several locker clubs in town where sailors could keep civilian clothing. I had one on the second floor at the bus station. I had two sets of clothes consisting of jeans and sport shirts, also socks and a pair of shoes, loafers. I kept a duffle bag in the locker. When I decided to go away for the weekend, I would go to the locker club and pack the duffle bag, then catch the bus, if I could afford it, or hitchhike.

My two brothers lived in St. Petersburg, Florida, about three hundred miles from Jacksonville. Sometimes I would hitchhike down US Highway 301 on Friday night and return on Sunday afternoon. I really enjoyed those weekends. I always wore my uniform when hitchhiking. Other times, I would go to Jacksonville Beach and play in the surf. I never tried to use a surf board, just swam in the shallow waters, or walked in the sand along the beach. Some weekends when I didn't have any money I would stay on base and see the movies. The base movies cost ten cents. Popcorn was a nickel.

The Base Commanding Officer held personnel inspections one Saturday each month. That meant that we had to be in our best dress uniforms, properly cleaned and pressed, along with highly polished shoes. Our only little ribbon had to be placed, precisely as prescribed, over our left breast pocket. We had to be clean shaven and our hair had to be cut to the proper military length and style.

Getting a haircut at the barber shop was a real experience. There was usually a long line and few barbers. A long bench lined two walls of the shop. As you walked in, you took a seat on the bench at the farthest end from what was known to be the number one position. The bench held about twenty men. As a barber's chair became vacant the man in the number one position would get up and move to that barber's chair. One didn't have a choice of a particular barber. The men on the bench would all shift along the bench until the number one position was filled. Sometimes it took a half day to get a haircut.

The inspections lasted all morning long, requiring great stamina to stand at "attention" or at "parade rest" as the inspectors went up and down each rank looking over each man. Some of the men didn't know how to endure. They would lock their knees, which cut off proper blood flow, and fall out unconscious. I always tried to flex my knees when I didn't think anyone was watching. I never passed out while standing personnel inspection. Liberty commenced after the inspection was completed and we were marched back to the barracks. A person who had failed inspection was denied liberty that weekend.

In August, I was eligible to take the test for advancement to Airman. Sure enough, I passed the exam and was advanced to Airman (AN) on 16 August 1953. My base pay was increased to seventy-three dollars per month. Upon completion of the school, I was assigned a designator of AE to go with that promotion and was then known as Aircraft Electrician Mate Airman (AEAN).

I completed the school on 8 October 1953, with a grade point average of 80.07 and a class standing of 7 in a class of 55. Again, I was in the superior group of the class. All of us were glad the course was over and each was looking forward to going to our new duty station assignment.

It was then time for the fleet assignments to be passed out to each man. The orders to various duty stations were handed out in this manner. The orders were to several duty stations throughout the world. All the places were listed on the blackboard. The number one man in class standing had first choice of the assignments. The class leader, regardless of his GPA or class standing, was given the second choice, and then the rest of us could choose according to our class standing, to a certain point. Some of the billets were required to be filled and others were not. So, at some point, if all the required billets had not been chosen, then those men with the lower standings would be required to choose one of them.

There were two assignments to Utility Squadron One (VU-1) and five assignments to Air Transport Squadron Eight (VR-8). A guy named Eickoff from Nebraska held the number six class standing. He asked me if I would choose one of the billets to VU-1 if he chose the other. We had no idea where this squadron was located, and it didn't matter to me where it was, either. So, I told him that I would. Even though we had made a selection of choice, we could change with someone else if the change was made before noon and the personnel office was notified of the change.

A man named Kearns from California had chosen VR-8. He went to the personnel office to find out where each of the assignments was located. He learned that a VU squadron was located in San Diego, but forgot the number of the one I had chosen. He wanted to be stationed in California so very much. He just knew that was where I was to be stationed. He asked if I would trade orders with him. He said that he had found out that VR-8 was located in Hawaii. I first told him "no" and then he said he would give me a full month's pay if I would trade. It didn't matter to me where I was going, so I told him that I would. I needed the money anyway to help me to go home on leave. Eickoff was a little put out with me for switching with Kearns.

We all were issued our orders and sent on our way, first to home on leave, and then to our new duty station. Airman Bullock, from Dallas, told me and another man that we could ride to Dallas with him for twenty dollars. He had a 1951 Mercury. That saved us money over a bus ride and we would arrive in Dallas before the bus. We left Jacksonville at 1500 in the afternoon and arrived in Dallas about 0700 the next morning.

While in Jacksonville, I had been faithful in my correspondence with Lila Faye. One day, I received a "Dear John" letter from her telling me that she was getting married. I was somewhat upset, but not totally surprised. I wrote her to send my high school ring either to me or to my sister Alice there in Dallas. She did neither. When I got home, I went to her house and had a time getting the ring from her. When I finally did, it was too big for me. Her husband had it stretched to fit him. That really perturbed me. I asked to meet her husband, but she kept telling me he was at work. I later learned that he was serving time in prison for a crime that he had committed. I got over Lila Faye soon after that. Then I called Diann and started a more steady relationship with her.

AEAN C. E. Hudson and Mother, Goldie Mae Hudson, October 1953
Home on Leave between Duty Stations at the Rock House near Anna, Texas

AIR TRANSPORT SQUADRON EIGHT HICKAM AIR FORCE BASE, HONOLULU, HAWAII

November 1953 to December 1955

R7V Super Constellation
VR-8 LOGO

After ten days at home on leave, it was time to head for California for further transportation to VR-8 at Hickam Air Force Base in Hawaii. I was to report to Treasure Island in San Francisco for transportation to Hawaii. I had a bus ticket from Dallas to San Francisco, and I thought I had plenty of money for food and snacks on the trip. It would take three days and three nights to get there. It definitely was a very long ride. The route took me from Dallas to El Paso, to Tucson, to Los Angeles and, finally, to San Francisco.

I don't know where my money went, but when I arrived in Los Angeles at 1400 hours, I had one silver dollar left in my pocket. I was tired and hungry, but really didn't want to spend that silver dollar. Somewhere along the trip to San Francisco, I bought something to eat with most of the money. When I arrived in San Francisco at 0600, I had fourteen cents in my pocket. I inquired about transportation to Treasure Island where I had to check in, and was told that the "A" train cost ten cents. That left me with four cents. Coffee cost only a nickel, but I could not afford to buy a cup.

Also, I was about fourteen blocks from the train station and I could not afford the transportation cost, either, so I had to walk all the way carrying my sea bag. That was the longest hike I had ever taken. That sea bag felt like it gained ten pounds each block. I spent the dime for the train ride to Treasure Island and caught a navy bus, which didn't cost me anything to ride, to the duty office to check in from leave. I was a day early and had only four cents in my pocket. I knew I was there in plenty of time to eat breakfast in the chow hall, but I needed a meal pass, which would have to be issued when I checked in. The Duty Officer decided that since I was checking in from leave, that I should have money to buy some food at the snack bar, so he would not issue me a meal pass. I had to wait until I had checked in with the personnel office and until noon to get anything to eat.

I was told to wait in the lounge until my name was called for classification and instructions as to my stay at Treasure Island. I was in my dress blues, having just returned off leave. Shortly, a Second Class Petty Officer asked me for my ID card. I thought that I was being taken into an office to complete my check in, but instead he said, "You are now on work detail." I told him that I was just checking in and in my dress blue uniform and dress shoes, so I couldn't be on a work detail. He told me that he was in charge and for me to get a swab and start mopping the area. Again, I started to protest, but someone warned me that was the way things happened at Treasure Island and that if I continued to protest, I could be put on report and go to Captain's Mast, and given a punishment for disobedience. I grabbed a swab and went to work.

It wasn't long until another man walked up to the second class holding my ID and asked that my ID be given to him. I had no idea of what was taking place. The second class told me to follow this man, that I was wanted in the classification office. The man led me around through several office spaces and then handed me my ID. The man was the same person that I had caught stealing things in boot camp, but wouldn't turn him in if he gave all the stolen items back. I had kept him from ruining his life. It was payback time, he thought, he got me out of that work detail. Classification wouldn't call me for another couple of hours. The man even bought me a cup of coffee after I told him of my plight.

Finally, classification called me into an office and explained that I would be transported to Hawaii on a troop transport ship whenever there was a full load. In the meantime, I would be assigned a berthing place and to the galley for work detail. The barracks was a large complex with several dorms with bunks stacked five high. I was given the fourth bunk up. That meant three men were under me and one over me. The work assignment consisted of cleaning the galley in all areas, from scrubbing the food trays and placing them in the scullery, to sweeping and swabbing the deck. In the navy, a floor is called the deck whether on a ship or in a building. My work hours were from 0330 to 2200 hours, but it was every other day. Those working in the galley could do most whatever they wanted on their days off. This went on for twenty-one days until I was assigned a boarding date. After we were assigned a shipping date, we were given shots for all sorts of diseases and lectures about conduct aboard the ship. While waiting one day, I was in line with another C. E. Hudson. I don't remember his first name. He was from Washington State. We had to muster several times a day until finally told to load onto a bus and be taken to the ship.

We were assigned berthing areas before going aboard, but didn't know that we had already been assigned work details, also. Again, I was assigned to work in the galley. The trip across the Pacific Ocean from San Francisco to Pearl Harbor in Hawaii would take six days. Most everyone was on the main deck as we sailed under the Golden Gate Bridge when leaving San Francisco Bay. It was an exciting time of my life, being the first time on a ship and the first time at sea.

I met some of the people who were going to the same squadron as I. There were five AEANs going to VR-8: Charles A. Fisher from Vermont; George B. Griner from Georgia; Dwayne Spence and Douglas Wausom ("Po Go"), both from California; and myself from Texas. Fisher, Griner, and I became good buddies and chummed around together. Working in the galley made the time go fairly quickly.

On our days off, we would try to stay on the outer main deck whenever possible, watching the waves roll by. One day we were at the rail looking over the ocean waves, when I noticed a man start heaving his breakfast over the side. I grabbed Charlie and George and shoved them away from the rail. Those still at the rail got splattered, but my reaction saved us. My buddies were sure happy with me for saving them. The sea got pretty rough after that and the Captain would not allow us out on the deck for about two days. You talk about a foul ship. Most everyone was getting seasick. Luckily, I didn't. It was hard to keep the food tray in one spot during mealtime. During those rough seas, we didn't feed very many men. I hated it when someone lost it there in the galley, because I had to clean up the mess.

For entertainment, they would show movies on the open deck at night. In the afternoon, they would have bingo games on the open deck. I didn't get to go much because of my galley work assignment, but, one time I won a travel alarm clock at bingo. I didn't have a clock, so I knew this would help me a lot. I kept that clock for more than twenty years.

It was a happy day when the ship pulled into Pearl Harbor. It was about1000 hours on 8 December 1953. There were many different types of ships docked in the harbor. It didn't take very long to get off the ship with all my baggage, along with all the other men who were going to Hickam Air Base. They loaded us on a bus for the short haul. In fact, there is only a chain link fence separating Pearl Harbor and Hickam, but the gates are a little way apart.

There were several people on the bus, but not all were going to VR-8. Also on Hickam was VR-7 located just down the flight line from VR-8. Personnel of both squadrons were berthed in the same general housing area and were fed in the same galley facility. Those reporting to VR-8 were checked in at and given a week of indoctrination of the rules and regulation of the life we could expect while in Hawaii.

The berthing here was fantastic. The air force really knows how to treat their men. Instead of an open eighty-man dorm in a barracks, I was placed in a room with only one other person. I couldn't believe my luck. The other person was AMS2 Snyder. I don't know where he was from, but at least he was likable and compatible to live with. We each had our own side of the room and it was up to us to make sure our space was kept clean and would pass inspection once a month. Yes, I hadn't gotten away from the inspections, both living spaces and personnel. Sometime later, I moved into a single room. It was great. I could arrange things to suit myself and I didn't have to be concerned about another person's privacy. Besides the bed, there was a table (shown), a chest of drawers, a chair, and a built-in closet.

I also still had four-section duty. The Airmen had to walk a four-hour beat, come rain or fair weather. The Third Class Petty Officers stood Duty Officer Messenger watches. They usually sat in the duty office reading comic books. I promised myself that I was going to get promoted to PO3, so I wouldn't have to be out in the rain.

After the week of indoctrination, we five AEANs were sent to check into the electric shop. Chief Miller was in charge. He told us that two of us would be sent to three months of TDY (Temporary Duty) and the other three would get to stay in the shop. One would go to the galley for mess cook duty and the other to barracks cleaning detail. He made us draw straws to see who was going TDY. Charles Fisher drew the shortest straw and went to mess cooking duty, Wayne Spence drew the next shortest and went to compartment cleaning. I considered myself lucky because I was checking into the electric shop. Chief Miller said the rest of us would get our chance. Two of the remaining three would have to relieve Fisher and Spence.

The shop had about sixty-three men assigned, which were split into four sections, except for four men who were in the instrument shop. Two of the sections worked the day shift from eight to five. One section worked the swing shift from four to midnight and one section worked the graveyard shift from midnight to eight. The squadron as a whole, worked twenty-four hours a day, seven days a week, but each individual only worked eight hours a day, five days a week. I don't know how many men were in the whole squadron. I met some of the people whom I came in contact with in VR-8 at other places where I was stationed later in my career. Chief Miller assigned each of us to a different shift. I was assigned to the swing shift. Chief Matherly was in charge of that shift.

Some of the people who were in the squadron who had significant impact on my career or I would encounter later in my travels are: Chief Miller, Chief Krause, Chief Matherly, AE1 Rogers, AE2 Bill Chestnut, AD1 Van Pembroke, AM1 Montgomery, AEAN Oberloe, and AEAN William Jack Partain. Charlie

Fisher, George Griner, Po Go, and I went on liberty together most of the time. That is, until Po Go got introduced to wine one night and then that's all he wanted.

This Is Me in My Dress Blues in My New Room

I'm on Waikiki Beach in Front of the Royal Hawaiian Hotel, 1954

Charlie Fisher and George Griner
On Waikiki Beach in Front of the Royal Hawaiian Hotel, 1954

Hawaii was a beautiful paradise at this time in history. There were only seven large hotels in the Waikiki Beach area. The Royal Hawaiian, the Beach Comber, the Out Rigger, and the Mauna Loa were situated on the waterfront with the other three on the side streets. We would go and lie in the sand in front of the hotels or swim in the surf and no one bothered us. Of course, we couldn't change into our swimsuits in the hotels. We had to use the facility at Fort DeRussey for that purpose, but it was just down the beach a way. It had been an active army fort during the big war, now it was just a rest area for military personnel. Po Go and I both bought Argus C III cameras and went sightseeing a lot. We took lots and lots of pictures. We liked to travel to the other side of the island and go surfing. The windward side was much prettier than the side where Honolulu was located. Whenever possible, we would drive by Hanauma Bay, Blow Hole, Long Beach, and Rabbit Island on the way to the windward side.

Hanauma Bay

Blow Hole

Long Beach

Rabbit Island

Sometimes we would go up Nuauna Street over the Palli Road to get to the windward side. The Palli is a Hawaiian historical site with lots of history about King Kamehameha conquering the Island. From the Palli Overlook one can see the north shore and Konioai Bay. The road leading from the Palli Lookout was very steep and curvy.

The Palli Lookout

The Palli Lookout

Sometimes, instead of going all the way to the Palli, we would detour from Nuauna Street to go to the Hawaiian National Cemetery, the Punch Bowl. It always seemed so beautiful and peaceful, and yet, humbling at the same time with all the crosses on the graves. A huge cross was always erected at the lookout site on Easter. One could see Diamond Head and the Waikiki area from the lookout and downtown Honolulu.

The Hawaii National Cemetery (The Punch Bowl), 1955

Punch Bowl Lookout   *Diamond Head and Waikiki*

I was just like most other young men during those times. Several of us would go out on the town, patronizing the local bars. In some places, it was easy to get into trouble due to the rowdiness of the type of people who patronized them. I stayed clear of those places. We didn't like to go to the EM Clubs because of all the sailors off the ships and they didn't care much for Airdales (a term to describe people of the navy aviation branch). I went to a place called Bill Leader's Bar on Hotel Street in downtown Honolulu. Then we started going to a place called the Hookila, closer to Hickam. In fact, we could walk to that place. I met a barmaid named Edith Bunbury.

The squadron had sixteen R7V Super Constellation aircraft with a mission to ferry cargo and personnel across the Pacific from California to the Far East. Captain B. M. Strean was the Commanding Officer. I had never been on such a large aircraft, so I needed a lot of indoctrination of the various systems. Chief Matherly assigned me with AEAN Marsh that first night at work. The job was to repair a heater problem. Marsh was to teach me where the heater components were located, as well as how to repair the discrepancy. The heater was located in the wing, but behind a panel called a "Hell Hole," in which only one man could see the unit. Marsh was on a stepladder with his head and shoulders inside the hole. Therefore, I was on the ground and Marsh was in the Hell Hole. Chief Matherly came up to me and said, "Hudson, my policy is that the first thing you do each night is go to the tool room and check out a red rag and a flashlight." I hadn't had time to respond when Marsh said, "Chief, the tool room is out of rags and flashlights." The Chief, who was already walking away, turned back and said, "You do not talk back to me in that tone of voice; when I tell you to do something, you do it. Do you understand?" I hadn't said a word, but I said, "Yes, Sir." Then the Chief made me go to the tool room. Sure enough, there were no red rags or flashlights available for me to check out. I made it through that first two weeks without any other trouble with Chief Matherly.

VR-8 Electric Shop

R7V Super Constellation

After fourteen days on the swing shift, I was rotated to the graveyard shift for fourteen days. One of the things I liked about those shifts was "mid rats." I was allowed to eat a meal at midnight. I usually had a breakfast-type meal of bacon and eggs. I would go to work, and then several of us would ride over to the mess hall in the shop jeep. No one ever told us that we couldn't. By eating mid rats, I could eat four meals a day, not that I needed them, but since I had a meal pass, I would make the regular breakfast and also the noon and dinner meals, as well. It's a wonder I didn't gain hundreds of pounds.

I struggled with my finances during this period of my life. I had not learned how to manage my money. With my pay at seventy dollars a month and me sending twenty-five dollars home each month, I was living from payday to payday. I would borrow fifteen dollars to get me through the end of the month and pay it back when I got paid. I am grateful to George Griner for his willingness to loan me a few bucks most any time that I asked. I had started borrowing thirty and each month I would stretch my money a little closer to pay day. Each month I would have to borrow a little less than the month before. Finally, there came a time when I still had money left from my last paycheck on payday. I had learned how to manage my money. It sure was a good feeling not to have to ask someone for help.

I knew that I was eligible to take the Third Class Petty Officer test in February, if I completed the required correspondence courses by certain dates. I completed G.T.C. for PO3, 2, and 1, and Chief Petty Officer, NavPers 10602-A on 13 December 1953 with a grade of 4.0. Well, I took the PO3 exam for promotion to AE3 on 16 February 1954. There were several men within the shop who took the exam, including Fisher, Griner, Spence, and Po Go. Even though I needed only one course for advancement to PO3, there were several needed for advancement to higher enlisted pay grades. I continued to work on and complete the other courses for advancement to PO2, PO1, and CPO. By May 1954, I had completed five additional courses.

In March, it was time for Fisher and Spence to be relieved of mess cooking and compartment cleaning duties. That meant that two of us original three men would have to relieve them. Again, Chief Miller had us draw straws to see who would get to stay in the shop. I lucked out again and drew the longest straw, so I stayed in the shop, Griner went compartment cleaning, and Po Go went mess cooking. Chief Miller said for me not to fret that I would relieve one of them in June. Of the five, I was the only one that had passed the exam and was promoted to PO3 on 16 May 1954. Third Class Petty Officers didn't clean compartments or do mess cooking duty. So, I remained in the electric shop all the time I was stationed in VR-8.

After I was advanced to Petty Officer Third Class, I thought I had plenty of money. My base pay was $142 per month and I could afford to buy a car. I hadn't thought about insurance and other expenses. I bought a 1940 Ford convertible from Marsh, who was being transferred to another duty station. The car was pink with a white top. It sure was a pretty thing, I thought.

The base outdoor theater was in the back with the Hawaiian mountain range in the far distance. It seemed that every time we were watching a good movie the rains would come down out of the mountains

I was working the swing shift at the time. One morning, about a week after I had bought the car, I felt someone shaking me and talking by my bunk. I opened my eyes and there was a person I had never seen before. Without introducing himself, he started telling me that he had run into my car. I couldn't believe him since I knew the car to be properly parked in the lot and that the parking lot was plenty big. Sure enough! He had decided to back out of his spot all the way across the lot before another car came by and rammed into my car. It never got repaired properly and it lost the luster and excitement. I sold the car shortly after that.

1940 Ford Convertible

AE3 Charles E. Hudson, 16 May 1954

One day PO3 Hendricks asked me if I would like to go deep sea fishing with him and eight other men. I really didn't think that I could afford the cost of a fishing trip, but he told me that ten dollars was all it cost. I agreed and it was arranged to be at the boat just before 0600 hours. I asked him about breakfast and food for the trip. He said that the ten dollars covered everything, including the food. I arrived at the boat in plenty of time and we got under way on schedule.

I had never been deep sea fishing before and didn't know what or when to do anything. There was plenty of fishing gear for everyone. At about 0800, I started getting hungry and wanted something to eat. I asked Hendricks about breakfast food. He said that all he had brought was baloney, cheese, and bread. He said that I could make a sandwich any time I wanted. I made the sandwich without mayonnaise, since Hendricks didn't bring any, and commenced eating. I asked him about something to drink. He said that he had bought a case of beer for each person on the trip. Man! I didn't want a beer for breakfast, so I asked him about water. He looked at me kind of funny and said that he knew that he was forgetting something. He had forgotten to bring any water. All we had to drink for the entire day was beer or go without. I had to have something to wash the sandwich down, so I opened a can. All the others on the trip joined me in making a sandwich and drinking beer. We did not get but one strike all day and by 1400 hours, most everyone on the boat was sick and heaving over the side. The boat captain trolled most of the day, only bottom fishing for a short time. Luckily, I didn't get sick. It would have been a great time had we had proper beverages and some water. I enjoy the sailing around on the ocean, but not this fishing trip.

I also thought I knew how to play "Poker." One night, I heard about a game that was going on up in the instrument shop. I figured that I could afford to lose twenty dollars, but with a little luck, I could also win a few bucks. I headed for the place of the game and arrived just in time to hear one of the men say, "…and I raise you fifty dollars." I kept my money in my pocket and watched while I decided that I really didn't know how or could afford to play Poker.

I thought I would get out of walking the post watches when I was advanced to PO3 and be assigned to the ASDO messenger watches. Man, was I ever WRONG! There were so many men advanced to PO3 that there were not enough Airmen left to man all the post watches. So, the PO3s were made to stand the post watches and the PO2s stood the ASDO messenger watches, and I was still walking in the rain sometimes. Later when I was advanced to PO2 in July 1955, the watches were reverted to the old ways and I was now standing duty as POW (Petty Officer of the Watch, not prisoner of war) and had to walk around all the various posts checking on the men standing those watches, sometimes in the rain.

In September 1954, Chief Miller asked me if I would like to go to "C" Schools at North Island, San Diego, California, for the G-2 Compass System, the P-1 Auto Pilot System, and the Glide Path Control System. He told me that normally those were reserved for E5 or above, but I had longer time remaining in the shop than most of the other men and he thought I was a good candidate for the schools. Sure I accepted. Man! That was the greatest thing that could happen to me! It gave me a big jump in my career. To be that junior and be selected for those types of schools was mostly unheard of in those days. There were three First Class Petty Officers, PO1 Manning, PO1 Monique, and PO1 Stimmel, and myself, a lowly PO3, who were ordered to the schools. It would take five weeks to complete all three schools, which I didn't mind at all. The Chief would even allow me to take a fourteen-day leave after the completion of the schools.

The evening before the day of my departure for San Diego, Airman Smith came by my room and wanted me to go to the EM Club with him. He said that he would be transferred to another duty station before I returned from school and he might never get to see me again. He told me that it was nickel beer night and that he was treating. Like an idiot, I went with him. He was a beer drinker and I wasn't. Naturally, I got drunk and Smitty had to put me to bed. The next morning, I awoke lying in the bed with my civilian clothes still on. I looked at the clock and only had forty-five minutes before reporting time at the OOD's office. Man! Did I ever get a move on! In thirty minutes I was showered, shaved, dressed, and standing in front of the OOD's office, ready to go. I think I learned a valuable lesson that morning. Had I not gotten there at the scheduled time, I could have been awarded a court-martial for missing movement. One doesn't party the night before going on a mission.

We flew from Hickam Air Force Base in Hawaii to Travis Air Force Base in California. It was up to us to arrange our own transportation to San Diego.

I did not have the experience that the others had, so I let them do all the arranging. We went to the Federal Building in downtown San Francisco and Stimmel had the Duty Officer make the arrangement for a flight. It took nearly all day, which caused us to have to spend the night. The Duty Officer even made reservations for hotel accommodations. We arrived at North Island without further delay and commenced the schooling for the three courses. AE1 Bill Chestnut had been transferred from VR-8 to Fleet Aviation Electronics Training Unit (FAETU) Pacific, the "C" School system for fleet personnel, and had been promoted to Petty Officer First Class. I encountered him at the school. I don't remember what my grades were, but I completed the courses and went home to Anna, Texas, for ten days leave.

By this time, Daddy and Mama had moved back to Eck Brown's place, but this time in what we called the "Rock House." There was much celebration. Not only had I come home, but it was also Christmastime. I had met Diann before I had joined the navy and we had dated on and off over the last three years. She and her mother still lived at 4500-1/2 Junius Street. While on leave this time, I asked her to be my wife, would she marry me? She accepted, but now it was time for me to leave to go back to Hawaii. I did give her an engagement ring, though. My cousin Leonard Allen helped me purchase it from Zale's Jewelers in downtown Dallas. Leonard had a business of his own and was able to get the ring at a wholesale price. It sure made the cost easier for me.

Engagement of Ed Hudson and Diann Henley, November 1954

I had to report to Travis Air Force Base for transportation back to Hawaii. It seemed there were a huge number of people in transit at that time. There was a backlog of flights. I was there three days and still no flight. One night I was reading a book and fell asleep without checking the bulletin board for a flight list. The next morning a flight was listed on the board that had left at midnight and my name was on it. Man, I had missed movement! That was a court-martial offense. Sure enough, I was summoned to Mast to explain why I had missed movement. The officer dismissed me because there had been only an hour's notice given for the flight and about thirty other men had missed the flight also. My name went to the bottom of the waiting list. I spent two more days in Travis before getting a flight back to Hawaii.

When I got back to Hawaii, Chief Miller had been transferred and now Chief Matherly was in charge of the electric shop. It was also time to get my recommendation submitted for advancement to Petty Officer Second Class, PO2. I had all my courses completed and all I needed was the recommendation in order to take the exam. I asked him if I was going to be recommended. He said, "You have to show me what you can do before I can recommend you." I said, "Chief, I've been working for you for a year." He said that I had been gone for seven weeks and that he didn't know what I could do. I really felt dejected. He assigned me a task, which gave me direct access to Division Officer, Lt. Schappels, without having to request to see him. I had to inventory the plant equipment for which the Division Officer was responsible and report the conditions directly to him. While we were going over the report, he asked me if I was taking the PO2 exam. I told him what the Chief had said about my recommendation. He said, "You have been here over a year now and the Chief should know what your capabilities are." About that time the Chief walked in and Lt. Schappels asked him if he was recommending me for advancement. Again, the Chief said the same thing about not knowing what I could do. Lt. Schappels said that since I had completed the inventory in record time that I should be recommended, and Chief Matherly didn't object. In February 1955, I took the Second Class PO exam. Lt. Schappels was one of the monitors. He came by a couple of times to see how I was doing. One time he asked me if I was sure about the answer I had given for one of the questions. I told him that I was sure.

After returning to Hawaii in December 1954, Diann and I started saving our money to fly her to Hawaii so we could get married. I did not know all of the problems we would encounter in trying to accomplish this feat. It would cost quite a bit for the air fare alone. I had started smoking cigarettes when I was a teenager. I found that working in aircraft maintenance, I could never finish a cigarette that I had started. Just about the time I lit one, the Chief would tell me to go work on a plane. Of course, there was no smoking around the planes, so I would snuff it out and get on with the task. In December 1954, I had a cold and the cigarettes didn't taste good, even though I thought I wanted one. Finally, I decided that I would lay off them for a while. That decision helped me in saving money to get Diann to Hawaii. I did not smoke another cigarette until January 1956.

Diann graduated from high school in January 1955, at nineteen years old. By March we had enough money to get an apartment and her plane fare to Hawaii. In 1955, all the planes were propeller-driven aircraft. The movie, *The High and the Mighty*, had just been released and was showing in the theaters. I had seen the movie and was both anxious and concerned about her flight.

I leased an apartment in the Waikiki area at the Trade Winds Apartments, 1720 Ala Moana Blvd., Honolulu, Hawaii. The lease was ninety-five dollars per month with the utilities included.

Diann arrived on March 8 about midday. She did not know a soul in Hawaii, but me. I wanted us to have the wedding and a reception, but no arrangements had been made at the time. We went to the apartment and then down to get the marriage license. We knew there was a three-day waiting period, so we were planning the wedding date to be 12 March. The woman at the License Bureau asked Diann for a letter of consent to get married, which she did not have. Women in Hawaii could not get married until twenty years of age without a letter of consent. We frantically forwarded a telegram to her mother to send us the letter. We told her that both mother and father had to sign it.

After that we started trying to set up the arrangements for a wedding and a reception. We went to the Hickam Base Chapel and set the marriage arrangement with the base Chaplin. I found a place that would make us a wedding cake for a price that I thought I could afford. Then we started looking for a place to hold the reception. I went to all the EM Clubs, but there were none to be had. I put an invitation card on the bulletin board inviting all the electric shop personnel to the wedding, but still didn't have a place to hold the reception. I thought that I should invite all the Chiefs verbally. As I was in the process of inviting Chief Matherly, he stopped me and said that he would be busy that day. I hadn't gotten to the point of telling him the date. I guess it didn't matter the date, he was going to be too busy to come to my wedding.

One day, Chief Krause stopped me in the shop and said that he and his wife would like to have our reception at their house, if we didn't mind. DIDN'T MIND! Man! That was a godsend, a prayer answered. I readily accepted. I told Diann and she couldn't believe that anyone would be so generous. Charlie Fisher was to be my best man, but Diann didn't know anyone in Hawaii to ask to be bridesmaid. I asked Edith Bunbury, the barmaid, if she would be Diann's maid of honor and she accepted. Edith was a French lady and the wife of an air force staff sergeant.

Well! That telegram shook Diann's mother up so much that she sat down and wrote a letter of consent right then, and located Diann's father and had him sign it. She then mailed it without getting it notarized. The letter arrived in Hawaii on 12 March, the day that we had wanted to be married. I looked at the letter and told Diann that the woman at the License Bureau would not accept it because it was not notarized, but we went down anyway. Sure enough, she wouldn't accept it. We had to send another telegram telling Diann's mother the circumstance and to be sure to have it notarized this time.

We frantically started the cancellation of all previously made arrangements for the wedding. We were both disappointed, but there was nothing we could do about it. I was sure glad that everyone understood, especially the bakery about the cake. The new letter arrived the morning of 15 March, but didn't have Diann's dad, Mr. Henley's, signature. However, it was notarized. The woman didn't want to accept this one either, until Diann told her that her parents had been divorced since she was a little girl. We had to get an affidavit swearing that this was, in fact, true about the divorce before the woman would consent to issuing our marriage license. She referred us to a lawyer, who gladly agreed to make out the affidavit. When he was finished he told us that the price was $150. Man! The look on my face must have told him that we didn't have a dime, much less $150. Then he said that would be $1.50. That's a whole lot less than $150. We went back to the License Bureau and the lady issued the license. It was 1100 hours. I asked Diann if she wanted to get married that day. She said, "Yes, let's do it before anything else goes wrong."

A man in the electric shop named Freddy (don't remember his last name) had loaned me his car for the week. So, we started making the rounds, making the arrangements all over again. We had set the time at 1730 hours at Hickam Chapel No. III, and asked all the participants to be there. Diann was staying in the apartment in Waikiki and I was staying in the barracks at Hickam. I went to pick her up in the afternoon early enough to get to the chapel on time. When we went to the car in the parking lot, it had a flat tire. There were three spares in the trunk, which were also flat, and there was no place close-by to get one repaired. So, we had to take a cab to the base. By this time, it was just about time to start the ceremony. All the people were there, except the best man, Charlie. I had loaned him a suit of clothes and had told him that I would bring a tie. I got PO3 Marrell to take me to the barracks to get him. He was sitting in his room completely undressed, waiting for me to get there with the tie. By the time he got dressed and we got to the chapel, it was about forty-five minutes past the time of the ceremony. The Chaplin announced us man and wife at 1830 hours.

The reception at Chief Krause's house was fabulous. Most of the men from the electric shop were there. There was food and drinks along with all kinds of presents, which was totally unexpected. Most everyone stayed late and had such a good time. Diann and I departed about 2200 hours. I had taken a week's leave for our honeymoon.

Wedding Ceremony of Ed and Diann Hudson, 15 March 1955

Edith Bunbury	*Chaplain Luther C. Goebel, Capt. USAF*	*Charles A. Fisher*
Maid of Honor	*Officiating Chaplain*	*Best Man*

Sealing the Wedding Agreement with a Kiss

Charlie Fisher and Edith Bunbury
Best Man   Maid of Honor

Cutting the Cake

Wedding Party Reception at Chief and Mrs. Krause's Home

Two days after the wedding Freddie called, saying that he wanted his car returned. Diann stayed at the apartment while I went to deliver it to him. I was driving up Nimitz Highway a little too fast and a policeman driving parallel to me on Kam Highway was clocking me. I got a ticket for going 45 mph in a 35 mph zone. I didn't know how much the fine would be and I only had ten dollars on me. I stopped by the police station on the way home to settle the ticket. The fine was fifteen dollars. I had to call Diann and tell her to come to the police station to bail me out of going to jail. She did not have any idea where the police station was or how to get there. After giving her directions, she arrived in about an hour. We could not afford many stupid mistakes like that.

Making ends meet was something of a miracle. After the government took $60 out of my pay toward Diann's allotment check, that left me with $35 per paycheck twice each month. Diann's allotment would be $137.50 per month, but she would not receive her pay until the first of June. Approaching the payday on the first of April, I told her that I didn't know how we were going to be able to pay the rent. Since we were married on the fifteenth of the month, I received half of her allotment on my paycheck. I received $125. We paid the rent and went grocery shopping at the Richard Street Commissary. Sure enough, on the fifteenth of the month I received $35, which we used to buy groceries. Then on May 1, I again received $35 and the rent was due. Diann had gotten a letter from her mother and in the letter was her income tax return of a $120. Again, we paid the rent and had a little extra, so we splurged and went to a movie. We didn't count going to Bingo as splurging, because it was basically free entertainment. Then June 1, Diann started receiving her allotment check and we had no more difficulty paying the rent.

We still didn't have very much money and had to rely on public transportation to get from one place to another. I would catch the bus each day at the corner of Ala Moana Blvd. and Kalakaua Ave. to go to work. It was usually a long day by the time I arrived back home. Taxis were too expensive to ride, but the buses only cost ten cents. On weekends, we would walk along the beaches or lie in the sun and watch the tourists go by. Sometimes we played cards for entertainment, always for fun, because we couldn't afford to gamble our money away, even if we condoned gambling.

Although all five of us who had arrived in the squadron together were now Third Class Petty Officers, I was the only one promoted to second class. On 16 July 1955, I was promoted to Petty Officer Second Class, AE2. My basic pay jumped from $145 a month to $165 per month and Diann's allotment increased from $137.50 to $157.50. We had so little each month before that increase; we now thought we had money to burn. Actually, we remained frugal with our funds except that we found a car we could get for only $100. It was a 1941 Plymouth sedan. I think gas was seventeen cents per gallon. Now, on weekends, we would go for a drive around the island of Oahu.

We stayed in the Trade Wind Apartment until September 1955, and then moved to 926 Lunalilo St., Apt. #5. It was an efficiency apartment with one big room as living room, bedroom, and dining room, plus two smaller rooms as kitchen and bathroom. The rent was only seventy-five dollars per month and we thought we could save money. Wrong! We now had to pay our utility bills, which in fact cost us more than the twenty-five dollars we thought we were going to save.

926 Lunalilo Street, Apt. # 5

While as PO3, I was assigned to perform electrical maintenance on the aircraft. The R7-V Super Constellation Aircraft was equipped with four Pratt &

Whitney 3350 engines with Hamilton Standard Propellers. I soon learned to perform inspections and repairs to the various systems of the aircraft. VR-8 was a C and D activity, which helped in learning how to service and repair electrical components. The electrical shop was authorized to disassemble and repair the equipment. Chief Matherly had me build a component test panel that improved my knowledge of electrical systems.

After I was promoted to PO2, Chief Matherly designated me as the Shop Materials Petty Officer. I had the responsibility of ordering and receiving all supplies and parts for the entire shop. Anyone needing something from the Supply Department had to report their needs to me and I in turn, ordered and picked up the material from Supply. The only time I could work on the aircraft as an electrician was on my duty nights, which was every eight days. As duty electrician, I was responsible for completion of repairs to the electrical systems of the aircraft on the next day's flight schedule. Captain Music had relieved Captain Strean, and several men had been ordered out of the squadron. There were not enough people to man three shifts. Therefore, four duty sections were formed with one duty section handling the maintenance of the aircraft at night. On my duty days, I would alternate between watch duty and duty electrician.

There were three occasions that I had to finish repair jobs that were started by Chief Matherly, and that did not make him any too happy. On each occasion, I proved that he didn't really know how to make the repairs. Actually, I lucked out in discovering the root of the problems and in making the repairs. The first one involved an auxiliary power unit that would not start. The Chief and a Petty Officer First Class (PO1) had worked on the discrepancy for two days before my day of duty. That evening as the Chief was turning the shift over to the duty section, I asked him if there was anything of major concern to which I should devote my time. He said there was nothing left to repair except that power unit gripe and he knew that it was beyond my ability to repair it. He left for home. The only other person in the shop with me, because all other men in the duty section were on a watch, was AEAN William Jack Partain. So, he and I took our tools to the aircraft and commenced to analyze and access the problem facing us. The first thing we noticed was that every part of the power unit had been disassembled. Neither of us knew anything about the system. We had to go by the manual step by step to reassemble the unit until we got to a point where we could attempt to start the engine. We first checked to determine if there was electrical power available and found none. So, we started tracing the circuit until we found the open connection, which prevented power from reaching the unit. After we made that repair and determined that there was power available to start the unit, we put everything back together and, sure enough, the unit started and worked as it should. The Chief could not believe that we had found and fixed the problem. The other two times were similar in nature. The Chief and a PO1 had worked on each one a day or two before my day of duty. Each time William Jack and I made the repairs during the night.

Most of the men in the shop did not like Chief Matherly. He had some peculiar managerial ideas that were misunderstood. To me, his ideas were negative in nature. When the men were sitting around in the shop, he would order a First Class Petty Officer to get a broom and sweep the shop. The First Class POs would comply and start sweeping. All the juniors would either leave the shop or get out of the way. The Chief would also leave the shop. One day AEAN Veau and I were in the shop. I needed to go to supply to get some parts that had come in, but had not started to move in that direction. Chief Matherly ordered me to get a broom and sweep the shop. I knew that I had to go get the parts from supply. So, I picked up the broom and walked over to Veau and handed him the broom and told him to sweep the shop. He said, "The Chief told you to sweep the shop!" My reply was, "Yes, and now I'm telling you to because I have other things that have to be done and, besides, I'm senior to you." Chief Matherly looked at both of us and then went out of the shop. I went to supply and picked up a package, and was returning to the electric shop when Chief Matherly stopped me. He asked why I had told Veau to sweep the shop when I was the one he had ordered to do it. I told him my reasons, one being that Veau was the junior, and two was that the part was at supply ready to be picked up. He said that was what he had hoped the first class would do. That it was not his intentions to have them sweep the shop, but have them delegate the task to a junior. To me, this action was a negative approach to leadership.

As a punishment for infractions, the Chief would tell the person to paint the shop door. I bet that door was painted every two weeks. Of course, the old paint was never scraped off before applying the new coat. If a person failed to complete the necessary paperwork when completing a maintenance action before leaving the shop, the Chief would leave orders with the duty office to have that person come into the office at midnight to complete the paperwork. It only took one time for him to get the point across. I made sure I completed all paperwork before securing to home.

Since I was now a Second Class Petty Officer, I was eligible to go to "B" School, which was also located in Jacksonville, Florida. I thought if I could get "B" School, I would have a very good chance in getting a job as an electrician when I got out of the navy. My enlistment was up in November 1956. I applied for the school and was selected, but my orders did not arrive in time for me to finish before my enlistment expired. In order to accept the school, I had to agree to extend my enlistment one year.

To enhance my knowledge of my profession and to further my education, I was most always working on correspondence courses. During my tour with VR-8, I completed the following courses:

Date Comp.	Course		Grade
12/13/53	GTC for PO 3, 2, 1 & C	NavPers 10602-A	4.0
5/9/54	Aviation Electrician's Mate, Vol. I	NavPers 10319	3.49
5/9/54	Aviation Electrician's Mate, Vol. II	NavPers 10320	3.77

5/13/54	Basic Electricity	NavPers 10622-B	3.48
5/13/54	Aviation Supply	NavPers 10394-B	3.56
5/13/54	Aviation Electrician's Mate 3 & 2	NavPers 10316	3.81
7/16/54	Aviation Electrician's Mate 1 & C	NavPers 10055	3.58
12/17/54	Aircraft Instruments	NavPers 10333-A	4.0
12/17/54	NTC for AE1		3.60

Diann and I departed Honolulu, Hawaii, in late November 1955, just after Thanksgiving Day, headed for Jacksonville, Florida, with thirty days leave and ten days travel en route. We flew on an air force C97 Prop-driven plane from Hawaii to Travis Air Force Base in California. When we tried to get transportation from San Francisco to Dallas, we were told there was none available. We didn't have very much money, so we couldn't afford to stay very many days in a hotel and still have enough to pay for the bus, train, or plane ride. We went to several travel agents and each told us the same thing that all buses, trains, and planes were filled and there were no seats available. Finally, one of the agents said he had one seat available on a plane to Dallas. We said we would take it. I planned to send Diann on that plane and I would start hitchhiking. By the way! Diann was pregnant with Gerald at the time. The man told us to check into the Shaw Hotel and if there was a cancellation he would give us first chance. We had just got back to the hotel and the man had already called. We were two happy people knowing I wasn't going to have to hitchhike to Dallas.

We went to see Daddy and Mama at the Rock House in Rosamond. While we were home, Daddy said he knew where he could buy a pig to raise for slaughter. Diann and I bought the pig for him. It cost us ten dollars. We went with him to pick it up in a 1935 Chevrolet. Daddy put the pig in the trunk, but the trunk had a broken latch. We were going down the road when I saw a pig running in the field along the side of the car. I asked Daddy if that was not the pig we had just bought. Sure enough, the pig had gotten out. We chased that pig for fifteen to twenty minutes before we caught it. Both of us were ready to give out by the time the pig was put in the pen. We also went to see Diann's mother, but in Waco, not Dallas. She had been divorced many years before I had met her and Diann, and was dating a man named Lefty. After she made sure Diann was happily married, she and Lefty were married in July 1955. They had moved to Joey Drive, Waco, Texas.

Pictures around Hawaii in 1955

Aloha Tower, Honolulu Harbor

King Kamehameha

King Kamehameha on His Day

Eilonie Palace

Diamond Head, Waikiki, and Honolulu Waikiki Beach and Hotels

AE ("B") SCHOOL, NATECHTRACEN JACKSONVILLE, FLORIDA

January 1956 to November 1956

After my leave was nearly over, Diann and I headed for Jacksonville, Florida. We flew out of Dallas Love Field on a Delta Airlines aircraft. We arrived in the afternoon of 31 December 1955. I had no idea of what we were in for. While waiting for our luggage, I decided to call a cousin, Lovus Bowie. The first thing he asked was where we were staying. When I told him that we had just arrived and were going to find a hotel, he said that he would come get us and we could stay with them while we looked for an apartment. He said that today is "Gator Bowl Day" and that there isn't a room to be found anywhere in town. All motels and hotels were filled with college kids there for the big game. I didn't even think about the fact that this was New Year's Eve or the Gator Bowl football.

In order to enter "B" School, I had to extend my enlistment contract. I had to have at least one year of service remaining between the time I entered "B" School and the end of my enlistment. Because of a delay in receipt of my orders, I only had eleven months remaining. On 4 January 1956, I went to the base and signed an agreement to extend my enlistment for two years.

Diann and I lived with Lovus and his wife, Dolores, for about three weeks. There were not many apartments to be found that we could afford. Besides, Diann was pregnant and couldn't help in the search. Plus, I had to check in and start school on 6 January 1956, which meant that we could only go apartment hunting on the weekends. I didn't have a car, so we had to ride the bus to look for an apartment and to get to and from the base each day. The bus stop was about seven blocks from the Bowies' house. Luckily for me, it did not rain during the time that I was walking to and from the bus stop.

On 17 January 1956, Diann began having labor pains. We checked her in at the Naval Hospital that morning and she labored all that day and night. Of course, I planned to take a ten-day leave period, which would set me back in school to the next class that would start in February. At about 1000 hours on the 18 January, Gerald Lynn was born. The baby was two months premature and had several things wrong or incomplete. He lived for only about three hours. Gerald was buried in the Jacksonville Cemetery on 20 January 1956. In order to take care of the arrangements for the burial and also to be with Diann while recuperating, I took eight days leave from the 20 to 27 of January. Because of all the stress and anxiety of the events, I started smoking again. This time I quit after about two months.

During the period from the time Gerald was buried to the starting date of my next class, we had plenty of time to look for an apartment. We found one at 2784 Forbes St., Jacksonville, Florida, near Five Points. It was located completely across town from the Bowie's, but closer to the base. The building was a multiplex unit containing four apartments that each had a living room with a "hide-away" bed, a bedroom, bath, and a kitchen with a breakfast nook. The hot water unit was the most antiquated that I have ever seen. The water flowed through a coiled 3/4-inch pipe mounted above an open flame gas heating element and then into a pressurized holding tank. It is now outlawed from use. Our apartment was on the second floor. By today's standards, the apartment would be considered a fire hazard. There was only one way in and that was up a single flight of stairs. I still had to ride the bus to and from school, but the ride was much shorter than when we were staying with the Bowies. The bus stop was only two blocks away. Diann and I still walked or rode the bus to wherever we wanted to go. I started to school all over again on 10 February 1956.

2784 Forbes St., Jacksonville, Florida
Ed and Diann at the Entrance to Our Apartment, Which Is the Right Door Upstairs

Even in 1956, the buildings on most bases were still of the WWII vintage without air conditioning, equipped only with attic fans for cooling. In order to cool the rooms, the windows were raised about six inches to allow the attic fan to draw the air in. Most of the buildings had asbestos siding. "B" School students were allowed to smoke in class, but "AN-P" and "A" School students had designated smoking areas outside.

I still had duty every fourth day. As a PO2, I would have to muster at 1600 hours, but was free to go home until the time for my watch. I would stand either Master at Arms (MAA) duty at the EM Club or Petty Officer of the Watch (POW). One time, when standing MAA duty, I met Earl Duer, a person I had graduated with from Anna High School in 1952. He had joined the marines and was attending the Marine "AN-P" School. He was E3 and was amazed that I was already E5. We visited whenever I could get a free minute, which was not often. I never heard from or about him again. Another time while on duty at the EM Club, I met a girl by the last name of Smallwood, who had gone to Anna High School with my sister Elsie Marie. She knew of me, but not very well.

One Friday night, I had the 2000 to 2400 POW. I went to check on the post watch that was out by the perimeter fence. The post was fairly large and the man on watch was on the far end of the post. I had gotten out of the vehicle to locate him when I noticed two men under a street light about a block away. They separated and each man walked toward the opposite sides of the post. I stood concealed and stopped the man who had come to my side of the post. It just so happened that the man on watch detained the other individual. I asked the man in my custody what his intentions were and he said that he was a friend of the man on watch and had come to visit him. That was a NO, NO! So, I decided to confront the watch. He brought the other man in his custody to my location and we both questioned the culprits. The man on watch said that he did not know either of the men in custody. I knew that to make a report of the incident would require many hours of questioning and paperwork for both me and the man on watch. Our time on watch was almost over and I really didn't want to spend late hours filling out paperwork. I took the initiative and told the men, after writing down their names and living quarters, that I would give them a break. They could start walking back in the direction from which they had come and when I saw them pass under the street light where I had first seen them, then I would forget the incident and so would the man on watch. They did as I had suggested. Later I was telling my relief, AE2 Kemp, about the incident and he said, "Get in the truck and let's go look." I didn't know what to look for until he said that the two men had probably thrown a bottle of booze over the fence and were on their way to retrieve it. Sure enough we found their bottle, a pint of bourbon. I was riding with Kemp because I didn't own a car then, and had to wait until he had stood his watch in order to go home. We drank the evidence on the way home after Kemp's watch was over. It demonstrated how inexperienced I was at this time in my career. I had not been exposed to this kind of behavior before.

I was eligible to take the First Class Petty Officer exam, which would be given on 16 February. With the death of Gerald and with us looking for an apartment, I didn't take the time to study as I should have. However, I was awarded the Navy Good Conduct Medal on 14 February 1956 for service ending 19 November 1955, which gave me extra points toward promotion. I now had two ribbons to wear on my work uniform and two medals to put on my dress uniform. They were the National Defense Service Medal and the Good Conduct Medal. Promotions were determined by multiple points accumulated from awards, conduct, performance marks, number of years in service, number of years in pay grade, and test scores. Since I had only three years in service and only one year in pay grade, I had very few accumulative points. So, the Good Conduct Award sure would help. I took the test 16

February, but would not know the results until early May. I did feel somewhat confident about the test, although I had not studied for it.

AE "B" School was a thirty-three-week course with instructions on many subjects. The first three weeks was a math class consisting of simple addition, subtraction, multiplication, fractions, algebra, geometry, and trigonometry. I had algebra and geometry in high school, but the trigonometry was new to me. I first encountered the slide rule during this period. The instructor was a Marine Tech Sergeant named Smith. He was tenacious in teaching us about the exponents, mantissas, and logarithms. I had some difficulty, but completed that portion without failure.

One of our classes was in a building by the Marine AN-P School with their smoking area between the buildings. We were taught generator and motor theory in this class. One day while sitting in the classroom, I noticed a skunk beneath a window of the AN-P School building. About that same time the smoking break bell sounded for the marine students. As one marine came around the building to the smoking area, he also saw the skunk. He picked up a brick from the yard and clobbered the skunk. Of course, the skunk immediately sprayed the area. The attic fans drew the fumes in through the window, polluting the whole building. It was comical seeing all of the instructors exiting that building from all doors to get away from the odor. They held classes outside the rest of that day. I don't know if the identity of the one who threw the brick was learned, but I'm sure the whole class was punished for that act.

In May, the results from the February exam were in. I was not on the list for promotion. A man whose name was on the list stopped me and said I had almost made the list. I don't know where or how he came across the information, but he had a test score of 54 and was being promoted. He said that my test score was 53. I had missed it by only one question. I would have to take the test again in August, so I decided to make sure I would study harder and be more prepared for it next time.

I was always trying to better myself and applied for every program that could enhance my education and career. During this time, the navy instituted a program whereby they would pay for a four-year college tuition at Purdue University. I applied and was considered eligible to take the entrance exam. There was only one other person in the entire "B" School who was eligible. We both took the exam, which was four hours long. Each portion was a timed test. When the results were announced, he was selected and I was not.

During the seventeenth week, we were taught magnetism. AEC E. E. Weeks was the instructor. He tried his best to teach us all about the properties of magnets. He told us about gausses, maxwell, and oersteds. What was most memorable about his class was his statement at the end of each session. He would ask, "What does that teach you?" Then, he would always say, "It teaches you to put a keeper on a horseshoe magnet." The purpose of the class was to prepare us for the next class about transformer theory. I was an "A" student to this point. For some reason, I could not grasp or comprehend the transformer theory. I ended up failing that course and was set back to the next class and had to go through the course a second time, which was three weeks later. Because of my previous high grades, all the instructors accused me of failing the course on purpose. I tried to assure them that I had not. I had held third place in class standing when I flunked that course and when I was placed in the new class, I still held the third place standing.

There were two other individuals with better standings in grade point than I. One was a marine and the other was AE1 Bill Purcell. Purcell was one pay grade ahead of me. He was a First Class Petty Officer and I was a Second Class Petty Officer. I started studying harder at night and it wasn't long before only hundredths of a point separated the three of us. I was striving for the first place position. In the end, they both beat me out, with the marine getting the top honors. I still had the third place spot.

Although I had signed an agreement to extend my enlistment contract in January 1956, it would not go into effect until 20 November. I could reenlist up to three months early, which was 20 August. Diann and I talked it over and it was decided that I would reenlist. So, on 27 September 1956, I reenlisted into the US Navy for a period of four years. As a bonus for reenlisting, the navy would give me three months base pay, plus I could sell up to sixty days leave and the State of Texas would give me $300 mustering out pay. I received $800 base pay, $429.78 for fifty-eight days of leave, and the $300 for a total of $1,529.78. Until this time, we did not have enough money to buy an automobile.

After I had been in school for a little while, some of the men asked if I would be in a carpool with them. Since I didn't have a car, I would give ten dollars a week to cover expenses. Gas at that time was fifteen to eighteen cents per gallon. I was in the pool with AE2 Davidson, AE1 Paulette, AE2 Kemp, and AE2 DeRoucher. After I reenlisted, Diann and I went to a Ford dealer and bought a 1956 Ford Custom, light blue and white. We paid $1,600 for it. I couldn't afford the extra expense for the Fairlane. Now I didn't have to pay them the ten dollars because I could drive some of the time. The only problem with the carpool was that Petty Officer Davidson always wanted to stop at some bar on the way home each Friday and have a beer. So, when it was his week to drive I was always late in getting home from school. If I had any money for a pay phone, I would always call Diann to let her know I was going to be late. There had been many times that I didn't have any money.

While Diann and I were living in Jacksonville, we would spend our weekends according to our money situation. Sometimes we went to Jacksonville Beach. That would be an all-day affair. It was a good distance, so we had to take a bus to get there. Other times, we would go to a movie on base. We enjoyed ourselves, even though we didn't have much money. One day we were at the beach with some friends. The man and I were playing with a rubber ball in the surf. He threw the ball one time and I tried to catch it, but missed. The ball stripped my wedding ring from my finger. We searched for that ring for a long time before giving up. We were both upset about it. After

I was able to buy a car we could go farther. We went to St. Petersburg to see my brother and sister in-law, George and Jean; then to Daytona to see another brother and his wife, Herman and Betty.

My father-in-law and mother-in-law came to visit during the Fourth of July week. Babe and Loraine Toon came with them. I could only visit with them at night or on the weekend. So, while I was in school, they and Diann would go to the beach or other places. That was a fun time while they were there. Luckily there were two beds in the apartment, but still Babe and Loraine slept on a pallet in the living room.

The only other visitor we had was Harvey Perry, my brother-in-law. He was working for TEMCO on some missile program and they sent him to Jacksonville to work on the planes. I never knew exactly what. We enjoyed his visit very much.

I completed AE "B" School on 19 October 1956. Because I had been on sea duty prior to the school assignment, I was eligible for shore duty. When my orders came in they were for ATU 614 in Hutchinson, Kansas. The day I checked out for my new duty station, I drove 1,100 miles, straight through to Dallas. However, somewhere along the way we did stop to get a couple of hours of sleep about two in the morning. Diann did not know how to drive at that time.

AE "B" School, Jacksonville, Florida, July 1956
Top Row: Unknown,   Unknown,   AE2 Davidson
Second row: AE1 Purcell,   AEC Smith,   Unknown,   AE2 Marquette
First Row: AE1 Ewald,   AE2 Kemp,   AE1 Paulette,   AE2 Hudson

AVIATION TRAINING UNIT 614 NAS HUTCHINSON, KANSAS

November 1956 to April 1958

Navy P2V-4

On transit leave on our way to Hutchinson, Kansas, we went to see Daddy and Mama, who still lived in the Rock House. Lillie was going to school in Westminster. One Friday night, I took Daddy to meet Lillie at a football game at the Westminster School. I was in my new 1956 Ford automobile. Eck Brown was there. He seemed really surprised that I could afford a new car. Daddy seemed really proud of my accomplishments and happy that night. November 1956, was the last time that I saw Daddy alive. After Diann and I had moved to Hutchinson, Kansas, Daddy, Mama, and Lillie moved back into the house on the hill. It was where they lived when Daddy went to be with the Lord.

Diann and I arrived in Hutchinson, Kansas, on the afternoon of 19 November 1956. We found a little motel on the east side of town and checked in. The next morning we bought a newspaper and started looking for a place to rent. We didn't care if what we found was an apartment or a house. We just knew that it had to be one we could afford. I checked into the Duty Office at 2000 hours on 20 November 1956. I wanted to see the Duty Yeoman. The Chief of the Watch wanted to know why. I told him that I wanted the Duty Yeoman to check the promotion list to see if I had passed the test and was cited for promotion to First Class Petty Officer. He came back and told me that I had passed with a promotion date of 16 November 1956. That was good news to me. Now I would be checking in as an E6 instead as E5. Also, on 20 November 1956, I completed four years of service. Both of these feats meant an increase in pay.

AE1 Skislack was in charge of the electric shop when I checked in. He said I would be happy with my promotion to first class because I would have less duty watches to stand than the second class did. I got my new stripe sewn on before being assigned to the electric shop. One of the first persons I met was AD1 Van Pembroke, who had been stationed in Hawaii when I was there. He knew how long I had been in the navy and told me that I had not been in long enough to be a First Class Petty Officer. "Ski" was the only other first class in the shop and also the highest ranking individual. He said that he would give me two weeks to get orientated and learn the P2V aircraft electrical systems, and then I would be assigned as the Night Crew Leading Petty Officer.

We stayed in the motel for about a week before finding a house to rent at 816 West Fourteenth St., Hutchinson, Kansas. Mrs. Lear was the landlady who lived two houses down. We shared the driveway with Mr. and Mrs. Byroad next door. There was a detached two-car garage, which we also shared. The house had a basement, living room, one bedroom, a bath, and kitchen with a breakfast nook. There was a big backyard and a garden spot beyond that. Also, just after we moved into the rental house, I registered our car. The license number was RN 9910.

816 West Fourteenth St., Hutchinson, Kansas

I was there one week when Ski said that he had to assign me to the night crew the next day. The Maintenance Chief wanted me in there now. I knew now what Van Pembroke was saying, I didn't have the experience to be in charge. I was only twenty four years old with only four years of service and now in charge of several men and with the responsibility of ensuring the work for the whole shop during the night shift. Although I had been through both "A" and "B" electrical schools, I had worked on only one aircraft. I did not know the systems of the P2V-4 aircraft. So, I had to get myself indoctrinated in a hurry. I soon learned that the P2V-4 had Pratt & Whitney 3350 engines and Hamilton props, the same as those on the R7V Super Constellation, which I had worked on while in VR-8. It wasn't so hard after all.

There were six men in the shop on nights. Two of the men had a little knowledge of the aircraft electrical systems, but the other three men did not. In fact, they were fresh out of "A" School and had never worked on any aircraft. Their names are Leo Rosenberg, Robbie Robinson, and Ollie Olson. Our mission was to ensure the availability of aircraft to meet the next day's flight schedule, plus ten percent. Sometimes we worked from 1700 hours through the night to sunup. However, there were times when the crew could go home early because all the work had been completed. I usually released the men without checking with the Maintenance Chief. One night, Chief Smith asked where I thought I was going. I told him, "Home." He had just been assigned as the Night Maintenance Chief. From that time on, I had to get permission before I could release the crew.

The primary mission of the Training Unit was to train naval officers in navigational skills. Most all flights were extended flights from Hutchinson to Shreveport, Louisiana, to Tucumcari, New Mexico, and then back to Hutchinson. As a first class electrician, I was on authorized crew member flight pay for the purpose of performing maintenance tests of electrical equipment during flight. In order to qualify to receive the pay, I had to complete a minimum of four flight hours each month. Sometimes there was no need to perform any test of equipment, so I would go on a flight just to qualify for my flight pay. I would be assigned the task as lookout on those flights. I would watch the surrounding sky for other aircraft that might come into the vicinity of the plane. I was to alert the pilot of such aircraft. I really liked those times. The country below was always so fascinating. Just to observe the change in the terrain as we flew over it, always amazed me.

For some reason, I always trusted the pilot and never thought about the possibility of an accident. I remember only one flight when a problem occurred where there was the possibility of having to ditch. We all got into our ditching stations, but the crew members got the problem corrected, so all was okay. On every flight there would be some kind of emergency drill for training purposes. Those drills would teach the crew members what to do during an actual emergency. During my tour in the unit, there were only two aircraft accidents. There was only one where the crew had to bail out. The other made a crash landing on base. I was not on either of the planes. The aircraft were P2V-4s, which had the wing spar in the middle of the fuselage that separated the forward and rear compartments with a big hump. In order to get from one compartment to the other, one had to lay on their stomach or back and slide over the hump. I was always in the rear compartment. The bad thing was that the rear compartment didn't have a heater. I had to really bundle up during the winter flights. The pilots knew how cold it could get in the rear compartment and would let us slide over the hump into the forward compartment to get warm every so often. I always dreaded going back to the rear after getting warm.

During the holiday period, the night operations were suspended and the night crew worked days. I joined Ski and two others in a carpool. One day it was my time to drive and it began to snow while I was picking everyone up for work. By the time we arrived at the base, about two inches had fallen. By the time we had changed into our work clothes, there were about four inches on the ground and the CO had decided to close the base. Everyone who wanted to go home had to be off the base by 1000 hours. There were about six inches on the ground by the time we got off the base and on the highway home. It was fourteen miles from the base to town and I didn't have snow chains. The traffic was bumper to bumper on the road. I was able to stay on the road by being very careful, but several cars were already in the ditch. The way the snow was blowing, it didn't take long for them to be covered over. We were hoping that the people had gotten out and found a ride. I knew if I could keep the car moving, no matter how slow, it would make it through the snow. Once a car stopped it was hard to get moving again. The wheels would spin and start sliding toward the ditch.

About halfway to town, I saw the car about six ahead sliding sideways and the other cars stopping. I knew that if I stopped, I would not be able to get rolling again. I slowly pulled into the other lane and passed them. All the vehicles were going to town and none were coming from town. All my passengers were pleased with my driving ability in the snow. It took four hours to go fourteen miles and deliver everyone to their homes. I got home about three o'clock in the afternoon. We were snowed in for four days. I was lucky to get our car in the garage. During those four days, I built a snowman in the backyard. I put my neckerchief and hat on it to look like a sailor.

1956 Ford in Driveway

Snowman

During the holiday season of 1956, Diann and I just enjoyed our new home away from home. Ski and his wife, Jan, had us over for Thanksgiving Day celebration. They had five children, three boys and two girls. Christmas we celebrated alone, but New Year's Eve I had duty. The senior Watch Petty Officer considered Thanksgiving Day and Christmas Day as family times and New Year's as bachelors' time. Therefore, he assigned me the midnight watch on New Year's Eve. December 1956 was the second Christmas for Diann and me since we were married. Of course, we had to have a Christmas tree with presents for each other. I bought Diann a vacuum cleaner from Sears & Roebuck. Most would say that wasn't a present, it was a household item, but Diann was happy with it.

Ed and Diann, Christmas 1956

Shortly after the holidays, another first class named Raymond Johnson checked into the electric shop. His wife, Lee, was expecting their fourth child. Although he was senior to me and would normally be put in charge of the night crew, due to Lee's pregnancy, I was back on nights.

I was in a carpool with Leo Rosenberg. He was an Airman fresh out of "A" School at this time, but was advanced to Third Class Petty Officer after the February 1957 exam. It sure helped both of us with our finances, although gas was only seventeen or so cents per gallon. Some nights we would get off early and other times we worked until the wee hours in the morning.

There are two electrical problems that come to mind. One was a landing gear indication problem. It was a broken wire on a switch located on the landing wheel strut. The wire had to be soldered to a lug on the switch. It was bitter cold and the snow was about four inches deep. The aircraft was on the back line just about as far from the hangar as it could be. Another electrician and I were tasked with making the repair. It took more time getting wrapped up and prepared to do the job than it did to complete the job. Getting the soldering iron hot enough to do the job was a task unto itself. After the job was completed, I was so cold. I started running for the hangar. I didn't notice the aircraft tie-down cable and it caught me across the shins. I went tumbling into the snow and slid about twenty feet. I was so cold that I didn't feel a thing.

The other problem involved a generator problem. During a flight the pilot, for some reason unknown, turned off one of the generators; then it would not come online when turned on again. He pushed a test light to determine if the generator was putting out power and the generator came online. The pilot, being curious, turned off the generator again. The only way to get it back online was to push the test light. The problem was puzzling to me. I solved the puzzle while studying the schematic of the system. This was one of the few problems that I figured out without going to the aircraft. I told a PO3 to go to the hump in the aircraft, remove a panel cover, and reset a particular circuit breaker. He came back to the shop and asked how I knew that circuit breaker was tripped. The push to test circuit was wired in such a way that when pushed it would supply power to the generator control relay. This power would normally be supplied through the circuit breaker.

The winters in Kansas were much more severe than either Diann or I had experienced before. The temperature was a lot colder and the wind would just blow right through a person. In 1957, the word hypothermia was unheard of. After being stationed in Hawaii and in Jacksonville, it took some time for us to get acclimated. That year was also the year of the Asian flu. I contracted the flu in January and was laid up for several days. We had a nineteen-inch black and white television. I can remember lying on the couch with a 105 degree temperature and couldn't see anything but a blur. Luckily, it lasted only about five days and Diann did not catch it.

One night in late spring, we got off about 2300 hours. By the time we changed into our liberty uniforms and were out the gate, it was nearing midnight. About halfway to town there was a slight curve in the road. When approaching that section of the road I saw a flash of lights go up into the sky. I told Leo that it looked as if someone didn't make the turn and ran off the road. We came upon an auto accident involving a 1953 Chevrolet and a1954 Mercury. The Mercury, with four sailors who were returning to the base after a night on the town, had crossed the center line and was hit on the passenger side by the Chevrolet, with four air force personnel in it who were trying to get to town before the bars closed. All eight men were killed.

Leo and I were the second to arrive on the scene. Soon other cars were there. There was gasoline all over and the ignition switches were still on. The driver of the Chevrolet was bent over the steering wheel and had to be moved in order to get to the ignition. I pulled him back and his head rolled back against me, splattering blood all over my white uniform. I turned off the ignition and let the ambulance crew, who had just arrived, take over.

Diann was experiencing morning sickness in her pregnancy and I sure didn't want her to see me like this. She would think that I had been involved in an accident. When I got home I called her from outside and told her that I was okay, but looked terrible; then I told Diann what had happened and how the blood had gotten on me, before I went into the house.

My Daddy went to be with the Lord on 24 May 1957. I know that he must have been happy because the Lord took him while he was doing what he liked best, "FISHING!" Mama knew to contact the Red Cross, so they could send a telegram to inform the Base. I started making preparations to go to the funeral the day I learned of Daddy's passing, but I couldn't leave until the next day. That night it rained and rained. There were severe storms in Texas and Oklahoma with tornadoes and heavy rain that caused lots of destruction and flooding. Diann and I were traveling on Highway 77, somewhere in Oklahoma, in our 1956 Ford. We came upon one place where the water was flowing over the highway for about 300 yards. Not knowing how deep the water was, I was afraid to try to drive through it. While we were sitting there trying to decide what to do, a 1957 Ford drove up and stopped. The driver looked the situation oven then proceeded to drive through the water. We watched the car drive through without any problem. Our car was higher off the ground than the 1957 Ford, so I decided if they could drive through the water, so could I. We had gotten almost halfway through when a big semi truck came from the opposite direction. That truck made the biggest waves I had ever seen on a small pond. The water came up over the hood of the car and almost drowned out the engine. The motor was running on about two cylinders by the time we got to the other side. I could not believe that truck would not wait for us to get through.

We saw a lot of damage en route to Mama's. When we got to Mama's, the creek where Daddy had died was over its banks. Had they not found Daddy when they did, his body would have been washed away.

The year 1957 was a bad year for storms. Several times I had to shovel snow in order to get out of the driveway. Also, there were many thunderstorms that rumbled through the state that year. Besides the storm that had occurred at the time of Daddy's death, there was a bad one in July. This one produced a tornado that came right over our house. It happened just as we were going to bed. In fact, Diann was already in bed and I was just getting in. Diann was pregnant with Bruce at the time. The house had only one bedroom. We had shoved our bed next to the wall to make room for the baby crib. I had to crawl into bed from the foot. As I was doing so, I looked out the window and saw debris flying across the road. I told Diann to get into the basement NOW! The back door was open and she JUST had to close it. She turned around to go down the basement steps and the door flew open again, knocking her down the steps. She had a big black bruise where the doorknob hit her. I thought for sure she was hurt real badly, but the bruise was all she had.

The tornado came over our house at treetop level. I couldn't see anything out the basement windows, but knew that I should be able to. The next morning we found tree limbs piled around the house and a huge tree down across the driveway. It had broken down the garage door, but didn't damage the car. I couldn't get my car out of the garage. I called the base and they told me to stay home because there were power lines down all over town. All I had to cut the tree into pieces was a hand saw and a hatchet. It took me all that day to clear the driveway.

Sometimes our squadron flight crew would take extended training flights to places outside of the normal training area. Some of the flights would go to the Caribbean countries, including Cuba. When they went on these missions, they would bring cheap booze to anyone who had the money and asked for the booze. Olson had asked a person to bring him a case of whiskey. Since he lived in the barracks, he had no place to keep it. He asked me if I would keep the whiskey at my house. I agreed. One weekend I invited him and Robinson out for grilled hamburgers in the backyard. He opened one of his bottles for us to have some drinks. I had no idea that he was an alcoholic. He would not put the bottle down until it was completely finished. I would not let him have another one. He was out of his mind. Poor Robby! He stayed up all night with Olson. I gave them some sleeping bags so they could stay in the backyard. I was glad that the next day was Sunday and they didn't have to go to work. I took them to the base that Sunday morning and never invited them out again. When Olson was going home on leave, I let him have the rest of his whiskey. I learned from that mistake and never let anyone keep booze at my house again.

The plane that had brought the whiskey for Olson had gone to Cuba. During the trip, the crew encountered all sorts of mechanical problems. Someone went to extremes to depict the amount of difficulty they had experienced. A patch was placed on two propeller blades of one engine. Also patches were placed in various places on the fuselage. Everyone walking by the plane would stop and stare in amazement. The patches were placed there as a joke.

I don't remember the exact time of year, but William Jack Partain checked into the shop. He had also been in VR-8 with me. He had some wild tales about Chief Matherly that happened after I had left. One of them was the shop door. He had ordered someone to paint the door again. A coat was put on one side then opened to do the other side. The door fell off the hinges because of the weight of the amount of paint that had been put on through the years.

Jack was basically a good person. He was proficient as an electrician with high quality workmanship. However, he was not dedicated toward attendance. When he went on liberty, he sometimes would forget to return to the base on time. Sometimes he would be AWOL for days. When he did report, he knew that he was in for some sort of disciplinary punishment. The three First Class Petty Officers in the shop would take turns going to Captain's Mast with him. During the time he was there, he had been to mast so many times that the

Captain knew him by his first name. I can remember one time when I went to mast with him, the Captain said, "Well, Jack, let me hear your tale about this time; you always amaze me with your stories." He was an unforgettable character.

Another unforgettable person is Fred Bolls. I met Fred in Jacksonville in "B" School. We both went to Hutchinson from school, but were assigned to different units. He was in the first unit and I was in the third. One weekend, I invited him to our house for dinner. Fred was a First Class Petty Officer who was not married and lived in the barracks. After that first invitation, he would show up at the front door just at dinner time from one to three times a month. He never called ahead of time to ask whether we were busy or not. Diann and I began to dread knocks on the door when we were at the dinner table. Of course, we would ask him to join us although we may not have much to eat. We would never tell him that he was not welcome. This went on all year long. Finally, one day he came early, before Diann had started cooking the evening meal, and asked if we would join him for dinner at a restaurant. We both liked to have fainted, but gladly accepted. It was the first and only time that he took us out to dinner.

Mother-in-law and Lefty came to visit us in July. It sure was good to have company from home, but having only one bedroom made for cramped quarters. They had Fred and Beverly with them. Creba and Louis were in the process of moving from Dallas to Louisville, Kentucky, so they were keeping the kids. We made pallets for Fred and Bev; Diann and I slept on the foldout bed in the living room, and my mother-in-law and Lefty slept in the bedroom.

I always had the desire to further my education. So, in September 1957 I enrolled in Hutchinson Junior College for the fall semester. I signed up for algebra, English, and speech. I had no idea of how bad a decision that would be. I was working the night shift and attending classes during the day. Diann was pregnant with our son.

On 26 September 1957, Leo and Judy Rosenberg gave me a birthday party. It was my twenty-fifth birthday. There were several people who attended and all had a good time. Although there were alcoholic beverages, no one appeared to have enough to even get a hangover. I had ample myself. The next morning I got up feeling very good. In fact, I was planning on going to school that day. I went into the bathroom, brushed my teeth, shaved, and used the commode. When I reached back to flush the commode I noticed the stool was blood red. I thought to myself that I must be dying. Although I didn't feel anything, I am bleeding to death.

Diann was so far along in her pregnancy with Bruce that I didn't want to tell her. I didn't want her to worry. I went to work early and stopped by the hospital clinic to get checked out. The doctor was very nice and told me to take these pills and not to eat any solid foods for dinner, and to give myself an enema that night, again in the morning, and return to the hospital. I had to tell Diann now, so she wouldn't cook dinner for me. I did as told and the doctor located a hemorrhoid seventeen centimeters up my rear end. The hemorrhoid wasn't serious enough for removal and I was to reduce it with medication. Man! I sure thought I was a goner with all that blood in the stool.

On 17 October 1957, I took a night flight just to get my allotted time in order to qualify to receive my flight pay. Each person drawing non crew member pay (called skins) had to have a minimum of four hours each month. I had gone to work at regular time at 1700 hours, but the flight did not actually take off until midnight on the 18 October. I got home after the flight at about 0530 and into bed about 0600.

Diann awoke me at 0900, telling me that she had stomach pains. I asked her if the pains could be labor pains, but she didn't know. After a little while, she had another one that was more severe than all the others. She called the doctor while I got dressed; then we departed for the hospital. We arrived at the hospital at about 10:00. The nurse told me to wait in the waiting room until they got Diann prepped for child delivery and then I could go in the labor room and sit with her. I waited fifteen, thirty, forty-five minutes and no one came out to get me. I was getting anxious by now, and finally went to inquire why no one had called me to go to the labor room. A nurse told me she would check for me. She came back and said that Diann was in the delivery room having our baby. Bruce was born at 1053. It took fifty-three minutes for Bruce to come into this world from the time we arrived at the hospital. After I had determined that both Diann and Bruce were okay, I went home to get some rest myself. I still had to go to work that night. We had decided that I would not take leave from work until they came home from the hospital. When I got to the house, Mr. Byroad came over to learn all the details. He offered me a cigarette. He and I sat at the dining table and had a cup of coffee with the smoke. After he left, I went into the bathroom and vomited. I did not try to have another cigarette after that for years.

It was totally a new life in our house, since we now had the responsibility of caring for a baby. I was working nights, going to college during the day, and tending to a new baby. Bruce developed the colic, which lasted for six months. Diann and I would take turns getting up with him. Of course, when I was away, she had to take care of him by herself. It would take an hour to get him satisfied and sleeping. He would sleep an hour and need tending to again. Whoever had taken care of getting him to sleep last would stay in bed and the other would get up to tend to him. So, basically we slept two hours, then up for an hour, then back to sleep for two hours. One month of this schedule was taking a toll on my grades. I finally dropped the speech class. After another month, I dropped the English class. Finally, I just had to quit altogether.

Neither Diann nor I knew how to handle Bruce. In the daytime, he seemed to do just fine, but at night he wouldn't or couldn't sleep and neither could we. One week, Creba and Louis came to see us on their way to Waco from Louisville, Kentucky. The first thing Creba did was give Bruce one of George's pacifiers. George was four months older than Bruce. Bruce slept all night long. Neither Diann nor I could believe that we had stayed in bed all night. We had not had that much rest in months. When Diann was in town, she was sure to buy some pacifiers for Bruce.

Bruce at Three Months Old

In January 1958, the navy instituted a new program to motivate individuals to proficiency. In fact, it was called "Proficiency Pay," (pro pay for short). Those people who were recommended by their CO would be eligible to take the exam in February. I was one of the lucky individuals who were recommended. When it came time to take the exam, I found out it was the very same exam that other men were taking for advancement to Chief Petty Officer. AD1 Van Pembroke saw me and wanted to know how I could be taking that exam. He said, "Man! You haven't been in the navy long enough to be a First Class Petty Officer, much less a Chief. I didn't tell him that I was taking the pro pay exam.

After we got back to the electric shop, Ski, Ray, and I were talking over the questions on the exam. They were all multiple choice questions. During the discussion, I told Ski that he had not passed the exam because he had missed so many of the questions. He really didn't believe that I knew what I was talking about. He would read the question until he saw an answer that fit what he had read. He would not read the rest of the question. As it turned out, I was right. He didn't get promoted to Chief, but also the Pro Pay Bill had failed to be approved by Congress for that year and I didn't get pro pay, either.

Also in January 1958, Congress approved a change in the Social Security system and started withholding Social Security Tax from servicemen's pay each month. Prior to that time, men in service did not pay into Social Security, even though they had an SSN.

In order to improve my educational background, I continued working on correspondence courses. During my tour in ATU 614, I completed the following courses:

Date Comp.	Course		Grade
1/21/57	GTC for POs	NavPers 91203	3.75
11/20/57	Aviation Electrician's Mate, Vol. I	NavPers 91610-B	3.86
11/20/57	Aircraft Instruments	NavPers 91627-1A	3.63

In fact, to continue the education and proficiency of all the people in the division, classes were conducted whenever workloads permitted. Since I was in charge of the night crew, it was my responsibility to teach the lesson. Preparing for the lessons helped me in my promotion to higher ranks. I know that it helped Leo Rosenberg because I met him years later as a LTJG.

In January 1958, the station started a renovation of the streets of the base. We were all pretty happy about that because there were several bad potholes in the street, which we had to traverse to get to work. Several of the buildings were refurbished also. The enlisted barracks were much better for the men. Morale was very high at that time. But in March, we wondered why all that money had been spent to make the base a much better place to live and work because orders came in to close the base effective 1 July 1958. I still cannot understand the reasoning for wasting the taxpayers' money like that. Surely the CO had known about the base closure before the paving was started. Anyway, I received orders for ATU 601 in Corpus Christi, Texas, and checked out on 15 April 1958. The base did, in fact, close on 1 July 1958.

AVIATION TRAINING UNIT 601
NAS CORPUS CHRISTI, TEXAS

2 May 1958 to 19 December 1958

Beech SNB-5 Navigation Trainer

After only a year and a half in Hutchinson, Kansas, I was transferred in May 1958 to Naval Air Station, Corpus Christi, Texas, to finish out my shore duty tour. We had our household goods shipped and packed our car. We then turned over our keys to the house at 816 West Fourteenth St., Hutchinson, Kansas, to Mrs. Lear and headed for Texas. I had three days travel time, plus I took ten days leave, which gave us two weeks to get to Corpus Christi and find a place to live. As we passed through Waco, Texas, Diann and I left Bruce with his granny and grandpa, Lefty, on Joey Drive while we went to Corpus Christi to look for a place to live. Neither of us had ever been to Corpus Christi before so we did not have any idea of where to begin. We stayed in a rundown wooden motel on North Beach, bought a newspaper, and started looking through the ads for places we could afford. We found a duplex at 2707 Ayers Street with two bedrooms, a kitchen complete with stove and refrigerator, a bathroom, and a large living room and dining room combination. One thing about this house was the second bedroom. Now Bruce had his own separate bedroom. The house was large enough so that Bruce had plenty of room to move around in his walker/stroller. The rent was something we could afford and it was located conveniently near four large grocery stores. However, the down side, it was also located just across the street from a funeral home and mortuary. The house was also just a little way from Del Mar College.

2707 Ayers Street, Corpus Christi, Texas

Without checking in, we made arrangements to have our household effects delivered. After getting all of our furniture moved in, we went back to Waco to pick up Bruce. We had applied for on-base housing, but there was none available. The base was located about ten miles from downtown Corpus Christi. There were two ways to get to the base; along the water line, called Ocean Drive, or Staple Street to Padre Island Drive. Each of these roads went through a few miles of cotton fields. Ocean Drive and Alameda Boulevard intersected at the Oso Canal with only one road crossing to the base. Ocean Drive was such a pretty drive. The Padre Island Drive went across the Oso waterway and through the town of Flour Bluff. The base was located at the edge of Flour Bluff city limits.

Although we still had our almost new 1956 Ford Fairlane, Diann had not learned to drive and, therefore, did not have her driver's license. So, I drove to work each day and sometimes she would walk to the stores just down the street. I would drive her to the base and let her practice driving on the unused streets in the old housing area, which had been abandoned. I tried to teach her everything that she might encounter in taking a driving test. She became fairly proficient in driving, but not parking. She just could not get the hang of parallel parking. I got her the Driver's Hand Book, which she studied thoroughly. Finally, one day we decided she was ready to take the exam for a Texas Driver's License. Sure enough, she passed everything except parallel parking. The inspector let her get her license anyway. However, I still had to use the car each day because there was no one near with whom I could carpool and the bus line was too far away. In order to ride the bus, I would have to transfer twice. I would have to leave too early in the morning to get to work on time. Then, I would also be late getting home.

The base was considered a whole complex at that time. A Commanding Officer, who was a Navy Captain, was in charge of all the activities of the base except the Chief of Naval Air Advance Training, which was headed by a Rear Admiral. There were several Air Training Units (ATUs) on the base commanded by navy commanders. All the men and officers who reported onboard were assigned from a central personnel office. I checked into the administration office and was assigned to the electric shop of ATU 601. Most of the people who came from Hutchinson were assigned to ATU 501, but I wasn't allowed. I was told there were too many First Class Petty Officers already in 501. ATU 501 operated P2V aircraft, with which I was familiar, and P5M Seaplane aircraft. There were two other squadrons, ATU 301, that had A4U aircraft, and ATU 401 that had US2C utility aircraft. The ATU 601 had SNB aircraft. It was a small two-engine, seven-passenger plane. Again, the primary mission was navigator training.

I checked into the electric shop to find a Chief in Charge, AEC St. Ones, and one other First Class, AE1 McCreedy. But, this time, I was the senior First Class. Man! I didn't have all that much time in service, yet, I'm the next senior man in the shop. Only the Chief was senior to me. There were four Second Class Petty Officers and I can't remember how many Third Class Petty Officers and Airmen in the shop. Again, I was assigned flight pay for maintenance testing purposes. The aircraft was the SNB, which was so small and basic that it didn't take long to learn all the systems. I soon became friends with the first class, a second class, and a third class and settled into the routine.

One of the peculiar discrepancies I remember was with the aircraft flaps. The gripe read that the flap would creep after the switch was turned off. The Chief and the other First Class Petty Officer worked on the gripe for a couple of days before I got involved. Looking over the schematic, I determined that the system had dynamic braking. Someone had replaced the flap control relay with a landing gear control relay. They looked the same, but were different electrically. The reason that the wrong relay was installed was that there were no flap relays in the supply storage. I discovered that the landing gear control relay would work if one of the terminals was shorted to ground. I made a short jumper wire and installed it. There were never any more problems with that system. It took months before the correct relay was available. No one ever knew that this particular plane had a modified landing gear relay in the flap control system.

The duty section was also the night crew for the shop. Being the senior man, when on duty I was also responsible for getting all the work completed. One day we had a lot of aircraft needing work in order to meet the next day's flight schedule. One of the Second Class Petty Officers told me that he had football practice and would not be available for work that night. I let him know that, in my books, work came before play; that there was too much work and he could not go to practice that evening. He told me that he was on Admiral Clifton's team and that he could not miss practice. Again, I told him that he couldn't go. A while later, my name was called over the hangar PA system, stating that I had a phone call in the duty office. A voice over the phone was very loud and gruff saying, "How dare you keep one of my men from football practice." I tried to explain the situation with the amount of work; the man wouldn't listen to me. He said that if the second class was not on the practice field in ten minutes, I would suffer the consequence. I let the second class go. The man on the phone said that he was supposedly Admiral Clifton himself, but I never knew for sure. The next day, I was telling the Chief and others in the shop about my experience the night before. The Chief told me that it was most likely the Admiral and it was good for me that I let the second class go to practice. Sports, was one of the Admiral's most prized interests. I guess aircraft maintenance was on the lower end of his interests.

I had been there about two months when I saw a person that had been in Hutchinson, Kansas, with me. He was a First Class Petty Officer in Hutchinson, but now he was wearing Airman stripes. I asked what had happened. He said he was found guilty of making a fraudulent statement and was reduced in pay grade to Airman. He said that he had applied for travel pay too early. He and his family had stopped off at his mother-in-law's house on the way from Hutchinson and that his wife had decided to stay there while he found a place to live. Before going back to pick her up after finding a place to live, he had filed for travel pay for his whole family. Had he gone back to get his wife first, there wouldn't have been a problem. But since he didn't, he was charged with falsifying his wife's travel and filing a fraudulent claim. His wife came on down to Corpus Christi immediately after hearing of the charge. He had filed a rebuttal and was hoping for a reinstatement to First Class. About a month later I saw him and he was wearing First Class stripes again. Hearing his story, I was glad that Diann and I had made the trip together.

One of the things I liked about Corpus Christi was the fishing. There was no license required to fish in saltwater. Although I didn't always catch much, I still liked to go. I would nearly always go to the base and fish off the piers. There were bait stands along the way and it wasn't all that far. It was a pretty good drive to the Gulf Coast. The first time I went fishing in saltwater was an unforgettable experience. Petty Officer Renfro asked me if I would like to go with him one Friday night. Naturally, I accepted the invitation. We went to the causeway to Padre Island to fish in the inner coastal canal. We stopped to buy bait at a bait stand near where Renfro wanted to fish. While at the bait stand, a man asked us what we were hoping to catch. Renfro told him anything that was edible. The man said that he had thirty-two fish already cleaned and on ice that we could have if we wanted them, that he was getting tired of messing with them. We readily accepted the fish. Since those fish were on ice, we put them in our cooler, but still wanted to fish for ourselves. Renfro caught the first fish, which was a golden croaker. It's edible. Then he caught a speckled trout, which is also edible. Finally, I caught one, but when I pulled it in Renfro said,

"Oh, Man! That's a dog fish!" It was the ugliest fish I had ever seen of course, inedible. Renfro caught a couple more good fish and then I caught a sea robin, another inedible ugly fish. I then caught some hardhead catfish and a stingray. We fished all night long and Renfro caught six edible fish. I caught several fish, but none that were keepers or edible. Renfro declared me a jinx.

There was a first class mechanic who lived on the base with his large family. I don't remember his name. In order to feed all of the family, he would fish most every day. He would tie a string on his finger and bait a small hook with dough bait. He would drop the hook along the seawall to catch piggy perch to use as bait on another line that he would cast a way out for bigger fish. I was observing him one day when he caught a big fish on the main line. He was trying to reel it in moving his hands in jerking motions. That motion kept bobbing the dough bait line. About a sixteen-inch skip jack snagged the dough bait and took off. The tension on the line tightened the loop on his finger which was quite painful. He didn't want to let go of the main line because it was a good fish, yet he couldn't reel it in with one hand. The fish on the bait line was also a good size fish and he didn't want to let it go either. It took him a good while to get one of the fish in where he could use both hands to land the other. That was a funny sight watching that skip jack swimming around with the man's finger pointing at it.

Another time I was fishing off the Coast Guard pier using shrimp for bait. One of the Second Class Petty Officers from the shop, named Schroeder, came down to fish, too. Neither of us was having much luck. The sea gulls were all over the place. We were constantly shooing them off our bait. The gulls were so daring that as soon as we turned our backs, they would fly down and snatch a shrimp from the bait pail. Schroeder was making a long cast to see if there were fish farther from the pier than where we had been fishing. A sea gull dove, snagged his bait in the air, and got hooked. That was a very funny sight; Schroeder trying to reel in the gull and the gull putting up a fight while flying all around. After he had landed the gull, there was another battle in trying to get the hook out of the gull without killing it. I couldn't be of much help because I was laughing so hard.

Sometimes I would go fishing at night. One Saturday night, the only bait I could find was squid. I fished until about midnight, but didn't have any luck. I had tried every spot that I could on base and still didn't catch any fish. I finally gave up, packed all the gear in the car, and went home. I was tired and decided that I would leave everything in the car until the next day. I forgot all about the squid. I slept in the next morning. The day turned out to be sunny and hot. About 1000. Diann decided to go somewhere. She came running into the bedroom yelling at me to get up and wanting to know what that terrible odor was in the car. I knew immediately. I had left the squid in the trunk. I used everything I could think of to remove the odor. It took all day before we could even stand to ride in the car.

Bruce Age Eleven Months in Side Yard at 130 Ave. K, Naval Air Station, Corpus Christi

In September 1958, we moved on base to live at 130 Ave. K, Naval Air Station. We considered ourselves lucky because this was a single dwelling. Most everyone I knew in navy housing lived in duplexes. Chiefs and Officers were assigned single houses. However, a Chief had just moved out of this one and I was the most senior man on the housing waiting list, so it was assigned to us. It was a two-bedroom house with a living room, a bathroom, and a kitchen big enough for a dinette table and chairs. This was our first experience in living in government housing. We really enjoyed the convenience of living on base. The commissary was just about two blocks from our house. I could get to work by walking and didn't have to be concerned with traffic. The Navy Exchange was also very close-by. We could even take in a movie at the base theater for a dime each. AE1 McCreedy and family, plus AE2 Veasey and family lived close-by. Now we had someone with whom to socialize.

The one thing I didn't care for about the assignment at the Naval Air Station, Corpus Christi was the monthly personnel inspection. Rear Admiral Clifton was the Chief of Naval Air Advance Training and Captain Wilson was the Commanding Officer of the Naval Air Station. I don't know which one was so "Gung Ho!" for the personnel inspection, but whomever it was, held one every month, rain or shine. All the units of the base had to participate. It was known as the Captain's Personnel Inspection, but I think Admiral Clifton was the one who initiated it. All the men and officers would have to put on their best uniforms and shined shoes and fall in for inspection. The ceremony was always on a Saturday morning and lasted from 0800 to 1200 hours, four hours long. When it was hot, several of the men would faint from heat exhaustion and would be carried off the field. I never fainted. The Captain would come by and inspect each man and officer. If there was something amiss about the uniform, shoes, or hair then the person with the discrepancy would be placed on report and be punished for the infraction. I never had anything wrong with me. After we were inspected by the Captain and his crew, we would be ordered to "Pass in Review." The march helped get the blood circulating after having to stand in one place for so long. At the end of the march, we would be dismissed for the rest of the day. My mother-in-law loved to come watch these inspections. She thought everything looked wonderful. Even Diann enjoyed the inspections and parades. They would have thought differently had they been the one required to stand them.

It was at this duty station where I began to understand the value of one's performance evaluations. Each enlisted man was graded every six months and a performance evaluation was placed in his service record. I always tried to elevate myself whenever I thought I was eligible for a promotion. To become a Navy Warrant Officer, a person had to have six years of service, a high performance evaluation, and be recommended by the Commanding Officer. I completed my six years of military service on 20 November 1958, plus my performance evaluations were pretty good, so I thought, so I applied for the Warrant Officer Program on 21 November 1958. The test would be given in March 1959, but the recommendation had to be submitted prior to 1 December 1958.

I knew that I had been sent to Corpus Christi to finish out my shore duty tour. I was expecting to receive orders to another sea tour at any time. Because I had not been onboard a ship, I would most likely receive orders to one. I asked Diann where she wanted to live during the time that I would be gone to sea, at home with her mother or where the ship would be home ported? She said she would go to wherever the ship was home ported. She had lived with me long enough by now that she would be able to handle the conditions wherever she lived.

I received my orders to Patrol Squadron Forty-Five in December. I went home to Diann singing the song, *Down in Bermuda*. She said, "You received your orders and we're going to Bermuda?" I told her that was right; I wasn't going aboard a ship after all. So, we started making preparations for our move to Bermuda. We learned that she and Bruce could not go to Bermuda until I had found and rented an approved house to live in. However, I did have ten days travel time and thirty days leave before having to report to my new duty station. We departed Corpus Christi on Christmas Eve for my mother-in-law's house in Waco. I also learned that I could not ship my 1956 Ford to Bermuda because it was considered too large to have on the island. I was told that I would have to store it someplace for three years or sell it. I sold it in Waco for $925 with less than 30,000 miles. Diann and I used the money to open a savings account with Waco Savings on Waco Drive. It was the first time we had enough money to do something like that.

PATROL SQUADRON FORTY-FIVE (VP-45) NAVAL STATION, BERMUDA

10 February 1959 to 22 February 1962

VP-45 Squadron Emblem

P5M-2 Marlin

Diann and Bruce did not have travel approval to go with me when I had to report to Charleston, South Carolina, Naval Receiving Station to await transportation to Bermuda. On the way to Charleston, I stopped in Atlanta, Georgia, to see George B. Griner. George and I were together in VR-8. He had gotten out of the navy and was now working for Delta Air Lines. He was a station attendant. He had also gotten married since I last saw him. I spent the weekend with George and Caroline. She was a pharmacist, working for Walgreen Drug Store. Both George and Caroline had to work that Saturday, and I didn't have anywhere to go. I couldn't go with George to the air field, so I spent the day with Caroline at the drug store. Most of the time Caroline was working behind the drug counter and I sat in a booth reading books. I became interested in one of the medical books. I started looking up the effectiveness of various contraceptives. There were several types, condoms, diaphragms, and a variety of gels. I did not know that there were so many. Caroline came over and asked what I was reading. When I showed her she also became interested in the subject. We got a big kick out of the information, especially when we told George that evening. I left Monday to continue on my way to Charleston.

I didn't know it would take three weeks before I'd be able to get a flight to Bermuda. Since I was a First Class Petty Officer, I didn't get assigned to the base work details. Each morning I had to fall in ranks for roll call and then was free to lounge until meal time. I really didn't care to go out on the town, except to look around. Plus, I didn't have all that much money to spend. One morning my name was called. Someone had decided to assign me to a detail of taking prisoners from the base to Washington, DC. A Second Class Petty Officer I'll call John because I can't remember his name, was also assigned to the detail. He and I spent two days at the firing range learning to shoot a .45 pistol. On the third day, about 1300 hours, we picked up eight prisoners and only four pair of handcuffs plus a .45 pistol with two clips. The prisoners were just a bunch of young men who were more mischievous than bad or mean. Our instructions were to keep our guns unloaded and let the prisoner go if one started to run. That really made a lot of sense since we had just spent all that time learning how to handle our weapons. Also, if there was any trouble, we were to handcuff two prisoners together.

A bus took us to Shaw Air Force Base, about thirty miles from the receiving station, to catch the prisoner plane that made runs from Key West, Florida, each week. We had two hours to kill before the plane arrived, a scary time for me and John. We had to keep eight prisoners occupied for two hours. They entertained themselves by telling stories of their jail time. One of the stories was, for entertainment they would have crab races on the windowsill, crabs they had gotten from a prostitute.

The plane arrived at about 1700 hours. In order to board, we had to turn the pistols over to the pilot. Basically our worries were over at this time, although we were still responsible for the prisoners. We arrived in DC about midnight. From there, we were relieved of the prisoners and free for the night. The next day we were flown back to Charleston. It was an experience and an assignment that I will always remember, but don't want to do again.

Finally the day came when I was called and assigned transportation to Kinnley Air Force Base in Bermuda. The flight was on a C121 Super Constellation, the same type of plane I had worked on when I was in VR-8 in Honolulu, Hawaii. Upon arriving, I boarded a bus bound for Naval Station Bermuda to report into Patrol Squadron Forty-Five. The date was 2 February 1959. I was assigned to the electric shop and berthed in the PO1 dorm in the barracks. Chief E. E. Weeks was in charge of the shop. He had been my "B" School instructor in Jacksonville, Florida. CDR Durham was the Commanding Officer and Chief Smig was the Maintenance Chief.

I was in the shop almost a month when ordered to report to Fleet Airborne Electronics Training Unit, Atlantic, Jacksonville, Florida. I was to attend the P5M-2 Aircraft Power Systems Course 510 that commenced on 2 March 1959. It was a four-week course on the P5M electrical system. The primary subject was the AC generator system and related components. I met an AE2 there named Kovach, also from the squadron, but taking a different course in school. Also, while I was walking down the street one day, I spotted Bill Purcell. He was now a Chief Petty Officer, one pay grade ahead of me, again. He was now stationed in Patrol Squadron Forty-Nine, VP-49, which was just across the base in Bermuda from VP-45.

March in Jacksonville is very cool, but coming from Bermuda it was cold to me. Shortly after arriving, I contracted a rash known as pita-rhizopus-rosea (misspelled). The rash looked like ring worms. My body was completely covered except where exposed to the sunlight. If I sun bathed, the rash would disappear, but it was too cold to lie in the sun by the time I got out of class. Diann flew down from Waco to be with me for a week, but due to the rash, she didn't want to get close to me. The doctors told me that it wasn't contagious, but that didn't impress her at all. I must have used ten gallons of calamine lotion just to stop the itch. The doctor told me that it would run its course in two to three weeks. Those weeks lasted two months it seemed. On the weekend, I would lay in the sun hoping to make the rash go away sooner. I was glad when it did. During the time Diann was there, we stayed with Lovus and Dolores again. Diann returned to Waco and I completed the course on 27 March 1959, with a grade point average of 93.6, and then went back to Bermuda.

Again, I was living in the First Class Dorm in the barracks, eating in the mess hall, and trying to find a place to live. I didn't have a car, but it wasn't that far to the electric shop, so I walked. There were several First Class Petty Officers living in the dorm. Liquor was cheap and readily accessible in the clubs. A lot of the first class were on the verge of becoming alcoholics or were already. I remember one first class metal smith by the name of McCord, who was married and lived off base. He stopped by at evening mealtime one payday, a Friday, on his way home. He had a case of booze with him. He offered us a drink. Abbot and I declined, because we were on our way to the mess hall for the evening meal. There was a lot of chaos in the barracks when we returned. I don't know all the details other than that McCord lost his first class crow over that event. The Skipper, CDR Durham, had a policy of "NO Booze in the barracks!" The Master at Arms (MAA) was trying to get McCord to leave, but he wanted someone to have a drink with him. He was too drunk to know what was happening, so the MAA had no choice except to place him on report.

Another man, AE1 Columbonie, was a flight crewman who had a late Friday night flight and was trying to get some rest. A radio was playing and he asked someone to turn it off so he could sleep. After asking about the third time, he put a crash axe through the radio. I didn't trust him with my life after that incident. Nobody messed with Columbonie.

One Saturday, AM1 Abbot asked me if I would like to go to Kinnley Air Force Base with him on his motorcycle. Since I didn't have anything else to do and I had not been there shopping before, and he had said that we would be back by 1600 hours, I accepted. We did some sightseeing on the way over and back. I got to see some of Bermuda that I had not seen. On the way back, he wanted to stop by to see a friend who lived in Warwick Parish. Since I was riding with him, how could I object? The friend was another AM1 from the other squadron. When we got to the friend's home, he and his wife were eating an early dinner of enchiladas. They were drinking straight Scotch whisky with their meal. They invited us to join them in their meal, but we declined. Abbot said he would have a drink with them, though. Well! I had a drink, too. I was then ready to leave, but Abbot wanted another drink. Then he had another one and another one. He was now too drunk to operate the motorcycle. I had no idea of where we were or how to get to a place so I could catch a cab to the base. Abbot went into their living room and fell asleep on their couch. About ten o'clock the woman told me to walk down a certain road to the main highway; that I could get a taxi. When I started out the door the man decided that he would go with me and stop at a pub at the bottom of the hill. Then his wife decided that she would go, too. We all left the house with Abbot sleeping on the couch. I had to go into the pub to call a cab. While I was on the phone the man ordered us all a drink. I told him that I didn't want one. Then he asked what I expected him to do with the one he had ordered for me? I said that he could drink it. Then he wanted to get into a fight if I didn't drink it. I finished it just as the cab arrived. I was glad to get away from that guy. I never went anywhere with Abbot again, either. I didn't mind going out with people, but I wanted to know that I had a way home after the party.

On Friday and Saturday nights, if I didn't have to work the next day, I would go to the EM Club, First Class Lounge for social activities. Sometimes we would get into a "Liar's Poker" game with one dollar bills. That was a weird game. All the numbers in the serial numbers on all the bills were used. The winner collected all the bills from the other players. Other times we would play Pinochle. It was something to do until Diann came to Bermuda.

In order to go look for a place to live, I had to rent a small motor bike, called a MoPed. It took me a while to get used to the roads in Bermuda. Bermuda is a British Colony and the British drive on the opposite side of the road than those of us from the US. One evening after work I had gone to look at a place in Summer Set and was returning to the base in the late evening. A taxi cab was coming toward me with the horn blaring. I could not imagine why that taxi was driving on my side of the road. Just before meeting head-on, I realized that it was I who was driving on his side of the road. That little episode almost cost me my life, but it did get my attention. From then on, I had no more problems with driving on what I considered to be the wrong side of the road.

Housing was scarce in Bermuda. I would go looking at all leads that were given to me each day that I could. On the days that I had section leader duty, I couldn't leave the base. Diann and Bruce could not come to Bermuda until I found a suitable place to live and got it approved by the Navy Housing Authority. Although I was eligible for government housing, there was a one-year waiting period before I would be assigned one. I finally found a place in Warwick Parish. Addresses were hard to find for Americans. All the houses were listed by the name of the people who either owned them or had built them. There were no street numbers. The one I found to rent was called Francis Martin's Place, Spice Hill Road, Warwick Parish. It was located about seven miles from the base. The way to get there was to take the main road to Hamilton, then in Warwick take a right up a steep grade and through a narrow one-lane gorge called Khyber Pass, at the top take a right past two roads and take a right up Spice Hill Road. It was also a steep grade. The house was pink, with a white roof, on the left-hand side of the road behind a stone wall. All the roads in Bermuda were lined with stone walls. Each time we invited someone to our house, we had to draw a small map of directions.

Another thing about living in Bermuda, there was no public water supply "system." Each house had its own built-in cistern with the roof being the water catchment area. Most all the roofs were whitewashed to trap the rain and drain it into the cistern. Each system had a pump and a pressurizing tank. Water was piped to the kitchen and bathroom from the tank. Everyone ensured that the cisterns were maintained in proper working order and in sanitary condition. That was for drinking, as well as for all other purposes. If it didn't rain often, it was time to start conserving water. Bermuda is a coral island. When building a house, the builder would carve the coral into blocks from the lot site. The hole from which the coral was removed would be covered with stucco and a sealer, which would be used for the cistern. Then the house would be built over the hole using the blocks of coral that were carved from it. After the new house was built, everyone prayed for rain to fill the cistern before anyone moved into it. The bases did have a water system with the rain catchment area being a large hill that was covered with stucco and a sealer and then painted white. The reason for the cisterns was that all the ground water was brackish and unusable, except for flushing commodes. Even then, the plumbing had to be corrosive resistant due to the salt content of the water.

After renting the house and getting approval, Diann was given permission to come to Bermuda. Bruce was eighteen months old and had just started to walk. She had to take the flight to La Guardia Air Field in New York and change planes to go to Bermuda. They arrived in May 1959, but I do not remember the exact date. The plane was a four-engine, propeller-driven plane. Again, I was reminded of the movie, *The High and the Mighty*.

The furniture was already delivered and set up in the house by the time Diann arrived in Bermuda; however, we did not have an automobile. In order to go someplace we had to take a taxi, which was expensive, or ride the bus. The bus did not come up through the pass, so to ride the bus we had to walk about a half mile down the hill through Khyber Pass to the main road. The main road ran the full length of the island, which was twenty-two miles long. It was always scary walking through Khyber Pass. The Pass was very narrow, only one lane for automobiles. I always tried to look all the way through the pass to the main road before going in the Pass. The Bermuda bus was not allowed to go on base. We would get off at the intersection of the main road and the street to the base. After we were through the gate to the base, we would catch the base bus. The bad thing about having to ride the bus was taking the groceries home after shopping in the commissary and then having to carry them the half mile up through Khyber Pass and up the steep Spice Hill Road to the house. Spice Hill Road was almost 35 degrees uphill. It was only about 500 yards long that dead ended at the top of Spice Hill. We lived about halfway up the road.

Doing the laundry was an adventure and an all-day chore. Because of the water situation, a clothes washer could not be used in its normal automatic mode. The washer was mounted on a base with rollers. When not in use, it was pushed to one side of the kitchen. In order to wash clothes, the washer would be rolled to the kitchen sink and hooked up to the water supply. All the clothes were carefully sorted according to their colors and fading. The washer was filled for the first load, the white clothes first. When the load had completed the wash cycle, the machine was turned off. The clothes were hand squeezed and laid in the sink, leaving the water in the washer for the next load. The lighter colored clothes were put into the washer and the above step repeated. The procedure was followed until all the clothes had been washed in the same water. Sometimes it would be necessary to add hot water, which was boiled on the kitchen cook stove. After all the clothes, except the last load, had been hand-squeezed and laid in the sink or bath tub, the last load would be allowed to spin dry. Those clothes would be removed from the washer and a previous load of clothes would be put in to spin dry. For the spin cycle, the white clothes would be spun last. This would save time when starting the rinse cycle. The rinse cycle was a repeat procedure of the wash cycle.

The conservation of water was a must. If for some reason someone ran out of water, the military would bring that someone two thousand gallons of water for their cistern. The next time that person ran out, they would have to buy water if they could find anyone willing to sell any. During dry spells, there usually wasn't any water available to buy. I remember one time our cistern was getting low and it wouldn't rain on our house. We got very concerned. We could see clouds pouring rain out on the ocean and we would pray, beg, and plead for the cloud to come over our house. In fact, we only flushed the commode when absolutely necessary. We used a lot of disinfectant and Pine Sol to cover up the odor. We learned to conserve the water whether rainy season or not. We really knew that WATER is a precious commodity.

Besides getting used to the water system, there were some other things that required some adjustment to our lifestyle. Our finances were such that shopping at the base commissary and exchange retail stores was a necessity, even though I was now a First Class Petty Officer with a base pay of $180, plus receiving sea pay, housing, and cost-of-living allowance. The stores and shops in Bermuda were very expensive by our standards. Plus, the British currency was the English pound instead of the US dollar. All prices in the Bermuda stores were quoted in the pound and the currency exchange rate changed on a daily basis. The food prices at the local grocery store were atrocious. Therefore, we did all our grocery shopping at the base commissary. Our taste buds had to undergo an adjustment to get used to eating the food and drinking the milk. Most everything came in the powder form. The milk could be bought either in the powder form, which came in a box, or the recombined form in a carton. The recombined form tasted the best, but spoiled at a much faster rate. When the milk had a horribly bitter taste, you knew that it had gone bad. One tiny taste and down the commode it went. Never down the kitchen sink. The commode and kitchen sink were on two separate septic systems. And the bread! The texture was coarse and the taste was bland. It seemed that most of the food had a bland taste. After we had lived there awhile, we learned that we could get milk and bread from the Mainland US by squadron planes. When word was passed that a plane was going to Norfolk, everyone who wanted to could submit an order to the flight crew who would bring back all they could. Most everyone limited the amount of their order, so that more people could benefit because there was a limit to the amount a plane could carry. We had a freezer and we usually ordered one six pack of milk, half gallon size, and a case of bread. Everyone called those flights "the milk run."

Another thing that was of constant concern was mildew. It seems that everything stayed damp all the time. We aired our clothes and bedding often. We thought we had found the remedy to the clothes mildew problem. We did for the mildew, but the remedy created another problem. We put a lamp in the closet. The heat generated by the lamp did prevent the mildew from forming, but the bright light bleached the clothes. Finally, putting a cover over the bulb to block out most of the light did the trick.

Entertainment at the Bermuda night clubs was too expensive for my pocketbook. On weekends, we usually entertained ourselves by either inviting friends to our house or going to a friend's house for a card game or party. If we played cards with the Lightcaps, about a five block walk, it was always at their house. Bob and Kathy had a little girl who was handicapped, which prevented them from going out at night. The Banilies, an Air Force Tech Sergeant and family, lived in front of us on Spice Hill. Fred and Bee had two little girls. Of course, we only had Bruce. Most of the time, we played Canasta.

Fred was a funny man. One night we were at his house playing cards. We had a round of beer. Fred left to go to the bathroom. He was gone a long time, so I asked if anyone would like to have another beer. Fred called from the bathroom and said to get him one, also. I got two out of the refrigerator and opened one in the kitchen. It started spraying all over the ceiling. Fred started laughing, but I didn't think it was funny. Before going into the bathroom Fred had shook up all the beer cans so that they would spray when opened. I don't know what Bee thought of his antic, but Diann would have killed me if I had done that at our house.

Bruce in Side Yard of Francis Martin's House

Rhonda Banilie on the Wall along Spice Hill Road in the Front of Their House

Bruce in side yard Francis Martin House

There was a deep drop off between our house and the Banilies' house. I had to put up a fence to keep Bruce from running over the edge.

Diann had been in Bermuda less than two months when, in July 1959, the whole squadron deployed to Corpus Christi, Texas. This was where I had been stationed just six months previous. When I learned of the deployment, I wanted to carry some of the cheap booze back home to Lefty, my father-in-law, in Waco. I was DUMB and NAÏVE! I thought each person could declare a full gallon of liquor through customs when entering the US. I asked some of my friends if they weren't declaring any booze, if they would declare a gallon for me. I wanted to carry three gallons back home to my father in-law. Two of them agreed so I bought whiskey, rum, scotch, and gin. I even bought some of the expensive stuff—Crown Royal, Ole Smugglers, Jack Daniels, etc. The whole squadron flew all the way to Corpus Christi before entering the US as far as customs was concerned. When we started through customs in Texas, the custom agents told us that Texas Law would accept one quart of booze per person not a gallon. I thought I was in big trouble then. I didn't have enough money to pay the duty on one gallon much less on three gallons. There were several people who had brought a gallon; however, not everyone had booze to declare. After some head counting and booze counting the customs agent told everyone to declare a quart. There were more people in the squadron than there were quarts of booze. I got the three gallons through by the skin of my teeth.

It was the Fourth of July and we were given three days liberty. I packed the liquor in my suitcase and hitchhiked 300 miles up Highway 77 to Waco from Corpus Christi. When I got nearly to the circle in Waco, I called my father in-law, Lefty, to come get me. I was tired of carrying all of that booze. Mother-in-law was in the hospital at the time. That was probably a good thing, because she probably would have killed me for bringing all that liquor into her house. I made it back to Corpus Christi on time and decided to never do a stupid thing like that again. The squadron stayed in Corpus Christi six weeks and then returned to Bermuda.

C. W. Wilkerson at Home on Joey Drive, Waco, Texas, and Ed Hudson, 4 July 1959

Bruce and I with Our 1959 Ford Popular Auto

Finally, we decided that we could afford to buy an automobile. This was about September 1959. Bermuda had some very peculiar laws when it came to owning and driving automobiles. They considered automobiles a luxury, not a necessity. The first law was that if you bought a new car, you must sell it at the end of three years or not at all. If you kept it longer than three years, you could not resell it on the island. If you bought a used car, you must sell it at the end of two years. After two years, it could not be sold on the island. Next were the inspections. The cars were inspected every year by appointment. Once an inspection date was set, the car had to pass the inspection within ten days of that date. If it failed the inspection the first time, then the discrepancy had to be repaired and inspected again within that ten-day period. I don't know what would be the consequence if that time frame was not met. There was an exception. If rust was found on the frame of the car, then the car would be declared unsafe for road use and the automobile would be cut in half with a cutting torch on the spot. The only way to prevent it from being cut in two would be to agree to ship the car off the island. Everyone kept their car in very good condition all year round. Due to the sea spray, corrosion was a major concern. Although we could afford a car, we could not afford an expensive one. We settled on the cheapest one we could find. Since we would be in Bermuda longer than two years, we decided on buying a new one. We went to the Ford Dealer and bought a 1959 English Popular. It looked like a 1936 Ford that had been squeezed in from the sides. The steering wheel was on the right side of the vehicle. While driving, you had to remember to keep left instead of keeping to the right as in the US. The car also had standard shift. Because of that, Diann did not know how to drive it and, therefore, never got her Bermuda driver's license.

To get into the driveway off Spice Hill Road where we lived was not easy. The hill was steep and the car had to be in low or second gear. Then there was a narrow gate at the entrance to our house. Besides steep, Spice Hill Road was narrow. Lucky for me not many people on that road owned a car. I always tried to be very careful driving up the street and turning into the driveway. One night I had a watch and got off at midnight. I went home tired and not paying too much attention to the narrow gateway. I heard the metal of the rear fender scrape the gate pillar as I went into the yard. I became fully awake at that time. Man! I was perturbed with myself. I straightened the fender and painted it with RUST-OLEUM paint. I didn't want corrosion to set in.

The laws concerning the owning of an automobile were not the only peculiar laws in Bermuda. Diann was with some of the neighbor wives who had walked down to the beach. They had taken the children with them. Bruce was in his stroller. A policeman passed them and gave them a look over. He stopped them and told Diann that her shorts were too short. He said he would allow her to go straight home to change into Bermuda shorts. There was a good possibility that if she had not had Bruce, he would have taken her to jail. We learned after that incident that there were several laws concerning apparel. Bermuda had a very strict dress code.

Besides myself, there were two other first class electricians in the shop. One was named Robert L. Lightcap and the other James Hilton. Hilton was a converted engine mechanic who had seventeen years in service. Lightcap had about ten years. Although I was the junior, I had more electrical experience than Hilton. However, my experience did not include the systems of the P5M aircraft. Lightcap was the most experienced electrician, but continued to ask me for opinions of corrective action to problems with various systems. I can remember my first experience was in troubleshooting a searchlight problem. He asked me if I thought it was the commutator wire or the arbitrator head. I had no idea what he was talking about. I knew then that I was going to have to hit the books hard if I was going to learn how to work on the P5M aircraft. The DC generator power system was no problem. It was the same system as all other aircraft that I had worked on, as was the Hamilton Standard Propeller system. It was the AC power system that I was most afraid to tackle. Besides being complicated, I had heard many wild stories about the destructive nature of things that could happen from the operation by inexperienced personnel. The P5M had two 40 KVA alternators, one on each engine, which were operated in parallel, meaning the alternators had to be operating at the same frequency and in phase with each other.

One day, I learned firsthand about a hazardous feature of the P5M. It had an ejector tube, called the RETRO, near the rear entrance about head high when parked on the ramp. The tube was used by the ordnance personnel to launch flares and practice depth charges during Anti-Submarine Warfare (ASW) operations. One day AE1 Hilton and I were walking by an aircraft when a flare came out of the tube passing our faces within a few inches. Luckily, the flare did not strike anything before landing in the water of the harbor. Had we been one step forward, the flare would have struck us both in the head and most likely we would have been killed. We entered the aircraft to find an ordnance man working on the RETRO unit. He said he didn't know there was a flare in the unit and he was, he thought, performing a dry run operation. We let him know our feelings and how close we came to being killed. We did not report the incident to higher authority, but probably should have.

VP-45's primary mission was patrol of the Atlantic waters around the Bermuda area in search of enemy submarines. The P5M-2 Seaplane was the type of aircraft flown by the squadron during my tour of duty. The P5M-2 was strictly a seaplane. It had no wheels and could take off and land only on the water. In order to get the plane on dry land, beaching gear had to be floated out and attached to the sides and then towed by a caterpillar tractor up a ramp. It had two Pratt & Whitney 3350 engines mounted on gull-type wings. A huge pontoon was mounted on the outer tip of each wing. A fifty million candlepower searchlight was mounted on the end of the right wing. When on dry land, the engines were about twenty feet off the ground. The appearance reminded me of a pelican, sort of clumsy in nature. In fact, the squadron was called the, "VP-45 Pelicans." A very big work stand had to be placed around the engine in order to perform any type of maintenance. It took several men to put the work stand in place. This same stand was also used to get to the searchlight. I hated to hear that a plane had searchlight troubles. That meant the electricians had to move that big stand.

VP-45 was a deploying squadron that flew missions to various areas in the Atlantic as well as patrolling the waters around Bermuda. Commander Palm had relieved Commander Durham as Commanding Officer. A three plane detachment was usually maintained in Key West, Florida, to patrol the water between Florida and Cuba. While I was attending school in Jacksonville, Florida, the squadron was deployed for two weeks to the Virgin Islands on what was known as "Operation Spring Board." After I had become familiar with the aircraft and the men, they would request that I be sent to make repairs on deployed aircraft. One of the planes in Key West was experiencing DC generator problems. A message arrived in the duty office that read, "Send a relief crew and AE1 Hudson."

When I found out the names of the two electricians on deployment, I asked the Division Officer, WO2 Alex Hilliard, why I was being sent. I told him that those two electricians would have the discrepancy repaired before we got halfway to Key West. He told me that I was going and that was that. I didn't take much money and no civilian clothes with me. When we landed in Key West, we had to wait for the ramp to be cleared by the plane that I was sent to repair. It was being launched to fly to Bermuda. When I saw that it was leaving, I told the pilot that was the plane that I came down to work on and, if possible, let me get on it and go back to Bermuda. He said he had not been told about the reason I was coming to Key West and he could not authorize me to get aboard that plane. I spent ten days in Key West with nothing to do and very little money. I read a lot of books those ten days.

As usual, I continued to try to improve my education and was always willing to take advantage of any school offered and completing correspondence courses. The CO decided to send AD2 Vorndran and me to the Naval Air Technical Training Command Mobile Training Unit, Norfolk, Virginia, on 29 November 1959, to attend the 34E60 Propeller Course. It was a ten-day course with five days of the electrical system and five days on the mechanical features. It covered the Hamilton Standard Propeller, with which I was well acquainted. I completed the course on 10 December 1959 with a grade of 4.0. I aced the course. When I was taking the final exam, I noticed one question that did not have a correct answer. The questions all had multiple choice answers. I called this fact to the attention of the instructors. They all thought I was a wise guy. When they finally decided to check, they found that I was right about there not being a correct answer. After some debate, they changed one word in the question and by doing so, one of the answers would be correct. After reading the question with the new wording, I told the instructors that their grading guide should also be changed because it would not reflect the correct answer. They wouldn't believe me this time. So, I told them that when they graded my paper it would show that I had answered one question incorrectly when in fact I had not. Sure enough, when they graded my paper, they said I had missed that one question. They had not changed the guide to reflect the correct answer of the newly worded question. The CO complimented me on my 4.0 grade.

We finally were notified that government quarters were available for us. The housing was not on the base, but closer to it and the rent would be cheaper. The rent was the same as my housing allowance, plus all utilities were included and water would be guaranteed. We moved to #9 Victoria Row, Ireland Island, in January 1960. It was a four apartment multiplex located about five miles from the naval station. Only US Navy personnel lived in the apartments. Parking was much easier. There were no hills to climb or narrow gates to go through and the lot was level.

Diann and Bruce,   *Apartment #9 Victoria Row, Ireland Island*

In February 1960, I was eligible and did take the test for advancement to Chief Petty Officer. I also applied for appointment to Warrant Officer, for which I was eligible. I had applied for appointment to Warrant Officer once before while stationed in Corpus Christi, but was not accepted. I was considered very junior as far as anyone taking the Chief's exam. In fact, I was the most junior first class in the squadron. Back in the summer of 1959, Chief Weeks had told all the first class in the shop that he would give us a list of books we could study and, if we did study them, we would make Chief. He said that all test questions had been formed from the information in those books. Of the list of seven books, only five were available in the VP-45 library. I talked to Lightcap and Hilton about us agreeing to only checking out one book at a time from the library. That way, there would always be another book for us to check out. One day, I needed another book. When I went to library, I found the other four books on the shelf. I read all five books over and over throughout that year until exam time, but Lightcap had read only one and Hilton didn't read any of them. The day of the exam, 16 February 1960, was an exciting day for me. The place to take the exam was in the galley. It was packed with men of all specialties. I went in with confidence and high hopes. We were given four hours to complete it. I had never taken an easier exam. It seemed that the answers to all the questions were right from the books as Chief Weeks had said. I completed the exam within about three hours. That afternoon back in the shop, Hilton, Lightcap, and I were discussing the exam and I got the feeling that I had done well. In March, news was that the Warrant Officer Program had been suspended. All who had applied would be considered for Limited Duty Officer (LDO), provided they met the eligibility requirements. I had less than eight years in service, but ten years were required for LDO. Only six years had been required for Warrant Officer. Therefore, I was ineligible to be considered for LDO.

The navy had approval to dole out pro pay to men in selected specialty ratings, provided they were recommended by their superiors and they were able to pass the pro pay exam. I was one of the few men in the squadron who was recommended and did, in fact, pass the exam. I started drawing P1 pay of thirty dollars extra per month on 16 May 1960. Instead of allowing that money to be added to my monthly paycheck, I had an allotment deposited in our savings account at Waco Savings in Waco, Texas. At last, Diann and I had started building our nest egg.

Chief Weeks had a philosophy about good electricians. He told the men, "A good electrician should be able to repair anything wrong on an aircraft." It didn't matter if the equipment was under the responsibility of the electrical shop or not. The electrician had to know the proper operation of all the systems on the aircraft in order to know when the malfunction was in the hydraulic system, mechanical, or electrical. If the electrician knew how all the systems functioned, then he should be able to make the repairs. I thought Chief Weeks' statement was true and applied that theory to my work throughout my career.

Sometime around December 1959, the XO's plane, LN 7, developed a problem with its number one engine propeller reversing system. The props could be placed in various positions, forward thrust, reverse thrust, or feather. To slow the plane down after landing the props would be placed into the reverse thrust mode. After the plane was slowed sufficiently, the props would be returned to the forward thrust mode. On LN 7, the left prop, when coming out of the reverse mode, would not stop until it went into full feather mode. The engine cannot run in the full feather mode. The first time this happened, I tried to get it to malfunction on the parking ramp, but it would not. I went to Maintenance Officer, LCDR Peterson, and told him that I could not find anything wrong with the system. He told me to run the prop in and out of reverse ten times and if it didn't malfunction, to sign it off as, "could not duplicate." I did not have engine turn up authority, so I had to get one of the mechanics to turn up the engines and operate the propeller controls. About two weeks later, the prop malfunctioned again. This time he told me to run it in and out of reverse twenty times and, again, I could not duplicate the problem. AD1 Schindler was the mechanic that performed the engine turn-ups for me.

In March 1960, it was time for another Operation Spring Board, this time to San Juan, Puerto Rico. The whole squadron deployed to San Juan. The *USS Albemarle*, seaplane tender, was tied up at the navy pier in the San Juan River. The ship was our home away from home for the next two weeks. All the planes were buoyed in San Juan Harbor. When LN 7 landed, the prop went to the feather position from reverse. I troubleshot the system and, again, could not duplicate the problem. LCDR Peterson and I taxied the plane up and down the harbor trying to get the prop to goof up again, but we couldn't. He was as baffled as I.

I stayed in the first class ward and ate my meals in the Chief and First Class mess hall. I could get off the ship whenever I wanted to. The ship was not only our living quarters, but also our working space. In order to work on the planes, which were tied up to a buoy in the harbor, we had to wait for a crew boat that would take us to the plane of our choice. Sometimes, it was difficult working on the plane with it swinging on the buoy. A wave would rock the plane, which caused some problems when handling screws, nuts, and bolts. When working over the water, you had to be extra careful not to drop anything. Anything dropped into the water was just plain lost.

USS Albemarle

Crew Boat on Way to Seaplanes

San Juan River

P5M-2 Mooring in the San Juan River

USS Albemarle

USS Albemarle

There was no swimming in the San Juan River because of all the filth. There was even raw sewage floating in the water. No telling what kind of disease one would catch from getting into the water. One of the planes had engine trouble, which resulted in changing the engine. There wasn't any ramp space available, so the engine would have to be changed with the plane floating on the water. The mechanics rigged the sea stands and removed the cowling from the engine. I was tasked to disconnect the engine electrical systems from the aircraft. That was the first time I had seen, much less been on, a sea stand. I could look straight down into the water. If a tool was dropped, it was gone.

Working on the sea stand was both scary and fun. Scary because the stands were so narrow and there was the possibility of slipping and falling into the filthy water. Fun because it was something new and different. After I had completed my tasks, the mechanics did their part and removed the engine. They installed the good engine and I was, again, tasked with the job of connecting the electrical system. A first class mechanic named Doddy had completed a safety wiring job and was really proud of his accomplishment. He decided to step back to admire his work. He forgot about the narrowness of the sea stand and stepped off into the water. It was funny, yet not funny. He had to stay in sick bay three days taking all sorts of antibiotics because of the contaminated water.

Because of the schedule and workload, I didn't get to do much sightseeing. However, one day several of us were able to take a tour around San Juan and up into the Rain Forest. San Juan and the surrounding countryside of Puerto Rico were pretty and clean. The beaches had white sand and were uncluttered. We would have liked to have had the time for a swim, but didn't. In the Rain Forest, we saw a lot of plant life, but no animals.

Rain Forest, San Juan

After two weeks in San Juan, the squadron returned to Bermuda. LN 7 still had the prop problem. Finally, one day I did get it to malfunction and discovered an open connection in a connector. I replaced both the male and female sides of that connector. That worked for about a month, then the same connector developed an open connection again. This time, I put a small piece of wire in the female slots and jammed the male connector into it. That problem never developed again.

In early April, the Chief's exam results came in. My name was on the list to be promoted to Aviation Electrician Mate Chief Petty Officer Acting (AECA) on 16 November 1960. That would be four days before completing eight years of service. The "Acting" part of the promotion meant that I would be in a temporary status for three years. If my performance failed or my military conduct became improper, I could be demoted for cause. I was the second man in the squadron to know that the results were in.

A Third Class Yeoman called me just after he had opened the mail. He was so happy that I was making Chief, but not because he wished me well. He did not like me because of my enforcement of the rules when I was the squadron duty section leader. I had made First Class in my first four years of service. I didn't want that promotion to be taken from me in one night for failure to carry out my duties of responsibility as section leader. I never hesitated in calling someone down for infractions of the rules. The CO had a rule that no alcohol was allowed in the barracks. What the yeoman didn't like was that he wanted to do as he pleased and keep alcoholic beverages in the barracks and I always would take them away from him and any others when I had section leader duty. By being advanced to Chief, I would no longer stand section leader duty. I would now stand Assistant Squadron Duty Officer (ASDO) duty. That's the reason he was happy, that I would no longer be in the barracks.

Not only the results of the Chief's exam came in, the results of all advancement exams had come in for all ratings. I don't know when or where the custom originated, but it was custom for the men whose name appeared on the list for advancement to be thrown into the water. I imagine it started aboard ship in the early history of the navy. When the Captain of the ship promoted someone to a higher status, his contemporaries would initiate him by throwing him overboard. All who were on the list tried their best to keep that event from happening, me included. All day long someone would be captured, carried to the sea wall, and tossed into the drink (water). I just knew that the men were lying in wait for me and I was doing my best to avoid being captured. I was in the electric shop at quitting time and found it odd that no one else was there. I decided to check with the Maintenance Control Office before changing clothes to go home. At that time in history, navy regulations did not allow enlisted men to wear dungarees off base. As I was returning to the shop, all the men jumped me and carried me to the sea wall. I am thankful to AE2 Ralph Holback. As they started to toss me in the water he told them to wait, the water was too shallow and I would be hurt. The men found a deeper area next to the sea wall and threw me in. Having been thrown in by several men, I knew they were all happy about my promotion and that I was well liked by all.

After the men threw me in the water, they all ran away and left me to get out on my own accord. The sea wall was very high and I had to wade and swim about 100 yards to the seaplane ramp in order to get out. By the time I arrived at the shop, no one was there. I changed clothes and went home. My work clothes were soaking wet. I went into the house carrying my wet clothes. Diann looked at me in a strange way. All of a sudden she screamed, "You've made Chief!" I told her yes I had and wanted to know how she knew. She said by your wet clothes.

Neither Hilton's nor Lightcap's name was on the list. They had failed to make Chief. The sad part was that Hilton had eighteen years in service and I had less than eight. AO1 Bridges asked me to come over to his shop. He had something to show me. He wanted to point out to me why I could not possibly make Chief Petty Officer. His name was on the list also to be promoted the same day as I; however, he had over sixteen years of service, twice as many as I. He went through all sorts of explanations on accumulative points and test points. Then he pointed out the statistics of last year's and this year's results. All 159 men who had passed the exam were promoted in 1959 for 100 percent advancement rate. On the 1960 exam, of 303 men who had passed, only 66 men were being promoted for a 22 percentile. When he got through, I pointed out one fact that he was overlooking. My name was on the list, it didn't matter about all the others facts that he had described. If I didn't make any mistakes, I would be promoted because my name was on the list. He couldn't argue about that fact.

By now, Commander Lee had relieved Commander Palm as CO and Commander O'Bryan was XO. Again, I was sent to the Naval Air Technical Training Command Mobile Training Unit, Norfolk, Virginia, on 25 April 1960 to attend the 4725 (MF-1 Compass) Maintenance Training Course. AE1 Calhoun was the instructor. There were supposed to have been four other people attending the course, but I was the only one who reported. I didn't receive very good instructions from AE1 Calhoun. He was senior to me at the time, but he had failed the Chief's exam and he knew that I had passed it. He knew that in six months, I would be senior to him. However, I completed the course on 29 April 1960.

I had heard about the Fleet Reserve Association from almost the beginning of my enlistment and how much good they did for the needy families of the sailors. Sometime in 1959, I decided to join the FRA. I paid my initiation fee and annual dues and attended the monthly meetings. The meetings were held in the EM Club. Although I paid my dues, I soon became disinterested in attending the meetings. It seemed that the officers of the Bermuda Chapter were more interested in partying than helping the needy.

One of the things I liked about living on Ireland Island was the fishing. Just a few blocks down the road, was a British Naval Yard and docks. I would go out on one of the piers and fish. Sometimes, I would get frustrated because the fish would not bite the hook, but I still enjoyed it. From the pier, I could see huge snappers swimming and I would always try for one of them. They were called lawyer fish because they would eat anything in the water except something that had a hook in it. I would even put a small hook in a piece of bread and throw it in along with some crumbs. The fish would eat all the crumbs, but not the crumb with the hook in it. Still, I would catch a halibut or a grouper, which we would have for a meal. One night when I was fishing from the dock, a British ship was anchored at one of the piers. Some of the British sailors came down to see what I was doing. One of them asked if I would sell him some line, hook, and sinker. I told him that I would give him the tackle, but I wouldn't sell him any. The next night I was fishing on the pier again. The British sailor came down and told me he had caught a big fish with the tackle I had given him. He asked if I would like a cup of tea and how would I like it. I told him I would like a cup, but no cream or sugar. He had not heard of anyone drinking tea straight.

British Ship Docked at Ireland Island Navy Yard
As Viewed from Our Front Yard

I liked to snorkel, but wouldn't adventure far from shore because of safety measures. One time I brought home a seven man life raft from the salvage yard. I would carry that down to the shore and launch out a little way and anchor. I would either fish or look at the various fish life and coral formations. I was always fascinated by their beauty.

I also liked to go deep sea fishing. The Navy Special Services had charter fishing trips, which we could go on. I took them as often as I could. Those trips usually went out twenty miles to the Bermuda Banks. The reefs were thirty fathoms deep. Sometimes it would require a full pound of weight to get the hook to the bottom on the reef. I would not know what had been hooked until the fish reached the surface of the water. It could be any kind of fish. I have caught groupers, snappers, halibut, mackerel, tuna, big reds, and even sharks.

Results of Deep Sea Fishing Trip on the Bermuda Banks, 1960

One time I went on a fishing tournament. The boat left the shore at midnight with instructions that we had to be in line to weigh in at 1700 hours. We went to the Bermuda Banks. About four in the morning, I snagged a big fish. It was really giving me a fight. I would get it almost to the top of the water and it would turn and dive. It was pitch black, no moon. I could determine that I had the fish fairly close to the surface by the amount of line that I had reeled in. The Skipper of the boat said that he would shine a light to see what kind of fish I had on my line. He did not want me to pull a shark into his boat. I saw a shark darting for the fish on my line, so I gave a big heave ho and jerked the fish into the boat. It was a big red that weighed thirty-five pounds. There would be a prize given for the biggest fish caught by each party. Man! I had the biggest fish, so far. I kept that lead until about three in the afternoon, just before time to head to shore, when another man pulled in a forty-two pound grouper. I was disappointed, but still had a good time and we had plenty of fish to eat when I got home.

In September, I decided that it was time to start accumulating my Chief Petty Officer uniforms. The uniforms were not available in Bermuda. I had to go to either Norfolk, Virginia, or to Jacksonville, Florida. I made a list of the different types that I would need. I did not know at the time there were so many. Up to this time in my navy career, I had only a few different types of uniforms to keep current. The uniforms were dress and working blues with the broad collar, whites and dungarees, plus the little round white hat, and only one pair of black shoes. Now, there were the dress blues; the whites, both dress and working; the khaki, both dress and working; plus, summer short sleeve shirts and winter long sleeve shirts; and white shirts, khaki shirts, and blue shirts. The types of shoes were increased to three pairs; black, brown, and white. Now, I was in the "Brown Shoe Navy." I also decided to get a set of the green uniforms. Only the aviation branch of the navy could wear the green uniform. Man! By the time I got the list made with the price, it was well over $500 that I would have to spend. I didn't have that much. I could get the work khakis in Bermuda along with the white shirts, so I would just get the basic blue, white, khaki, and green uniforms in Norfolk. I would get a $300 clothing allowance to spend toward the purchase of the new uniforms, but not until I was actually promoted. I made arrangements for a flight and spent the weekend in Norfolk getting the uniforms, so I would be ready for the day of my promotion.

On the flight back to Bermuda, I thought we were going to crash. The flight had left Norfolk shortly after noon, so it was after dark when we arrived at Bermuda. I was watching out the rear port hole as the plane was nearing the water. I could see that we were just about to the water, but the pilot was not reducing the air speed. After the plane touched the water, it kept sinking into it. The water was up to the porthole that I was looking out of. All of a sudden, the plane shot into the air for a couple hundred feet, and then it made a smooth landing. The pilot came over PA system with an apology. He said the altimeter showed the plane to be three hundred feet in the air when it touched the water. I knew something was wrong when the plane sank so deep into the water.

On 3 October 1960, Diann woke me at 0500, saying that she was having stomach cramps. I asked if they could be labor pains. She said that she didn't think so, but soon she had another one and this one she believed was, in fact, a labor pain. I got up and dressed and went next door to get someone to take care of Bruce while I drove Diann to the navy base hospital. Chief Weeks and wife, Quieta, lived in the next building, so I went to their house. Quieta came and stayed with Bruce. He would be three years old on the eighteenth.

We lived about five miles from the base. We arrived at 0600. Another woman was in the labor room waiting to have her baby. Her husband was with her, so the nurse had him leave to wait in the waiting room with me while they prepped Diann for delivery. In about fifteen minutes, they started taking a woman to delivery. I said to the man with me that it looked as though they were taking his wife to delivery. He said, "It's about time!" They had been there since five the past evening. But, instead of his wife who was being pushed up the hall by the waiting room door, it was Diann being taken to the delivery room. Carla was born at 0620 on 3 October 1960. It only took twenty minutes for delivery from the time of arrival at the hospital. With Bruce back in 1957, it took only fifty-three minutes for delivery from the time we had arrived at the hospital. I told Diann that if she ever got pregnant again I was going to learn how to deliver a baby, because I would not be able to get her to the hospital in time for a delivery.

The other man's poor wife could not deliver the baby through the natural process and the Naval Facility Medical Dispensary lacked the necessary equipment to perform a cesarean section. She was flown to the Air Force Hospital for the procedure.

Proud Mama with Week-Old
Daughter Carla

Proud Papa with Carla One
Week and Bruce, Age Three

The day I made Chief is an unforgettable day. I received orders on 15 November 1960, directing me to report to the Leading Chief's office at 0800, 16 November 1960. At 1230 hours, I was to report to the Chief Master at Arms, Naval Station Bermuda, Chief Petty Officers' Mess (Closed) for initiation and examination of my qualifications as a Chief Petty Officer. The orders stated that the uniform for reporting was enlisted undress whites with neckerchief, but required me to have a Chief Petty Officer's khaki working uniform on hand after completion of ceremonies.

I reported to the Leading Chief's office for my orders for the morning. I did not get to go to the electric shop to work, as I normally had done. Instead, I was put mostly in the Chiefs' Lounge performing idiotic orders given by the other Chiefs. Orders like, "Get me a cup of coffee." Or, go somewhere and fetch this or that. I bided my time and soon it was time to report to the Chiefs' Club.

I reported as directed and was I ever in for a treatment. Master Chief Petty Officer Zeb Gray was the presiding official. He had known me since 1958 while in Corpus Christi. There were eight men, including me, to be initiated that day. Seven of us were isolated in a back room while the first man was called to report to the JUDGE! We were not allowed to know what was happening during the initiation procedure until it was our time to be called. I was the fourth in line to undergo the initiation procedure. I was led blindfolded to the podium. I had on my round white sailor hat. When the blindfold was removed, the first thing I noticed were three sleeves from white jumpers with First Class Petty Officer chevron and hash marks on them attached to the podium. I knew then I was in for the long haul. Those sleeves had three or more hash marks. My sleeve only had one hash mark. That fact was immediately made known by the Master at Arms. My sleeve was cut off and hung with the others. A hash mark represents four completed years of military service. Someone said that must have made me hot under the collar and suggested that I be cooled down. Someone else filled my hat with ice cubes. Then someone else said that had cooled me down too much and that I needed a drink of something that would warm me up. I received a concoction of something awful tasting. Because I was so junior, the jury kept thinking of ways that I should be initiated. One of the things held against me was that I had purchased uniforms in September and had them in my possession at a time when I was not authorized to have them. Each time a charge was brought against me, my hat was filled with more ice cubes and I was given another awful tasting drink. They ended up spending so much time initiating me, that there was very little time left to initiate the other four candidates.

After all eight men had been initiated we had to change into our khaki uniforms and line up for pictures. Then it was time to eat. I was getting hungry by now. It was almost 1700 hours and we didn't even get lunch. The Master at Arms led us to the Hog Trough. All the food had been mixed together and poured into a trough that looked as though it had just been taken from a pig sty. On top of the food was a woman's Kotex with Worcestershire sauce topped with Heinz 57 Sauce and topped with ketchup. It looked as though it had just been discarded. The food didn't appear appetizing at all. Whether we wanted to or not, we had to eat out of the trough without using our hands. However, we only had to get our pictures taken with our face in the trough while taking a bite. This was to demonstrate our piggish desire to attain the rating of Chief Petty Officer; then the initiation was over. We were now considered to be Chief Petty Officers. For some reason, we were not given a copy of the pictures. With Carla being only six weeks old, Diann was not able to join me at the Chiefs' Club to celebrate the occasion of my promotion.

Shortly after my initiation, the official pictures were taken. My picture was added to the bottom of the Chief Petty Officers Roster located just outside maintenance control on the hangar deck. Now, it was official. I had joined the CHIEFS' RANKS! I was also now eligible to enter the Chiefs' lounge and have coffee, relax, and play "Acey-deucy."

VP-45 Chief Petty Officer Roster 1960

Chief Petty Officer Aviation Electrician's Mate

The Chiefs' Lounge

Shortly after I was advanced to Chief, AVCM Gray was transferred to Meridian, Mississippi; AVCM Weeks was the Master Chief of the Squadron; and AEC Meeker was now in charge of the electric shop. I was now second in charge, replacing Hilton, since he had failed the Chief's exam.

The Chief Petty Officers' Club had a lot more entertainment than did the First Class Petty Officers' Mess. Diann and I attended Saturday night dances, even though I did not know how to dance. We decided to take dancing lessons. We went once a week on Wednesday evening. We took lessons to learn how to do the waltz, the mambo, the tango, and the two-step. I could not get the rhythm. All I could do was shuffle around the dance floor. Diann did well and could dance with most any partner. Even today, all I can do is shuffle with no rhythm.

My pay was determined by various factors, such as pay grade (E1, E2, E3, etc.), longevity (number of years in service), and the number of dependents. Each time a change of one of those factors occurred, I would get pay adjustments. Because my number of dependents increased when Carla was born 3 October, I received increases in housing allowance and a cost of living adjustment. When I was promoted to Chief Petty Officer (AECA) on 16 November 1960, I again received pay adjustments in housing allowance and cost of living, plus a change in pay grade from E6 to E7, and an increase in sea pay. Then on 20 November 1960, I completed eight years of service, which entitled me to a longevity increase, plus increases in housing allowance and a cost of living adjustment. Diann and I thought we had hit a gold mind. We never had so much money before. My pay was now $340. Second Class Petty Officer Bently was the disbursing clerk in charge of maintaining my pay record. He called me one day asking me to report to the disbursing office stating that he wanted to show me something. When I arrived, he was mad because of all the work I had caused him during the last two months. So many changes had occurred that he had run out of room on my original pay record and he had to make out a new one. That fact did not bother me.

One of my most humiliating experiences occurred in December 1960. Shortly after my promotion to Chief Petty Officer, Commander Lee decided that there should be a compass rose on the base. A place where an aircraft's compasses are checked and calibrated, if necessary, is called a "Compass Rose." Well! CDR Lee decided that I should lay one out on the aircraft parking ramp. After examination of the area, I concluded that a compass rose would not be accurate in the available space on the ramp, due to all the metal buildings and structures in the area. My Division Officer, CWO2 Alex Hilliard, agreed with me. I informed the CO of my finding, but he was not convinced. He ordered me to continue with the project to lay out and paint a compass rose in the area he had designated. Warrant Officer Hilliard would not intercede for me. I got the survey crew lined up and had a circle laid out with the center point marked. Next, I had an officer take a Sexton reading to pin-point the coordinates of the north, east, south, and west directions. After that was accomplished, all that was left was painting the lines. I would not have any men under me do this. I did it myself. I was teased and ridiculed by all who walked by while I was painting the rose. Because of the metal in the area surrounding the rose, a magnetic compass would swing way off course from true north. It took a month of trying to calibrate the compasses of the aircraft before Commander Lee would agree that rose was unsuitable for aircraft compass calibration. Although I had proved my point, it was still a humiliating experience.

One of the things I would like to address, which most would not, is birth control. After hearing about duty station assignments from people with three or more children, Diann and I decided to plan and limit the number of children we would have in our family. Usually men with too many dependants were assigned unaccompanied tours of duty in either overseas areas or shipboard. Their dependants always had to stay behind in the continental limits of the US. Men with one or two children could get assignment to overseas areas. Although Diann and I had a happy and healthy sex life, after Carla was born, we used birth control methods to limit the number of children in our family. We did not want more than two children.

In January 1961, I was sent to Key West for a two-week deployment. I had been Chief for less than two months, but was responsible for the maintenance, service, and upkeep of the three aircraft during the deployment. After a few days, my khaki hat cover looked like a gray dish rag. It was covered with grease and oils. I needed to change it, but didn't know how. Another Chief named Bently, who had been promoted the same day as I, came into my room and saw what I was attempting and said he needed to change his hat cover too, but didn't know how either. We both struggled with our hats for quite some time when an "Old Salt" (a man with many years experience) came into my room. He laughed at the way we were trying to change our hat covers. He took pity on us and showed us how to flip the cover stay outside the hat, which released the tension. Now we considered ourselves to be "Old Salts." We knew something that the other new Chiefs didn't.

I returned from Key West to find Diann a total wreck. The day after I left, Bruce came down with the measles. He was sick most of the time I was gone. With a new baby in the house and me being gone, then Bruce getting sick, she really had her hands full. By the time I got home, he had gotten over the measles, except that he then developed trouble with his eyes. He had to start wearing glasses shortly after his spell with the measles. He had what is called "Lazy Eye." The pupil of his right eye would disappear behind his nose allowing him to see with only his left eye. In order to correct the problem, he was fitted with glasses and the left lens was covered so he had to use his right eye. He was just a little over three years old. He wore that eye patch for almost a year.

I must have proven myself during the Key West deployment. Shortly after returning to Bermuda, Chief Meeker was transferred to manage the Chief Petty Officers' Closed Mess and I was given charge of management of the electric shop. This was a very trying time for me. A lot of the men in the shop had more time in the navy than I, but I was in charge. Back in VR-8, Chief Matherly had demonstrated management by negative leadership traits, but I wanted to use positive leadership. I wanted to encourage rather than discourage. It wasn't long before I had the full support of all the men in the shop.

As mentioned previously, I stood duty as Assistant Duty Officer now instead of Duty Section Leader. One of the differences was an eight-hour watch rather than twenty-four hour day of duty. One night while standing the 2400 to 0800 hour watch, a secret message arrived at the duty office at about 0200, which only the Squadron Duty Officer, Lt. Shaw, was allowed to see and read. He called the CO and asked him to come to the office. He could not read the contents of the message aloud. When the CO arrived, they started discussing the actions with which the squadron was being tasked and how to proceed in implementing those actions. I soon learned the contents of the message and the orders that were given to the squadron CO. It seems that Trujillo, the Premiere of the Dominican Republic, had been assassinated and the US was concerned about a possible invasion from Cuba. The squadron was tasked with patrol duty of the sea between Cuba and the Dominican Republic. A liaison plane was to be launched as soon as possible to Guantanamo Bay, Cuba, to make preparations for the arrival of the squadron. The CO, Commander Lee, looked at me and said, "Go home and pack your bags. Do not tell your wife where you are going or how long you will be gone. You have seen the message, so you will be on the first flight."

When I got home and started packing my bags, Diann wanted to know what I was doing. I told her that all I could say was that I was going on a mission, but I couldn't tell her where, when, or for how long, and that I loved her and the kids and I would see them when I returned. That was the first time I had ever had to tell her that. Of course, I was going down to arrange for the maintenance spaces and aircraft ramp space. This was to be my first and only trip to Guantanamo Bay Naval Station, Cuba.

The plane launched from Bermuda around noon that day for the long flight to Cuba. Being a passenger, not a crew member, I was assigned lookout duty, which was rotated among other passengers. I sat in a window seat with headphones and watched the sky and water for anything of interest and listened to the pilot's, the copilot's, and radioman's conversation. Our estimated time of arrival was around midnight. About eleven that night, we ran into a thunderstorm. Sometimes the storm was quite severe. We had to fly around and not enter the air space until we got in contact with the plane on patrol at that time and were given permission to land. We went through one bad rainstorm, in which one engine was lost. We were now flying on a single engine, but still had no contact with the patrol plane.

Finally, the pilot got the approval to land, but he could not use the landing lights. He would have to fly and land by using the aircraft instruments. When in an aircraft, I have to put my faith in the pilot's ability and God's grace. I could hear the pilot asking the copilot if he could see landing strip buoys. Remember, this plane is a seaplane. It had to be set down on the water. The copilot's reply was, "No." I don't know how many times the pilot asked the same question, getting a "NO" response each time. The pilot said he hoped they could see the buoys soon because we were getting close to the water. About that time, there was big flash of lightning. The pilot yelled, "I see them! There they are and we're on the wrong side!" He banked the aircraft hard to the left and then back to straight and level and put the aircraft on the water in the sea lane almost immediately. I did not think too much about that landing at the time. It had been a long and tiring flight, plus I had stood an eight-hour watch the night before and I was ready for a bed. About ten the next morning, I was on the aircraft parking ramp looking out over the bay. That's when I became concerned about the flight the night before. On each side of the sea lane were huge posts sticking out of the water. A plane landing outside the sea lane would have been torn to pieces. God was watching over us on that flight. Because the landing lights could not be used during the landing, God gave us his BIG FLASH of LIGHTNING just at the right time to give us a safe landing.

The Naval Station at Guantanamo Bay was closed off from the rest of Cuba. There was a very high fence all around the base with marine guards posted to watch the perimeters for intruders. The US was not at war with Cuba, but considered Castro as a hostile enemy. Because of the insecurity of the situation with Cuba, we were restricted in our movement about the base. We were located at the seaplane side of the base and could not go to Leeward Point without special permits. The Chiefs' Club was a huge place, but I only got to go there one night. Even though we could not travel around the base, we had plenty to keep us entertained and occupied. Of course, work came

After the results of the accident report were published, everyone was wondering how such an event could have happened and what could be done to prevent it from happening again. I overheard First Class Structural Mechanic Smith discussing the accident with First Class Electrician Beardsley. He wondered if an alternate source of power could be provided to the engine instruments. When the primary power source failed, the engine instruments would automatically be switched to the alternate source. Since he was under my charge, I said to AE1 Beardsley that it sounded like a simple task so he should design a circuit that would work as the man had stated. I went home that night thinking about what the man had said. It wasn't long before I had designed the circuit myself, but I wanted to give Beardsley time to work on it. After about a month, I stopped Beardsley and asked how the circuit design was coming along. He told me that he had given up after a week because it couldn't be done. I told him that he hadn't tried hard enough to figure one out and that it could be done. If he didn't want to pursue it, then don't bother because I had one already designed and I would order the components for assembly.

I drew up the schematic of the circuit and assembled a prototype for test purposes. After I had everything working, I presented the idea to my Division Officer, now Lt. Hilliard. Lt. Hilliard was not only my Division Officer he was also a HAM radio operator and had been an electronics technician. I told him that I had designed an infallible circuit. He said there is no such thing. He took my design and schematic home and, after about a week, he agreed that my design was, in fact, infallible. He said I could now present my idea to the Commanding Officer. Commander Lee also had a background in electronics and was familiar with schematics. He looked over my proposal and liked what he saw. He could approve the installation of a prototype in one aircraft for test and evaluation purposes. He gave the okay for the installation in the XO's plane. It took me about two days to get the prototype installed. Every pilot who flew the aircraft commented favorably on my design. The CO was so impressed after making a flight in the plane he came to the shop and asked if there were any changes I could make to my design which could authorize him to have it put into his plane also. I worked on it a while and came up with the idea of a warning light that would come on when alternate power was in use. The crew would know the system was on alternate power. I then also put the circuit in his plane.

Then came the hard part! I was to draft a proposed "aircraft electronics service change." I had never done anything like that before and really didn't know where to begin. I checked out an actual service change from the Tech Library to use as a format guide and started from there. After about a month, I thought I had a good one drafted and presented it to Lt. Hilliard. He kept it about two weeks and returned it to me with all sorts of comments and faults. So, I started the drafting all over. It took another two weeks of work. Remember, I was doing the drafting of the proposal on my off time, not during normal working hours. Again, Lt. Hilliard chopped it all to pieces with corrections and comments. He would grill me on the exact routing of the wiring and procedures of installation. Finally, after about four months, he was satisfied and my proposal was forwarded to Naval Air Engineering Center for evaluation and approval. About three months afterwards, an Electronics Service Change was issued just as I had drafted it for installation in all P5M aircraft. That accomplishment netted me my first Letter of "Naval Commendation."

It was getting close to the end of my tour with Patrol Squadron Forty-Five. I had received orders to be transferred in February 1962, so I had to start thinking of selling our automobile. There were Bermuda laws that I learned about concerning selling an automobile to an individual who would be driving it in Bermuda. The car had to pass a rigid inspection. I couldn't just drive to an inspection station and expect it to be inspected within a few minutes or even hours. I had to make an appointment. I called for an inspection two months prior to my departure date. I could not get one until within two weeks of my departure date. Also, if it failed the day of the inspection, I could not make another appointment until two weeks later. I knew the normal things the inspector would look for: lights, tires, wiper operation, and, of course, for rust. I found a tail-light burned out, so I went to a service station, bought a new one, and put it in. I learned that not all service stations knew anything about car repair. They sold me the wrong bulb, but I didn't know it until the inspector flunked the car for it. That wasn't all that failed. I convinced the inspector to check the car out entirely, so that I would know what all had to be repaired for it to pass. Everything else was okay except the brakes. I nearly came unglued while watching him do a brake check. The inspector took the car for a test drive on a driving course. There was a white line painted on the pavement in the testing area. He sped the car down the white line at about thirty miles per hour, and then he put his left arm over the back of the seat and his right arm on the window of the door. He then slammed on the brakes to slide all four wheels and skid down the white line without holding the steering wheel. One wheel was not gripping the pavement as the others and the car slid sideways. He tried it again and the car slid sideways again. The car had failed the inspection with another fault. The inspector told me that the faults could be fixed at a garage and, if I could get them repaired, come back that afternoon. If I could not get it inspected that day, it would be two weeks before I could get another appointment. I was leaving the Island in ten days, so I had to get the inspection that day.

The inspector didn't think that I could get my car repaired and back in time to get it inspected that afternoon because of Bermuda customs. Every store and shop closed from noon until 2:00 P.M. for "Tea Time." No one would sell anything or do any work during that time. I went to the shop the inspector had recommended, although I knew it was too late. It was too late, it was 11:30 A.M. and they would not consider doing the work until 2 P.M. I went to the Service Station where I had gotten the wrong bulb, told them the story and they gave me the correct bulb. I borrowed a set of pliers and an adjustable wrench to adjust the brakes myself. I drove to a secluded area to do the adjustment. I did as the inspector had done. I slammed on the brakes to see how the car would slide. After a few times, I thought I knew which wheels to adjust. Within an hour, I had the car sliding straight. I returned the tools back to the service station and was back at the inspector's office by the time he returned from "Tea Time."

He looked at me and asked what I was doing there. I told him that I had the car repaired. He said that I couldn't have it repaired because all places were closed during "Tea Time." I told him that I had made the repairs myself, but he didn't believe I was capable. Anyway, I asked if he would check the car. He said that since no one else was there at the time and he didn't have anything else to do, he would give it a go. The light inspection was easy and passed. I anxiously watched as he drove to the brake test area. The car slid straight down the line. He tried it again and it slid straight again. He drove back to the office and apologized, said he didn't think I could have made the adjustment. The car passed the Bermuda inspection and I was now able to sell my car. I already had a buyer. I think that was the hardest thing to get done, in preparing to depart Bermuda.

Continuing my desire of improvement in the navy, I again applied for appointment to LDO as Electronics Officer. I submitted my application on 19 February 1962, just three days prior to my departure from VP-45. The application was forwarded from the Command to Bureau of Naval Personnel the day of my departure, 22 February 1962.

During my tour with VP-45, I completed the following correspondence courses:

Date Comp.	Course		Grade
6/1/59	Security of Classified Matter		3.70
8/31/59	Mil. Req. for PO1&C	NavPers 91207	3.44
5/11/61	Naval Orientation	NavPers 10900-3	3.80
12/18/61	Navy Regulations	NavPers 10740-A1	3.80

Three days before our departure date, the packers came to move our household effects. After the furniture and all the rest was moved out, we moved into a cottage set up by the navy as temporary lodging for departing families. I had already been relieved of my duties as shop CPO by AE1 Mullins and was awaiting transportation to the US. My orders were to Training Squadron Seven (VT-7) Meridian, Mississippi, with four days travel and thirty days leave en route. We spent three nights in the cottage. The cottage had a wood-burning fireplace. At night, we would make a fire with cedar logs. It was a very romantic atmosphere that made a fitting way to end our Bermuda tour. We departed from Kinnley Air Force Base on 22 February 1962.

Besides our luggage, we had a diaper bag for Carla and a Polaroid camera in a case, plus five bottles of liquor to carry on the plane. Each person entering the US was allowed a gallon of liquor to declare through Customs. Although each of us could declare a gallon, with all the other baggage, we could only handle one. We flew to Atlanta, Georgia, to go through Customs before heading for Texas. After going through Customs, we had a three-hour layover before boarding a flight for Dallas. George Griner was working at the air terminal as a Station Agent. I called him and he came right down to see us. Remember? George had been stationed in Hawaii when I was there. Also, I had stopped by to see him for a weekend on my way to Bermuda. Anyway, we had a nice visit by the time our flight number was announced for boarding. I started gathering up things for boarding the flight and discovered that the camera was missing. I had left it under the seat on the plane from Bermuda. George said not to panic and not to board the flight until he returned. He left and we sat. We were beginning to panic now. The PA system was announcing last call for our flight when George returned with our camera in hand. We were extremely grateful to him for locating the camera. George helped us get our belongings on the flight and we took off for Dallas.

Diann and Bruce had not been home for almost three years and I had not been home since that unforgettable trip in July 1959. Everyone was happy to see us. Mother in-law and Lefty had moved from Joey Drive to 3636 North 26th Street in Waco. We didn't have an automobile and needed one badly. I went to various dealerships in Waco and looked at many different ones. I found one that I really liked at Bird Kultgen Motors on Franklin Street. It was a 1962 Ford Fairlane, sort of burnt brown with a white top. I took it for a test drive out to show Diann. We decided it was the one. Lefty said he could help me get a better price at Kozelski Motors in West, Texas. He took me up there the next day and bought one just like the one I had tested for $200 less. I paid $2,700 for it, including taxes and license. We drove it to Meridian, Mississippi.

AVIATION TRAINING SQUADRON SEVEN (VT-7) NAS McCAIN FIELD, MERIDIAN, MISSISSIPPI

March 1962 to December 1964

T2A Buckeye

We arrived in Meridian, Mississippi, on 20 March 1962. We stayed in a motel on US 80 for about a week, while looking for a place to live. Interstate 20 had not been completed at this time. The base, NAS Meridian, was about nineteen miles north of Meridian, just a few miles off Highway 39. I checked in at 1400 hours on 23 March 1962. We found a place in the northern section of town at 2500 North 38th St., one block off Popular Springs Drive.

The place was a single dwelling with two bedrooms, living/dining room, kitchen, and large bath/laundry room. There were wooded lots all around the house, which gave the appearance that we lived in the countryside. There was a big shopping center with a grocery store, drugstore, a five and dime, and a "washateria" a little way from us. Diann and I settled into the community and started attending the Popular Springs Baptist Church. One of the men in my Sunday school class, I can't remember his name, owned a vacant lot next to where we were living. I asked him if I could clear a plot for a garden. We were able to have fresh vegetables most all the time we lived in Meridian.

The squadron operated and maintained T2J-A Buckeye aircraft. The primary mission was Student Pilot Basic Training in jet aircraft. Commander J. J. Brosnahan was the Commanding Officer, Marine Major R. A. Cameron was the Maintenance Officer, and, to my surprise, AVCM Zeb Gray was the Maintenance Chief. He had been the Leading Chief in VP-45 and also the one who acted as the judge at my Chief's initiation. Zeb assigned me to the electric shop. AEC Gene Warner was also in the shop. He was senior to me, so he was in charge.

Zeb told me that the squadron had a quota for CPO Leadership School in Pensacola, Florida, that must be filled. It was mandatory from the Chief of Naval Air Training, ADRM Clifton, that all Chief Petty Officers within his command attend the school. Zeb said my name would be added to the bottom of the list and when it came to the top, I would be going. I asked him where his name was on the list, but he wouldn't tell me. While in VP-45, I had made a trip to Pensacola on a liberty run. Chief Schindler was a student in the school. Chief Smig and I went to visit him one evening and he told us all about the school. He said, "If at all possible, don't get orders to this school." Now, here I am being told that I would be going to a place that I did not want to go, CPO Leadership School. There were fourteen Chiefs in the squadron and I made number fifteen.

VT-7 Chief Petty Officers

Naval Air Station, Meridian, was a sprawling station with the aircraft hangar area about three miles from the main gate. It was also known as McCain Field, named after Admiral John S. McCain. Much of the base was heavily wooded with thick undergrowth, almost impossible to walk through. The Navy Exchange, Commissary, Mess Hall, and living quarters were about two miles from the hangar area. After about a month to get myself orientated to the base, the squadron decided to send me to the T2J-1 Electrical and Instrument Systems Maintenance Course. It was a 56-hour course (7 days), which I completed on 8 May 1962. Next, I was sent to attend a 3-day Vertical Gyro Indicator Course, which I completed on 23 May 1962.

In November 1961, I had signed an extension agreement in order to get transferred out of Bermuda. I could reenlist for another four years, up to three months early, before the agreement went into effect, if I so desired. Since I had reenlisted 28 September 1956, I could now reenlist as early as 28 June 1962, which I did. There was an enlistment bonus given for the number of years of enlistment for a maximum of $2,000. On my first reenlistment, I had received a $982.80 bonus. For this, my second reenlistment, I received a $1,017.20 bonus. The very next day after reenlisting, Zeb told me that I was going to CPO Leadership School. He said it was because I had the money to buy new uniforms and was more able to get prepared for the school than any of the other Chiefs in the squadron. I was the most junior chief in the squadron, so I couldn't refuse. I found out later that it was him that I was replacing on the list. The school was five weeks long.

I told Diann about my orders and how long I would be in school. We decided that I would take her and the kids to my mother-in-law in Waco before going to Pensacola. I was to start school on 5 July. It was a long trip. Waco is about 500 miles from Meridian and Pensacola is about 700 miles from Waco. I didn't have much time to waste. I arrived at the school on the afternoon of 4 July 1962.

The CPO Leadership School was a concocted idea of Admiral Joe Clifton. I had run into that name in Corpus Christi in 1958. The school was worse than going through boot camp. The restrictions were horrendous. I was assigned to platoon one, room one, bunk one, with DTC Mulvaney in bunk two and AMC Sullivan in bunk three. Each of us was to assume Room CPO on a rotating daily basis. The room would be inspected daily and demerits for any infractions would be given to whoever was Room CPO that day. The first day of the school began on Friday. That day we were given instructions on schedules, maintenance of our room, conduct, personnel uniform inspections, and a host of other things. We had the weekend to get our personal gear in order. Monday and Tuesday would be demerit-free days. Warnings would be issued for any infractions incurred on those two days, but the demerits wouldn't count. Anyone receiving three or more demerits would have to appear before a board for possible disciplinary action. Accumulation of fifteen demerits warranted dismissal with a certainty of disciplinary action.

First Platoon

MC Sullivan suggested that we use the weekend to get our room in tip-top shape. That Saturday morning we went to the commissary and bought Pledge furniture polish to shine the floor and all the furniture. After we completed cleaning the room to everyone's satisfaction, we started shining our shoes. Being in the aviation branch, I was required to have a black pair, a brown pair, and a white pair, which had to be highly shined at all times. The two pair not being worn had to be placed under the bunk in a certain manner with demerits given if out of place. I had completed my black pair and white pair and was polishing my brown pair when I had an accident. As I was getting polish from the can, it slipped from my hand and landed upside down on the freshly cleaned and polished floor. My two roommates looked at me with daggers in their eyes. I told them that it was my fault and I would clean up the mess. The floor was covered with brown hardboard tiles. The more I wiped the brown polish, the shinier the spot became. The spot looked like a light in the center of a dull area. I decided to spit shine the whole tile. Now that tile looked like a lake in the dull land. All three of us spit shined the whole floor with brown shoe polish. We did not dare walk on the floor except in our stocking feet. I found an old blanket and cut it into pieces for us to shuffle on across the floor. This helped in keeping the floor shiny. My chest of drawers was next to the door, so I reserved the lower drawer for our shuffling rags. The floors were graded during the daily inspection as to condition. Any room with a grade of deck level five was awarded "Honor Room," which gave the occupants Friday night all-night liberty and excused them from locker inspection on Saturday morning. By late Sunday evening, we were satisfied that our room was in tip-top shape.

On Monday morning, school started with what was to be our daily routine. We had to fall in ranks and start marching at 0555 hours. We marched to the school building and dropped off our books in the classrooms, and marched to the mess hall for breakfast. We didn't have to eat breakfast if we didn't want to, but we all had to go through the chow line. After breakfast we could straggle back to the Q (barracks) and fall in at 0645 hours to march to the parade field. We would practice marching various formations for two hours and then march back to the Q. This was July in Pensacola, Florida. It was hot and muggy. Everyone was sweaty and in need of a shower after marching for two hours. We had fifteen minutes to get a shower, change clothes, and fall in for instructions and personnel inspection. While we were being inspected, inspectors were going through inspecting the rooms. After the personnel inspection was completed, we marched to the school building for classroom studies. This was to be our routine Monday through Friday for five weeks. This was worse than going through boot camp. There were sixty Chief Petty Officers in this class, all with eight plus years in service. It didn't seem right that we were subjected to this kind of treatment. Many complained, but I knew our complaints would go unheard. So, I just went along with the flow and did what I was told. I figured I could take it for five weeks and I wouldn't have to go through it again.

On Tuesday morning just before personnel inspection, the instructor announced that he did not know how room one could have gotten their room to a deck level five on the very first day of school. Anyone wanting to see what a deck level five room looked like should drop by room one and take a look. Room one was awarded "Honor Room" the very first day. Our work had paid off. We had Friday night liberty and didn't have to stand locker inspection on

Saturday morning. Room one was awarded "Honor Room" each of the five weeks of the school, all because of my accident the first day.

I did get three demerits during the time I was there. One of those demerits depicts the pettiness of the school. One day when I was Room CPO, we had thoroughly cleaned the room, we thought. After we had left, a mosquito flew into the room and died on the window sill. I received a demerit for gear adrift on the window sill because of the dead mosquito. Another demerit was caused by me closing my locker door in a hurry and not checking it before leaving the room. The plastic cleaning cover was protruding out the door as I was rushing to morning inspection. The third demerit was one of my shoes was sticking out from under my bunk by a fraction of an inch.

The daily drilling was sometimes downright funny. Each of us was given a chance to demonstrate our ability of marching a group of men in ranks. I did fair, but some of the men had zero ability. One such person was Chief Hreno. His every command was executed on the wrong foot. Especially during drills that required each squad to perform different maneuvers. The men would be running into each other. Also with column movements, he would get so concerned with doing it right, he would miss the spot of the turn and still give the command on the wrong foot. The drill instructor, Chief Smith, would scream and yell at him. I really think the instructor enjoyed yelling at Hreno because he had him marching us to and from the parade field most every day.

I can't say whether the school helped me in leadership skills or not, but I was glad to graduate and receive a completion certificate. I knew of Chiefs who had rebelled and either had to go through it again or be reduced in rank for failure to obey instructions. I did not want to go through that school again. I went back to Meridian without further ado, except first I had to go to Waco to pick up Diann, Bruce, and Carla. We arrived home in Meridian on 13 August 1962.

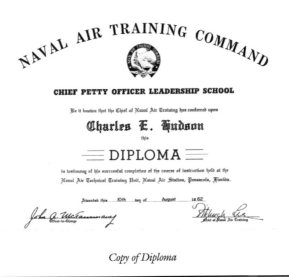

Copy of Diploma

TOP ROW: MC BRYDE, NEBERMAN, JONES, C.O.D., BEARD, STALLINGS, STEINKAMP, LAZARUS, ERVIN, HRENO, LUTZ, SULLIVAN, HUDSON, HANKINS, ROSETTE, WYLIE, AND MULVANEY

3RD ROW: GRACE, STONICH, BOYLE, BAILEY, BARRY, DENDY, KNOX, H. M., LOGUE, BLACKMON, WERBA, SMITH, WHITE, JONES, D. A., MORROW, AND HARRELL

2ND ROW: KUYKENDALL, COPSON, NIEMI, RIDGE, WYLIE, CARDWELL, BREWTON, THOMPSON, ADAMS, STAPP, MUNDY, PALERMO, WEEKS, YAKLIN, TIZZANO, AND COVAS

1ST ROW: GOEBEL, HICKMAN, KNOX, G.M., JOHNSON, BISHOP, CARTER, SAUNDERS, JONES, A.D., CAREY, SELLERS, PRIMROSE, AND CAIATI

CPO Leadership Class

All my life I have liked to hunt and fish. I heard that a logging company, Flint Co, offered to let men from the base hunt and fish on their property, provided they applied for a permit. It only cost a dollar per year. I didn't care as much about the hunting as I did the fishing. I got my Mississippi fishing license and applied for the permit. They gave me a map of the area to which I was allowed to go. It was about twenty miles north of Meridian with two small lakes in which were bass, crappie, blue gill perch, and catfish. Also, there were a few other places nearby where I could go fishing. One day while on a fishing outing, I met Lt. Stred and Lt. Strothers from the squadron, who were also fishing. We all agreed that if we had a boat, we could catch a lot more fish.

I decided I needed a boat, but couldn't afford to buy one. I bought a *Popular Mechanics* magazine that had a scale model drawing of a boat. It had detailed instructions on how to build your own boat. I convinced Diann to let me try my hand at it. I expanded the model layout and bought the materials listed in the magazine. A small shed was in the backyard where I would work on that boat 'til dark. It took me three or four months to build that thing. I saw Lt. Stred a while later. He said that he and Lt. Strothers had built a boat out of plywood and were having a great time fishing. I took him to my house and showed him the boat I was building. He was somewhat impressed. I had put a fiberglass coat on my boat. I had built it to last. I put special racks on top of the car so I could carry it to the lakes. Johnny Hybner, Bruce, and I would spend Saturdays up at the Flint County lakes.

I must tell about the time that I helped a man steal a boat. I was alone at the Flint County Lake one Saturday morning. A black man and his family came later to fish in the lake. I didn't have a boat then so I had to fish from the dam or the small pier that led out from the dam. There was a new aluminum boat chained to a tree next to the pier. I thought it sure would be nice if I could use that boat. The black man and I visited for a while and then went about fishing again. A while later, a 1962 Plymouth pulled up on the dam next to the boat. The driver took out a big set of keys and started trying to open the lock on the boat chain. He soon became frustrated with his inability to open the lock because none of the keys fit. He could see that both the black man and I were watching him. He made the statement, "That SOB gave me the wrong set of keys." With that he pulled a pistol from a holster and shot off the lock. While holding the pistol in his hand he said to me, "Here, help me load this boat." Man! I didn't argue. Then he called out, "Black man, get up here, and help load this boat." The black man said, "Yes, Sir." We put the boat on top of that new car and he drove off holding the boat with one hand. I was not about to refuse his orders, him standing there with a pistol in his hand. I was somewhat concerned that he might shoot us for scratching the top of the new car when we were positioning the boat on it. I packed up my gear and went home after that ordeal. I did not want to be there if that man returned.

ADC Stith worked in maintenance control as the logs and records CPO. He and Jane lived a short distance from us. One day, he approached me about joining him and two others in a carpool. It was nineteen miles one way to the base. I readily accepted. The others in the pool were Lt. Cheek, the Maintenance Control Officer, and AKC Woods, the Supply Chief. Lt. Cheek was a "Navy Mustang" also. The four of us taking weekly turns in driving saved a lot in gas money, plus the wear and tear on the cars. It also gave Diann the use of the car for shopping and getting out of the house. Later, AZ3 Johnny Hybner joined us in the pool. He worked with Chief Stith.

To further my education, I enrolled in Meridian Junior Collage for the 1962 fall semester. I signed up for algebra and physics. Unlike Hutchinson, Kansas, back in 1957, I had time to go to school and finish my study assignments without outside interference. The physics course was the one I liked most, although I had to work hard to complete the course. There was one unforgettable character in the class, Lt. Fields. He slept through most of the classes, yet he would always ace the exams. I asked why he bothered coming to class since he knew the material. His answer was that he needed the credits for his Masters and to receive them he had to attend the class.

It was 16 October 1962! J. F. Kennedy was President and Nikita Krushchev was Premiere of the USSR. The Soviet Union was building a missile base in Cuba. I remember the base being put on ready alert. Everyone's leave was canceled. Although the base had no retaliatory capabilities, all the instructor pilots could be ordered to combat duty if the US went to war over the "Cuban Missile Crisis." It was a grim two weeks. We were all glad when the Soviets backed down. None of the flight instructors were transferred to a combat-ready squadron during this ordeal.

Johnny Hybner and his wife, Flo, became good friends with Diann and me. We would get together on the weekends for cookouts and play card games. Johnny and I would go fishing and hunting together. In November and December 1962, Johnny and I entered into a business. There were many pecan trees throughout Meridian. The owners were letting the pecans go to waste. Johnny and I made a pact with the owners to gather them on the "halvsies." We would pick up the pecans and divide them in halves for the owner and us. We sold our pecans on the local market. With my basic pay being $350 per month, this income gave us a little extra for Christmas.

The Reason I Took Up Playing Golf: The Maintenance Chief, Zeb Gray, loved to play golf. All during the summer, Zeb would excuse the Maintenance Control Chief, ATCS Calloway; the Supply Chief, AKC Woody; and the Power Chief, ADC Parkas from work to play golf with him. Zeb would call down to the electric shop and order one of us chief electricians to come to man the Maintenance Control Office. There were two Chiefs in the electric shop, Chief Gene Warner, and myself. Gene would fume and fuss about us always being called on to man Maintenance Control every week. He claimed that we were never given a day off for any reason. We would also like to do some things during the week days. I told Gene that, in self defense, the only way we were going to get a day off is to take up golf. He said that he would never take up chasing a little white ball all over a cow pasture just to have a day off. One day Zeb called down to the shop for me to come up and man Maintenance Control. I asked him what he would say if I said that I wanted to go play golf, too. He said, "You want to go? Tell Gene to come up and man Maintenance Control, we need a fourth player. Go home and get your gear and meet us at the golf course." I had never played the game before in my life. I didn't have any gear except some tennis shoes. Zeb then said to go get my tennis shoes; that I could rent clubs at the Pro Shop and buy some balls and tees. Gene was really furious this time. He thought that I had deserted him. I met them at the golf course, rented the clubs, and bought a bag of tees and six balls. The first ball that I hit sliced over the fence, across a road, and into the woods. Lost it! Now I had five balls. When the game was over, I had a score of 136, two balls and some tees. I enjoyed the day so much that I was hooked on the game. Later, I was in the Base Exchange and bought a starter set of Northwestern golf clubs for thirty-five dollars. The set included two woods, a driver and a three wood, 3, 5, 7, and 9 irons, and a putter, plus a bag.

I didn't know if I wanted to play golf or go fishing. I enjoyed both outings. Diann and I became friendly with a family in the church named Bill and Kathy Sawyer. Bill worked for Phillips Oil Company. Bill liked to play golf as much as I, so we would go on Saturdays, whenever we could. He and I would get on the golf course as early as possible, because we knew it would take us all day to play a round. We were both real duffers and both sliced the ball off the tee something awful. The problem was that he was left-handed and I was right-handed. He would hit his ball into the rough to the left of the fairway and I would hit mine into the rough (woods) on the right. We had a hard time remembering where our ball went into the rough after we had helped the other find his. By the time we found both our balls several foursomes would have played through. At that time, I didn't know too much about the rules and neither did he. It took all day for us to play eighteen holes. When we hit a ball into the rough, which was every other shot, we would look for the ball until we found it. We didn't know there was a time limit on looking for lost balls. We would be on the golf course when it opened and leave at dark after the course had closed. Our wives would be so upset with us for coming home so late.

I mentioned that while in Hutchinson, Kansas, the day after my twenty-fifth birthday, I started experiencing hemorrhoid problems. The problem worsened while stationed in Bermuda. I tried to relieve my condition every way I knew how. I must have used a case or two of Preparation-H, which helped ease the pain, but did not shrink the hemorrhoids. By May 1963, I decided not to battle them any longer. I checked myself into the base infirmary for treatment. The doctor said my condition was beyond his capability. I would have to go to the Naval Hospital in Pensacola, Florida, to have them removed. It was thought that I would most likely be in the hospital from 21 to 30 days. Because I would be gone such a long period, I decided to take Diann and the kids to Waco, to my mother-in-law's house. I had the weekend to get to Pensacola.

We left Meridian after work on Friday evening. It was so late that we knew it would be about two in the morning when we arrived in Waco. We were stopped at a stop light in Bossier City at about eleven that night. Both Bruce and Carla were asleep in the back seat. Diann and I heard tires skidding on the pavement, but couldn't tell where they were. All of a sudden our car was hit in the rear and knocked completely through the intersection. Both Bruce and Carla were thrown off the rear seat onto the floorboards. Now they were crying and we were somewhat upset. The car that hit us pulled around us and sped off; it was a hit and run. Diann got the license plate state, but not the number. The car was a four door 1954 Ford from Oregon. I pulled to the side of the street and called the police from a nearby phone. It took about thirty minutes before a policeman arrived. After a few minutes we had given them all the information we had and they were satisfied that we had not committed any crimes. They told us that they would put out an APB for the car and for us to stop by the police station on our way back from Waco. I overheard one of the policemen telling the other one, "I sure would hate it if someone ran into me with that few miles on my car." There were just 6,000 miles on our 1962 Ford Fairlane. I knew that was the last we would ever hear from those guys. The hit and run car was from Oregon, we had Texas license plates, and we were in Louisiana. Only the rear bumper was damaged on our car, but it didn't make me feel any better. We drove on to Waco that night and I left for Pensacola the next day to have the hemorrhoid operation.

That operation was something else. I checked into the hospital on 14 May 1963 and spent three days in preparation for the operation. The doctors wanted me to be completely cleaned out on the inside of my body. I was put on a liquid diet of almost plain water. Then I had to give myself an enema on the second morning, another that evening, and two the next day. Plus, I could not have anything to eat after the noon meal that day. The morning of the fourth day, I was wheeled into the operating room for surgery. I was given a local anesthetic, which allowed me to know what was happening, and the operation began. It was over in about thirty minutes. The doctor brought three large masses in a jar to show me what had been removed from my rear end. They were about the size of my thumb. He asked if I wanted to keep them since they were already in alcohol. I told him that I had them long enough and he could keep them. I was taken back to what the hospital staff called the "Dirty Ward" to recover. I was told that I would be in the hospital for another two weeks.

The next three days were the worst of my life. I was required to sit in a sitz bath for thirty minutes at a time three times a day. I was to have the water as hot as I could stand it. Also, I was to have a bowel movement every day. Each time I moved, I was in pain. Yes! I was given pain killers, but they were ineffective most of the time. I sure couldn't sit in a chair. Once I got seated in the sitz tub and the pain had subsided, I didn't want to get out. But, I had to respect the needs of others in my condition and limit myself in the use of the tub. After all, there were only two tubs.

The first day, I could not make myself have a bowel movement. I tried once that first evening and it was like sitting on a bed of hot coals. I was also hungry after being on a liquid diet for three days. That evening after surgery I was given another liquid meal. The next day I was given a more solid food for breakfast. By evening of that day, I was back to the more normal solid diet. By morning of the second day, my stomach was full and I was beginning to get the urge for a bowel movement. I tried again and after only a tiny amount had passed, I thought I would faint. The pain was so bad that I had to have a pain killer when I got back to my bed. Each time I tried to have a bowel movement, it felt like razor blades were being extracted from my rear end, like I was being cut to pieces. On the third day after surgery, my stomach was really full. I knew I was going to have to make myself forget the pain and have the bowel movement. That afternoon a Marine was placed in the bed next to mine. He had just come from the operating room. He'd had the same type of operation as I and he too was in pain. He watched me all that afternoon going to the bathroom and returning without having accomplished my mission. My mission was having a bowel movement. About five that evening, I decided that I would take a sitz bath. Just as I sat down in the hot water, I got a strong urge to have a movement. I got out as quickly as I could and dried off. Quickly was about twice a snail's pace. I sat on the commode and had a movement about the size of a kitchen match stem, which felt like the Empire State Building. I sat there all tensed, unable to move because of the pain. The pain subsided after a few minutes and I began to relax. When I had relaxed just enough, an eruption occurred with such force that nearly blew me off the pot. I filled the commode with all that had been accumulated over the past three days. I felt like I had just given birth to a litter of half grown tigers. I thought I had experienced pain before, but it was nothing compared to the pain after the explosion. I sat there in a stunned state for a long time before I could move. I had to hold onto a rail to get back to my bunk. I asked for a painkiller and even that took several minutes to take effect. The Marine said that he was going to make sure he didn't have to go through what I had just experienced. Three days later I saw him holding the rail trying to get back to his bunk. He'd had his litter of tigers.

I checked out of the hospital to return to Meridian and report back for duty in VT-7. But, instead of checking in, I had to drive to Waco to pick up Diann and the kids. I took a few days leave and headed for Waco. It was hot and humid and our car did not have air conditioning. On Friday morning I called Kozelski Ford Motors in West and asked about installation of an air conditioner. It just so happened they had a special for that weekend. I went up that afternoon to get it ordered and set up for installation. After I arrived and had made the deal with the salesman, he discovered that the company was out of stock. I told him that it had to be installed by that Saturday because I had to return to Meridian. He called Bird Kultgen Motors in Waco and they had one in stock. He made arrangements for me to pick it up early Saturday morning. I set the alarm and was waiting for Bird Kultgen to open Saturday morning. All I had to do was sign for Kozelski Ford Motors to pick it up and head for West. As they were loading the air conditioner into the trunk of the car, the stock clerk noticed the damaged rear bumper. He asked why I didn't get a new bumper while I was there. I could get it at wholesale price since I was signing for Kozelski Ford Motors anyway. It only cost twenty-nine dollars wholesale. I jumped at the bargain. The air conditioner was installed on Saturday and we went back to Meridian on Sunday. It sure was nice to ride in a cool car. I checked into VT-7 on 6 June 1963. That next weekend, I put the new bumper on the car. I had a new set of tools from Sears. It took forty-five minutes from start to finish. Now we had a nice-looking, cool automobile.

I was not the only one in our family that had problems. Diann had experienced problems with her feet most of her life. She has what is known as "hammer toes" and "planter warts." She would soak her feet in hot water and I would trim the warts. She went to a foot specialist in Laurel, Mississippi, who operated on the toes of one foot. She had pins protruding from each toe after the removal of the middle knuckle bone. She hobbled around for two months in that condition, but her toes were straight. Finally it was time to return to the doctor for removal of the pins. The doctor did not give her a sedative, but proceeded to yank the pins out. I know it hurt. Both of us were shocked and upset with the doctor. After the pin removal, her toes returned to the original position of the hammer toe. She would never have the other foot operated on. Her feet are still in bad condition.

One day, I believe it was in July 1963, I came home to a dreadful sight. Diann was lying in the middle of the living room floor and Carla was sitting in a chair looking at her. I have no idea how long they were in that state. I called the base infirmary and they in turn sent an ambulance and she was put in the Meridian Hospital. All sorts of tests were conducted, even a spinal tap, but nothing was determined as to her problem. After about a week, she was released. After that first episode she would have a fainting spell every month. Still the doctors could find nothing. I started keeping track of the spells and her menstruation period. The record I kept reflected that she would start having blackouts about three days before her period. I told the doctors that her problem had to be female organ related as indicated by my records. They wouldn't listen to me. They kept doing brain scans and such and didn't look elsewhere. We became accustomed to the fact that she would have these problems every so often.

September 1963, was time to apply for LDO again. I submitted my application as usual. Gene said, "Are you going to apply for that again? I'm not applying this year. Both of us have been trying for several years and were never accepted." I decided to go for Aircraft Maintenance instead of Electronics. A review of the statistics indicated that more Aircraft Electricians Mates (AEs) were being selected as Maintenance Officers than any other specialty. Major Cameron was my interviewing officer.

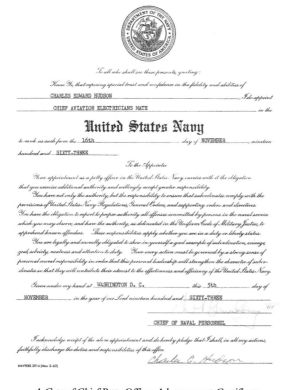

A Copy of Chief Petty Officer Advancement Certificate

At the time I was advanced to Chief Petty Officer, the navy had a policy that the promotion was a temporary appointment for three years. My three years of temporary appointment was up 16 November 1963. On 5 November 1963, the Chief of Naval Personnel signed the certificate changing my status to Chief Petty Officer, permanent appointment.

It was also time for Chief Cummings, who worked in the reports section in Maintenance Control, to retire. Since there was no need for two chiefs in the electric shop, I was moved into the reports section as Chief Cummings' replacement. This is one of the best things that could have happened to me. It allowed me to broaden my knowledge of the total aircraft maintenance spectrum. I soon learned that keeping track of all the squadron aircraft required many and various reports, for which I was now responsible. There were reports that were required by the CNO, NavAir, CNATRA, and CNABATRA. There were reports of aircraft flight hours, man-hours, and even reports on the amount of money spent for things, such as aviation fuel, flight clothing and shoes, and office supplies. The significant difference between the reports submitted in the 1960s and the 2000s is the reports had to be typewritten with no mistakes and no corrections. There were no computers for entering the data. I have spent hours trying to get a perfect report completed. There have been times that I would make a perfect report, then a mistake on the last line of a page and have to do the entire page over. After I had thought I had a proofreader would find a mistake and I would have to do the report all anew.

Diann and I had decided to spend Thanksgiving with Creba and family in Louisville, Kentucky. I had my leave request approved and was ready to go. President John F. Kennedy was assassinated that November 1963. The base was put on alert and my leave was put on hold until it was determined that there was not a National Security crisis.

New Year's Eve, 31 December 1963, was a day to remember. All the clubs had big plans for the New Year's Eve celebrations. I had already purchased tickets for the Chiefs' Club event and Diann had made babysitter arrangements. It was a Saturday and we needed to go shopping at the Base Exchange and Commissary. We arrived at the base at 0900, when the stores opened. We went to the exchange first. When we came out of the exchange, it was snowing. By the time we came out of the commissary the snow was about a half-inch deep. We still needed to stop at the service station for gas and we were nineteen miles from home. By the time we exited the main gate, there was about an inch of snow on the ground, and we didn't have snow chains for the car.

When we arrived in town, instead of turning on the street to go home, I told Diann that I had just heard on the radio that Gibson's, a discount merchandise store, had snow chains on sale and we were going to get some. Gibson's didn't have any chains the size for our car, so I bought the next larger size, hoping I could cut them down to fit. By now there were about three inches of snow on the ground. This was becoming a major snow storm and now the radio was broadcasting the depths of the snow, as well as warnings. Meridian being very hilly, we had a hard time getting home. I couldn't drive up the streets of the normal way home. I had to go on the one with the lesser inclines. By the time we finally arrived home, there were about five inches on the ground. After we had unloaded our groceries, I took the spare tire to the front porch that was out of the blowing snow and started working on fitting the snow chains. When I finished, about three or four P.M., the radio announced that there were ten inches on the ground. Also, the radio was announcing the cancellations of scheduled New Year's Eve parties. The EM and Officers' Clubs had canceled, but I didn't hear anything about the Chiefs' Club. I called and was informed that the party was not going to be canceled and there would be no refund for unused tickets. The party was scheduled for 1900 hours. After I had put the chains on the car, I told Diann that I was going for a test drive. The streets in the area were hilly. If I could navigate them, we could drive to the base, but if I ended up in the ditch, then I would not be very far from our house and I could walk home. It was fun driving in the snow, which was up to twelve inches now. Harry Wood and his wife, Pete, had planned to ride with Diann and me to the club, so I drove to their house to see if they still wanted to go. They were amazed that I was out driving in the deep snow. Harry said that if I would drive they would go.

At about six P.M., the snow stopped after dumping fifteen inches. This was a new record. Diann and I went by and picked up Pete and Harry then headed for the base, nineteen miles away. We were the first car on Highway 39 going north to the base. When we arrived at the club our car was the only one in the parking lot, but the club was full of people. They had walked from base housing. There were people dressed in everything from tuxedos, evening gowns, and fur coats to jeans and sweat suits. The band had not arrived. The band arrived about fifteen minutes later and said they were sure grateful to whoever made the ruts in the snow from town. The snow had filled the ditches along the highway. The only way I stayed on the road was watching the fence posts on each side of the road and keeping the car in the middle between them. As I said, "That was a memorable New Year's Eve."

January 1964, was the time to ensure my recommendation was approved to take the exam for advancement to E8. I took the E8 exam in February. The results of promotions from the exam were posted in May. I did not get promoted to E8 due to being commissioned to Ensign at a later date. Yes! The results of the LDO selection were also posted in May and I had been selected for appointment to Ensign, effective 1 October 1964.

ADJC R. B. Burge Retirement on 25 March 1964

I don't remember what month, but in 1964 three civil rights workers were killed in Philadelphia, Mississippi, which was located about twenty miles northwest of the base. The FBI came into the area to handle the investigation of the crime. The three men were missing and no one was talking as to their whereabouts. The FBI mostly took over the base. They ordered 400 sailors a day to go out in groups of thirty to search the entire community, so it was thought. Each squadron had to furnish 100 men and the Naval Air Station had to furnish 200 men. Commander Wikenheiser said that his Chief Petty Officers would not be assigned to tramp through the highways, byways, and fields. The 100 men from VT-7 made up of Junior Officers—Ensigns, Lieutenants Junior Grade, Lieutenants, and enlisted men below the rank of Chief Petty Officer—in order to reduce the workload of the white hats, were made available to the FBI for their search. I was assigned as Assistant Squadron Duty Officer (ASDO) from 0600 to 1800 for two months. Of course, I still had to make sure all the reports were completed and submitted on time.

One day, a Lieutenant came into the Squadron Duty Officer's office. He was hopping mad! He reported that he, along with twenty-nine other men, had to sit under a shade tree all day. His story is that they had ridden the bus to a certain road and been let off. The FBI agent ordered them to walk along a dirt road until they were out of sight from the paved road, then stop under a big oak tree. After a short time, the Lieutenant ordered the men to split into two groups; one group to search one side of the road, and the other group to search the other side. As they started crawling through the fence to commence their search, the FBI agent ordered them to return to the shade tree until he told them to move. They stayed there all day. It made the Lieutenant so mad that the FBI agent had overruled him. It was learned later that the FBI agents had already learned of the location of the three civil rights workers, but was only pretending to search in hopes that someone would identify the culprits. This activity went on for two months, after which we returned to our normal work routine. However, things were different. Most of the time, the men were discussing their involvement with the FBI.

I received orders 3 September 1964, to be commissioned Ensign (Limited Duty Officer- temporary) on 1 October 1964, and to depart in December to attend the Aviation Officers Indoctrination Course at Naval Air Station, Pensacola, Florida. I reported to the Commanding Officer's office, Commander Wikenheiser, as directed at 0800 on 1 October 1964. I was told to bring Diann with me. After the swearing in and accepting the commission, I was promoted to the rank of Ensign LDO temporary. I was in a white uniform. Commander Wikenheiser put one of the shoulder boards on my right shoulder and Diann put the one on my left shoulder. 2 Corinthians 5:17 states, "If any man be in Christ, he therefore is a new creation: old things are passed away; behold all things are become new." From the time of my swearing in and accepting the commission to Ensign, I became a new creation. This became my second new creation. My service number changed from 451 41 02 to 685956/6852. The 6852 was the designation as aircraft maintenance. One minute, I was a Chief Petty Officer and the next minute, I was an Ensign.

Commissioned Ensign (LDO) United States Navy, 1 October 1964

All my uniforms were a different style and I would be saluted by the enlisted personnel. I was now senior to the E8s and E9s when just moments before I was their junior. At that moment, I became a "Navy Mustang." Then CDR Wikenheiser ordered me to put on my hat. Now, it is standard protocol that navy personnel do not keep their hat on when in a building. I questioned that command, but I was ordered to put mine on anyway and then I was given an order of "Forward, March!" and was marched out the door of the CO's office. As I stepped out the door, Master Chief Zeb Grey gave an order of "Hand Salute!" There were twelve Chief Petty Officers in ranks to be the first enlisted men to salute me after being commissioned. It is customary for an officer to give a dollar bill to the first enlisted man that renders him a salute after his commissioning. The Master Chief had arranged with the CO in having me saluted first by all the Chiefs in the squadron at the same time. Man! I had to shell out twelve dollars for getting commissioned. Man! I had Side Boys at my commissioning! I guess it was payback time. I had worked under the Master Chief both in VT-7 and VP-45. I had told him that one day I was going to be his boss. Now that I was an Ensign and I was senior to the Master Chief. Although I was now considered a Commissioned Officer in the United States Navy, it was only a temporary commission. I still held a permanent enlisted status with the pay grade of E7.

Then Commander Wikenheiser said that he would give me two weeks to make my "Social Call." Man! What's a social call? I had much to learn about protocol. Lt. Cheek was also an LDO (a Mustang), so I relied on him for the information to keep me out of trouble with the CO. I had not known I needed an item called a "Calling Card." Those had to be ordered for both myself and Diann. Why did she have to have a calling card? She wasn't in the navy. It was then that I learned a wife could make or break a man's career. I soon found out that there were various social functions where my attendance was required. As an enlisted man, I could attend the social functions if I so desired, but it was not mandatory. I also learned that the Skipper could and would make a return social call without announcement and that I and my family had to be prepared at all times. But, it was not mandatory for the Skipper to make a return call. I did want my first call by the Skipper to be correct in every way. Chief Stith worked part time as a bartender at the "O" Club. I asked him to find out what the Skipper and Mrs. Wikenheiser liked as social drinks. I don't remember what Mrs. Wikenheiser liked, but CDR Wikenheiser drank Manhattans. I made sure I had all the ingredients and learned how to mix them the way he preferred. Today, I don't remember how to mix drinks. The Skipper never made any social calls to our house.

After getting all my uniforms converted, that I could convert, from Chief to Officer and purchasing the others that I needed, I was ready to act like an officer. Lieutenant John S. McCain III, who was a flight instructor, stopped me one day, and said, "Ed, let me tell you how to be a successful LDO. Always carry a piece of paper and walk fast. That will let everyone think you have a mission to perform and you have set out to complete that mission." I knew that may work on occasions, but it wouldn't work all the time. I still remember the advice from Lt. McCain, now Senator McCain from Arizona in 2011. The Skipper assigned me to the Line Division as Assistant Line Officer. I think Zeb had a hand in the assignment since I had made the comment to him, "You had better be nice to me, I may be your boss one day." He made sure that I was no longer in the Maintenance Control office.

About two weeks after my commission, I made my social call on the Skipper, as directed. I did not know what to expect. I had been told by Lt. Cheek to stay about fifteen to twenty minutes and excuse myself and leave. What I encountered was far from that which was expected. The XO was also at the Skipper's house. The first ten minutes went as expected, and then the doorbell rang. The XO answered the door and told the people at the door, "Bring it into the living room." To my surprise, the men were from the Line Division and carrying a sign that belonged to VT-9. It seemed that the two squadrons had a rivalry between them and pulled pranks on each other from time to time. I did not know of the rivalry. The removal of the sign was to get back at VT-9 for some prank that had been pulled on VT-7. Both the CO and XO looked at me and the XO asked what I wanted the men to do with the sign. "They're your men; what are you going to do with the sign?" Man! I was at a loss for words. I had no idea how to respond to their inquiry. They were having great fun watching me squirm under their bombardment of questions on what to do about the men who stole the sign and how I was going to explain to VT-9 about the missing sign. After about forty-five minutes, well beyond my intended stay, the XO said that he would take care of everything and that I could be excused. I'll tell you! My first social call was one that I'll never forget. As an enlisted man, I had always been taught that men of the officer ranks were aloof to such antics. Now, here were the CO and XO plotting pranks on a sister squadron.

Diann and I both were required to have "Calling Cards." She too had to become a "Lady" and attended most all social functions. Our first to attend was the Halloween Ball. We stayed the required amount of time and left well before midnight. After we had departed, things began to happen. The prank of the stolen sign began to backfire, so to speak. We were told that some officers from VT-9 had kidnapped the Skipper's wife, Mrs. Wikenheiser, and held her for ransom of the stolen sign. From the stories about that evening, I was glad that we had left the party early.

Ensign Hudson at 2500 38th St. Meridian, MS, October 1964

After I received my commission, we did not see Johnny and Flo. We didn't think too much about not seeing them socially because we were so involved in my learning how to be an officer. One day when I saw Johnny at work, I asked him why he and Flo had not been over on the weekends. He said that he didn't think we would care about him or his family now that I was an officer. I let him know that my being commissioned didn't mean that I had to give up being friends with him. He was a good man and I regarded him highly. I even tried to talk him into reenlisting, but he would not. He said that he was going back to Shiner, Texas, and become a dairyman. Johnny received his discharge from the navy and moved to Shiner, shortly after I left Meridian.

Every year from the time I was initiated to Chief Petty Officer, in Bermuda, I attended the Chiefs' Initiation function each time they were held. The initiations are always entertaining for those attending, but not so for those being initiated. However, the reason to attend is to encourage the new chief. I know that I was proud to be initiated and I think most are proud on the day they are initiated and happy to have so many at their initiation. I had attended only one after my initiation while in Bermuda. I had attended two in Meridian as a Chief myself. In November 1964, I was attending another one, but this time I was an Officer. Although Master Chief Gray was not the acting judge, I believe he put the judge up to this. My name was called out and asked to come to the podium. I could not imagine why I was being called on. The judge said, "You are hereby fined ten dollars for desertion. That is for deserting the Chiefs' ranks by accepting a commission." Zeb had done it to me again.

During my tour with VT-7, I completed six semester hours at Meridian Junior College in algebra (3 hours) and physics (3 hours) and the following correspondence courses:

Date Comp.	Course		Grade
10/5/62	Uniform Code of Military Justice	NavPers 10971-1	3.70
1/14/63	Military Justice in the Navy	NavPers 10993-3	3.70

Orders were received on 3 September 1964, directing me, upon acceptance of appointment to Ensign, to detach VT-7 in December and report to Pensacola, Florida, to attend an eight-week Aviation Officer Indoctrination Course. I departed VT-7 at 0300 hours on 30 December 1964, and reported into CNABATRA at 1712 hours on 2 January 1965, after taking Diann, Bruce, and Carla to Diann's mother's home at 3636 North 26th Street, Waco, Texas.

Throughout my career I had heard of Navy Mustangs. A person being promoted from enlisted to the rank of an officer is called a Mustang. This act is not a common occurrence and, therefore, is considered exceptional. I had always wanted to be a Mustang and now I was one.

AVIATION LIMITED DUTY
OFFICER SCHOOL
NAS PENSACOLA, FLORIDA

January 1965 to March 1965

I arrived at NAS Pensacola, Florida, and checked in at 1712 hours on 2 January 1965. My follow-up orders after completing the Aviation Officer Indoctrination Course were to report to UTRON FIVE at NAS Atsugi, Japan, for duty.

My class standing was 59 of a class of 62 men. The number was set by the LDO selection board. All the men in the class were ex-Chiefs. One of the men, Gene Ralston, had also been stationed in VR-8 when I was there in 1954 and 1955. He was a PO2 and I was PO3 at that time.

Although there were new BOQs at NAS Pensacola, we were berthed in the old wooden WWII buildings. The rooms were small and steam heated. It sometimes gets cold in Pensacola in January. I was one of a few men who had driven my car to LDO School. Sometimes, we were let out of class early enough to play nine holes of golf before dark. Most Saturdays, because I didn't have family in the area, I would play eighteen holes and sometimes thirty-six holes of golf. Some evenings, we would patronize the Officers' Club, but most times we patronized the Chiefs' Club in the evening, since we were ex-Chiefs.

Our day started with muster on the parade field along with all the Aviation Midshipmen at 0700 hours. The difference between us and the Midshipmen was that after muster they marched off to their various classes and we fell out and straggled into our classroom. Our curriculum consisted of everything from Naval History to Ward Room Etiquette with occasional gym.

As an enlisted man, I didn't have to know how to handle a sword, but now I did have to know. We were taught how to wear them, draw them from the scabbard, salute, and march with them hanging from our side. It did take practice to march and keep the point off the ground. I did not have a navy sword at the time. In fact, none of the men in my class had one. My sponsor in Japan wrote me that he had cups made for both myself and Diann and asked if I wanted him to order me a sword from the Japanese Sword Company. The cost was forty-five dollars for the sword, the scabbard, the knot, the belt and the carrying case. Plus, the sword would have my name engraved on it. I jumped at the price. In the Pensacola Navy Exchange, the sword alone cost ninety dollars, with additional cost for the other items.

The one thing that stands out during those eight weeks of school was the lecture presented by Commander Thornton. He had been a Korean prisoner of war. His topic was Survival in POW camps. His presentation lasted two hours with no intermission or interruptions. Those two hours passed so quickly because of his ability to hold our attention. The tortures that he had endured impressed upon me to not be captured and held in any POW camp.

The one subject I had the most difficulty with was the Speed Reading Course. I am a slow reader and could not comprehend the meaning or digest the subject matter at the speed the instructor required. I had to take the course over, but that was done after hours (at night).

On 10 February 1965, my orders were modified to proceed to Naval Air Facility, Naha, Okinawa, and report to Utility Squadron Five, Detachment Bravo instead of reporting to Utility Squadron Five at Naval Air Station, Atsugi, Japan. When Diann and I departed NAS Meridian, Mississippi, we had shipped our household effects to Japan. I now had to try to divert them to Naha, Okinawa. I could just see all of our furniture sitting in a warehouse somewhere in Japan and having trouble getting it delivered to Naha. However, the detailer assured me that everything would be diverted and all would be okay.

Sometime close to the end of the school, we were asked to stand and give a brief resume of our past duty stations and state where our next assignment was located. Everyone in the class had been stationed aboard a ship at some time during the past, except me. I was almost afraid to tell where all I had been. The location of my duty stations, besides boot camp, had been Jacksonville, Florida; Honolulu, Hawaii; Jacksonville, Florida; Hutchinson, Kansas; Corpus Christi, Texas; Bermuda; and Meridian, Mississippi. I was going to Naha, Okinawa. I had not been assigned to any ship. The only ships I had been on were six days on a Troop Transport en route to Hawaii and the *USS Albemarle* for two weeks in San Juan, Puerto Rico. I really took a lot of ribbing over that fact. Some of the men had orders to go back to the same ship where they had just been commissioned and I still was not going to a ship.

We all completed the school on 4 March 1965. A graduation party was held that night. Diann had come from Waco a few days earlier to attend the Graduation Dance.

I departed NAS Pensacola, Florida, at 0825 on 5 March 1965, to report to VU-5 Det. Bravo in Okinawa. Diann, Bruce, and Carla did not have concurrent travel orders to go with me. I had to report to VU-5B, find living quarters, and get approval before I could bring my family to Okinawa. I stopped at my mother-in-law's house in Waco, Texas, to see Diann, Bruce, and Carla before driving our 1962 Ford Fairlane to Oakland, California, for shipment to Naha.

I already had been assigned a flight number and a date to fly out of Travis Air Force Base, California to Okinawa, so I left Waco very early in the morning. The route took me along US 84 from Waco through Abilene and Lubbock, Texas, and Clovis, New Mexico, to Raton, NM, where I picked up Route 66. Interstate 40 was not in existence at that time. I was excited about my trek across the western states since I had not been on that route before. I can't remember all the towns and cities that were along the route, but I do remember passing through Albuquerque and Gallup, New Mexico. I topped a rise somewhere west of Gallup and spotted a hill or dome on the horizon. I wondered how far it was and if I would pass close to it. I checked and marked the odometer reading. As I drove along the highway, the hill continued to grow in size. That hill was Flagstaff, Arizona, and 200 miles from where I had first spotted it.

I spent the night in Flagstaff. It was about 1900 hours and I decided that I would get one of the cheap motels along Route 66. After all, all I wanted was a place to sleep. It didn't have to be elaborate. Rooms were six dollars per night, which I could easily afford. I filled the gas tank, ate a hamburger, and retired for a good night's rest. I had driven close to a thousand miles without sleep. Gas was about 27 cents per gallon, which was high compared to Waco at 19 cents. About one-thirty or two o'clock in the morning, a couple came into the room next door. It was then that I learned just how cheap this motel was. The walls were one board thick and every little noise made in the other room could be heard. The couple must have just come in from carousing and the man sounded as if he was intoxicated. They argued and fought for some time, which prevented me from sleeping. Things quieted for awhile and I went back to sleep. Then about three o'clock they started again. By this time I was wide awake, so I decided to check out and head for California.

There was a sign in Needles, California, which stated, **LAST GAS** for the next 110 miles, so I filled the tank at 33 cents per gallon, which was really expensive by Waco standards. I changed at Barstow and went through Bakersfield on over to Highway One and drove along the coast to San Francisco. I arrived there about 1700 hours. That night I stayed in the BOQ at Treasure Island. The last time I was at Treasure Island was in November 1954, when I was a Third Class Petty Officer. Now I was an Ensign.

The next day, I took my car to the Oakland Naval Ship Yard for shipment to Okinawa and went to Travis Air Force Base to catch my flight.

UTILITY SQUADRON FIVE
NAS NAHA, OKINAWA

2 April 1965 to November 1968

VC-5 Checkertail Squadron LOGO

F-8 Aircraft

M y first assignment as a commissioned officer was a learning experience. I had a lot to learn on so many subjects that are not common to enlisted personnel. What I had encountered during the short time at Meridian, Mississippi, and in LDO School was only a taste of what I would learn and experience in the next three-and-one-half years.

I arrived at Naha, Okinawa, Utility Squadron Five Det. Bravo at 2100 hours on 2 April 1965. LCDR Fred P. West was the Officer in Charge of the Detachment and LCDR Frank Krisman the XO. The Parent Squadron was VU-5 in Atsugi, Japan. Upon reporting, I was assigned as Assistant Drone Maintenance Officer within the Targets Department and commenced training for the position. LCDR Carl Bastin was my Department Officer. I quickly became known as the old new Ensign. I was the same age as all the Lieutenant Commanders in the squadron, but the most junior officer in the squadron. All the other Ensigns were my seniors. AEC Crawford was the Leading Chief. He had been a few classes ahead of me when going through AE "B" School in 1956 at NAS Jacksonville, Florida. He also was an AE2 at the time.

In addition to the training for Drone Maintenance Officer, I was also in training to become the Drone Ground Launch Officer during missile exercises. The Aerial Target Control Center and the Drone Ground Launch Facility were located at White Beach Naval Facility in Buckner Bay on the opposite side of the island, about forty road miles from the command. The maximum speed limit on Okinawa was 30 mph and in some places 10 or 15 mph. It took at least an hour-and-a-half of driving time from my house in Naha to White Beach.

The drones were manufactured by Ryan Aviation in California. Ryan representatives were located on-site to provide assistance whenever necessary. Mr. B. D Legg, Mr. Tim Mooney, and Mr. Provo were the Ryan Reps. Mr. Legg and I worked closely together in the ground launch phase of the missile exercise. The reps also provided the training for the Launch Control Officer and the Drone Flight Control Officer.

Since my family did not have concurrent travel orders, I started looking for housing right away. All housing for military personnel on the island, both private and government, was controlled by the US Army. Even if I found a house on my own, it had to be inspected and approved by an army inspector. In the meantime, I was berthed in the BOQ on Naha Air Base.

The daily routine for the detachment started with muster at quarters each morning for inspection and calisthenics, followed by a FOD (foreign objects that could cause damage to aircraft engines if ingested) walk down for the enlisted men, and Officers' Call. The officers were to report to the briefing room for the daily orders. On Friday afternoon, the Skipper would set the activities for the weekend. He would have the Parachute Loft display one of two flags out a window. One flag had TGIF on it meaning, "Thank God It's Friday." That meant the weekend was free, except for those in the duty section or who had assigned watches. The other flag had WWSS on it. That stood for "We Work Saturday and Sunday." This meant that the Detachment had received a request to launch drones for missile exercises during the weekend. My assigned duty station during those exercises was at the ground launch site at White Beach as the Ground Launch Officer.

Also on Friday afternoon, the Skipper would have an "Officers' Call" in the ward room. This was for the Skipper to pass along to us whatever information that was necessary and to have a training session on various subjects. After the training session, the Skipper would call to order "kangaroo court." The officers would tell of all the infractions incurred by fellow officers that had been observed during the week. The infractions were from petty to serious. The petty ones were usually uniform infractions, such as a button missing or unbuttoned, a torn uniform or un-shined shoes. The officer who had committed the offense would be judged and fined by his peers. The fine ranged anywhere from 25 cents to two dollars. The money went into a kitty called "The Happy Hour Fund." After the meeting was adjourned, all officers would be required to report for "Happy Hour" at the "O" Club. It was a mandatory appearance and without the spouse. At this time, there were no female officers in the unit. As an enlisted man, it was not mandatory that I go to the "Happy Hour." Most all rounds were paid for out of the kitty, but there were exceptions. To keep the kitty alive the dice cup was started around the table for the roll of twenty one aces. Each person rolled the five dice one time, counted the "aces," and passed the cup to the next person. When a certain number of "aces" was rolled that person had to put 25 cents into the kitty. Starting with the seventeenth ace, each ace rolled was removed from the cup and the person had to ante 25 cents. When the dice turned out to be the twenty-first ace, the person rolling it had to put a dollar in the kitty and the roll started all over again at zero. If a person, by chance, rolled five aces on one flop of the cup, he had to buy a round of drinks for the table out of his own pocket. Although it was mandatory in attendance, a person did not have to have an alcoholic drink, but he had to be drinking something, even if it was water. I had been to some wild parties at the EM and Chiefs' Clubs and seen various uncouth acts pulled by many people. I always thought officers were above any such actions. However, I was soon to learn that many of the Junior

Officers were spoiled brats who got away with a lot more things than those performed by the enlisted men.

I lived in the BOQ for about a month before finding approved housing on 5 May 1965, at D 21 Engineering Depot in Naha. My furniture, which had been in shipment since 30 December 1964, arrived the next day. It didn't matter what color it was supposed to be, it was now an icky green with mildew. It looked so bad I didn't know how to start cleaning it. Of course, I requested my family be allowed to join me as soon as possible. However, I didn't know how long that would take. I had the furniture placed in the proper rooms, but the boxes were stacked all over the house. There was a missile exercise the next day and I had to leave at four in the morning to be at the launch site on time. I just let it sit. I would unpack a little each day after work, but was making very little progress in getting the house in order.

The BQM-34 Ground Launch Crew, DTD May 1966

Launch Officer	Crew Chief	Crew
ENS Hudson	*AO1 McGraw*	*ADJ3 Jarvis, Unknown, AMSAN Shumaker, Unknown*

BQM-34 Drone Ground Launch Site, White Beach, Buckner Bay, Okinawa

When I first knew that I was going to Okinawa, I had asked for the address of my cousin John Alvin Hudson, and had written to him of my whereabouts. I asked that if he was ever in Naha, to be sure to look me up. One morning as I was going to Officers' Call, I saw a Second Class Petty Officer walking toward us. It was John. He was assigned aboard the *USS Mann*, which had docked in Naha Harbor. I got permission to take the day off and we bought a case of beer and went to my new home. The place was a mess, but we cleaned two chairs and sat to visit for most of the morning. John had joined the navy in August 1951, over a year before I joined. He was now a Second Class Boatswain Mate (BM2) and I was an Ensign. I asked him what he had been doing with his life. We compared our accomplishments, which were not anywhere near comparable. I had advanced rather rapidly and he had faltered.

While we were visiting, a young Okinawa woman named Kay Ko came to the door. She was looking for work. I could have hired her for a dollar a day. I was so confused with the mess that I told her I didn't have time to think about hiring anyone. After she left, John said, "Are you crazy? You need her." Too late she had gone. He took me aboard the *USS Mann* and showed me his living quarters, which was nothing more than a hammock and a storage locker for his personal items. He also showed me some of the work spaces. I had made an impact on John. He told me years later that the day had made him see his errors and he vowed to make First Class Petty Officer on the next exam and to make Chief before his retirement date. He did just that. He made Chief in 1972, twelve years after I had made Chief.

Lucky for me, Kay Ko came again the next day and I hired her for $1.25 a day. I put my trust in her and gave her a key to the house. She started to work at seven each morning and I had to leave for White Beach at five in the morning. I didn't want to leave the house unlocked. I couldn't believe the place when I came in from work that first evening. Kay Ko had already left for her home. She had several of the boxes unpacked and dishes washed and in the cupboard. By the time Diann, Bruce, and Carla arrived in June, Kay Ko had the home in tip-top shape. All Diann had to do was move in and enjoy her stay in Okinawa.

After I had found a place to live, I submitted the request for Diann's entry approval and travel orders. I waited about three weeks and wrote to Diann, telling her that if she had not heard anything concerning travel orders, to call a certain phone number. She had not heard and called. The person told her that she had missed several flights and wanted to know why. She told him that she did not have any travel orders. He made a search in his office and found that her orders had gotten buried in someone's "in" box. Then he told her to be at the air terminal at a specified time and her orders would be there. The family did not arrive until about 10 June. They got stuck overnight in Japan because of Typhoon Carla. When the supposed typhoon came through Okinawa, the winds were only 35 knots. I told everyone, "That was no Typhoon; it's just my little girl, Carla, arriving."

By the time Diann had arrived, I had made my social call on the Skipper, LCDR Fred West, and wife, June. He told me that he would not return the call until my family had arrived. Although I was only an Ensign, I was the same age as all the Lieutenant Commanders in the squadron. They had all accepted me as a friend into their social activities. One Sunday afternoon, LCDR Frank Krisman, the Executive Officer, and wife, Shannon; LCDR Bob and Shirley Hodges, the Admin Officer; and LCDR Carl and Joyce Bastin, Targets Officer; came to our home for a visit. The Skipper and June drove up to make the return social call. He had no idea the other officers and their wives were there and wanted to know the occasion for their visit. They told him that they just felt like visiting with us that day. It must have made a favorable impression with the Skipper in learning I had been accepted as a friend among all of his Staff Officers. My life in VC-5B was made easy from that day.

Life at D 21 Engineering Depot was interesting. The house had many geckoes (small lizards) running all over the place. They climbed around on the walls and ceiling. We could not keep them from going most anywhere they wanted to go. The yard had big snails, about the size of chicken eggs, slithering everywhere. Most everyone was trying to get rid of them. Sometimes I would carry a five-gallon bucket full of snails to dump in the ocean on my way to work. I did this about once every month. Then there were the homeless people who would come around at night and go through the trash cans. I did not like that, so I would go out and chase them away. They were pretty neat and did not leave a mess in the yard until I chased them off one night. From that time on, the yard would be littered with garbage every morning. I finally gave up and let them do as they pleased. To get them to quit leaving a mess, I gave a man some money one night.

Then there were the earthquakes. Man! Those things were scary. One evening we had just sat down at the table for the evening meal when the house started shaking. The dishes were falling out of the cabinet and the walls were reeling. I thought the ceiling was going to come down on our heads. We all got up from the table and went outside. People are creatures of habit. As we went out the back door we turned to go to the front of the house as we usually always did. I looked up and saw the overhead power lines swinging. The power poles were out of sync. One would sway to the left while the other was swaying to the right and vice versa. The wires would become taut and then slacken almost reaching the ground, then go taut again. I was sure they were going to break. To prevent being electrocuted if the wire did break we went to the back of the house. We wanted to run, but where? All the ground was rolling and looked like waves in water. I sure was glad when it stopped. We went back inside to find broken dishes in the kitchen and the living room and a cracked wall in our bedroom. However, the house was still livable, so the owner decided not to make any repairs.

All service members were warned not to pick up objects that could be a Japanese hand grenade left from WWII. One day I was in the back of the house when I discovered some strange looking object. Fearing the worst, I called the bomb squad. About four men came to look at the thing. They determined that it was a piece of discarded oil can pump. Even though they laughed about it, but said I did the right thing. I was glad that it was not a hand grenade.

Outside of a few service members living in the housing complex, all the neighbors around us were Okinawa natives. Carla was four years old at the time and wasn't in school. She played with all the little Japanese children in the neighborhood. One evening, she came into the house from playing with the other kids singing a song in Japanese. We were astonished by her ability to pick up the language. Sometimes we would have to tell her to speak English so we could understand her. It was easier for her to learn Japanese than to teach her friends English. Unfortunately, she lost the ability to speak the language shortly after we moved on base and she no longer had her Japanese friends to play with. Bruce was in the second grade of school. He rode the school bus to Naha Air Base each morning. Unfortunately for him, there were not many boys for him to play with in the area, so he did not learn any Japanese language.

Effective 1 July 1965, the name of the detachment was changed from Utility Squadron Five Detachment Bravo (VU-5 Det. Bravo) to Fleet Composite Squadron Five Detachment Bravo (FLTCOMPRON Five Det, Bravo). It didn't affect me all that much because I was relatively new to the Command, but all the letterheads and stamps had to be changed. Again, on 1 October 1965, the name of the detachment was changed to FLTCOMPRON FIVE Det. NAHA.

Effective 23 August 1965, I was assigned primary duty as Officer in Charge (OinC) of the Aerial Target Control Center (ATCC), White Beach. Lieutenant JG Lee Webb had been the OinC. My appointment was shockingly sudden and immediate. The assignment was made on a Saturday afternoon at a cemetery just outside of Naha. A PO2 from White Beach and his wife had lost their child during childbirth and there was a memorial ceremony being held that afternoon. Lee and I were visiting and LCDR Carl Bastin joined us. We chatted for a while and then the Skipper, LCDR Fred West, joined us. His first statement was directed to LCDR Bastin. He asked if Carl had told us yet and he said, "No, I haven't." Lee and I were puzzled by their conversation. The Skipper turned to Lee and said, "You are hereby relieved from your assignment as Officer in Charge of White Beach." Then he looked at me and said, "Ed, you are now the Officer in Charge (OinC) of White Beach, effective immediately." Then he told both of us to be in his office at 0700 Monday morning. Lee wanted to know what he had done to deserve the sudden change, but all the Skipper would say was, "I'll talk to you on Monday." I never knew the reason that Lee was relieved of his command. I was there on time to hear of my new instructions. I didn't want to make the same mistake that Lee had made, whatever it was.

There were two Chiefs and thirty-four men assigned to the ATCC White Beach. Fourteen men were in the Drone Launch Crew with AO1 McGraw in charge and twenty men in the Drone Control and Tracking Center with ETC Bishop in charge. ADRC Coe was the Chief in Charge overall. Prior to 23 August, I had only been associated with the Ground Launch Crew and Chief Coe. As the Ground Launch Officer, I had initiated several changes in the check-list and safety procedures that greatly improved the proficiency of the crew, which resulted in 100 percent of drone launches accomplished since my assignment. Now, my most immediate action was to get acquainted with the people in the control center and Chief Bishop, plus learn all I could about the drone control and tracking equipment.

There were several concerns that I had about the facility. One, it was remotely located and there were no mess hall facilities. Each man was given a subsistence allowance with which to buy food. Each barracks had a kitchenette and had assigned a person to keep food supplies available. Each man was to turn over his subsistence allowance to him for the purpose of buying supplies. I was concerned about the honesty of both the individuals; one man responsible with all that money each month, and the men willingly handing over their allowance to the mess manager. My concern was justified one month. PO1 McGraw came to me and said one of the men had not turned over the allowance to the mess manager. He had been feeding the slot machines at the EM Club. Gambling slot machines were allowed in both the military EM and Officers' Clubs on Okinawa as a form of entertainment. I confronted the man about his lack of compliance to the instructions on subsistence allowance. His response was that the machines in the White Beach EM Club were the best in Okinawa, they paid eighty percent. I had to teach the man a little bit about mathematics. Each time he put in one dollar he could expect to get eighty cents in return, if he was lucky. I had no more trouble after my lecture.

VC-5 Det. 'B' finished their two month long six team golf tournament on 18 September with Lt. Joe Enriquez capturing individual low scratch honors and Ens. C. E. Hudson and B. D. Legg winning runners-up low team handicap. Participating in the tourney were (from left) AEC M. D. Olander, Lt. J. Enriquez, B. D. Legg, AE1 R. R. Nadeau, Ens. C. E. Hudson, Ens. T. D. Gustafson, Lt (jg) A. H. McCleery, Ens. D. C. Hones, S. M. Uyehara and AEC R. C. Crawford, Missing from the photo are LCdr. F. P. West and T. J. Mooney.

Newpaper Clipping of Golf Team

I had taken up the game of golf in Meridian and continued playing in Okinawa. Usually, we would play on Saturdays. There were several courses on the various bases we could play. The only problem was we were navy personnel located on an air force base. There was not a golf course on White Beach Naval Station. It didn't matter that we had a "tee" time at the army or air force golf courses. If a person from that service wanted to play, we had to give-way and let them play through before us. It would make us so mad at times, especially if one of us had already teed off then we had to wait for them to go in front of us. Sometimes, there were tournaments in which we tried to compete. One was completed in September 1965, but our team didn't win anything.

I needed a second auto for transportation to and from White Beach. Our family had a 1962 Ford Fairlane, which we had shipped to Okinawa at the time of my assignment, but Diann needed it part of the time. A man named Farmer had a 1965 Mazda, which he needed to sell, so I bought it from him for $500. Now Diann had her own mode of transportation.

In the fall of 1965, there was a typhoon that came across White Beach causing minor damage. I thought we were lucky. Had it been any stronger, there could have been extensive damage. After things settled and all the repairs were accomplished, I formalized a new Typhoon Instruction Procedure to ensure better protection for both the crew and equipment. I established a Typhoon Watch Bill that would go into effect when condition II was set by the Okinawa Typhoon Commander at Kadena Air Force Base. I didn't allow typhoon parties in the men's barracks. There was a watch bill published assigning a competent Petty Officer in charge of each barracks to ensure the safety of the men. The next typhoon had stronger winds, but White Beach sustained less damage than the previous typhoon. The site had been secured according to the new instruction.

On 22 November 1965, I was assigned as Investigation Officer to inquire into the details of an assault on Petty Officer Shumaker by Seaman Croteau. I was to conduct the investigation in accordance with the JAG Manual. As an enlisted man applying for a position as an officer, I never dreamed that I would be performing functions of a JAG Officer. I don't remember all the details of the investigation, but there was another man on the sidelines who I thought had instigated the assault. However, Croteau ended up receiving two weeks restriction as punishment.

The instigator's name was Jarvis. I had many such investigations after this first one, all involving fighting. During each of the findings, Jarvis was in the background, although there was nothing that would indict him of any wrongdoing. Sometime later, Jarvis wanted to reenlist in the navy. The Skipper asked me for a recommendation. I told him that he was a troublemaker and that I would not recommend that he be allowed to reenlist. I told him that he was on the fence and that one day he would fall off on the wrong side. The Skipper had met Jarvis at several squadron parties, did not believe me, and reenlisted him anyway. About two weeks later, Jarvis was caught committing an offense, which warranted a reduction in pay grade. LCDR West told me that he sure wished he had listened to me; that during the investigation of the offense, the investigator learned that what I had told him was, in fact, true and that he should not have been allowed to reenlist. The Skipper had to explain to the Bureau of Naval Personnel why!

Chief Coe passed away on the night of 19 December 1965. I was appointed Summary Court Officer on 20 December 1965, to handle the personal effects of Chief Coe. I had no inkling of my duties as Summary Court Officer. After all, I was a lowly Ensign who was not supposed to know anything. My first act was to get the NavPers Manual and study the duties and responsibilities of the post to which I had been assigned. Next, I had to study the Supply Manual to learn how to dispose of a deceased person's personal effects. Chief Smith was assigned to assist me. We had to package all of the items for shipment to the next of kin, except for the food items. The perishable stuff had to be discarded into the trash. The canned goods and non-perishables were to be donated to a local charity. Then it came to the alcoholic beverages, which had to be opened and flushed down the commode. Man! That was a hard one. There were several bottles, which had never been opened. The Chief and I dumped all the bottles that had been opened, but we decided to keep the ones that hadn't. There were only two each for us. No one ever knew until this day.

LCDR West had many changes in mind for me to complete at the ATCC. There were two control sites, but not enough men to man both sites at the same time. One site was supposed to be the primary site and the other a backup. My job was to consolidate both of the control vans to a single site and close the site that was vacated. It was not an easy task, but I got it accomplished in early 1966.

I had only heard of an "Officer's Fitness Report," but had not actually seen one that was made for me. As an enlisted man, my semi-annual reports were "Enlisted Evaluations," known as "E-Vals." Each person was evaluated as to their performance, conduct, appearance, and military bearing. I was also ranked accordingly with my contemporaries. The grades could either make or break a person's career. I tried to ensure that I was graded in the upper end of the scale. The navy required the Commanding Officers to complete one for each officer assigned to their command. The Officer's Fitness Reports were far more important than the Enlisted E-Vals. If the Officer was in the command less than ninety days, a report of "Not Observed" was filed. Mine from both VT-7 and LDO School had been "Not Observed." Early March 1966, the Skipper called me to his office to discuss my Fitness Report. The report had already been sent to the Bureau of Naval Personnel and all I was allowed to do was read that which had been sent. I did not receive a copy of the report for my records. The only derogatory item was my ability to express myself. In other words, my grammar was bad. The Skipper recommended that I take a course in English. I enrolled in the University of Maryland USAFI (United States Armed Forces Institute). Later, I informed the Skipper of my actions and my next fitness report reflected an improvement.

Ensign Charles E. Hudson (The Bull Ensign), 1 October 1964

On 1 April 1966, I was promoted temporary appointment to Lieutenant (Junior Grade) United States Navy, LTJG. I had let the Skipper know of my eligibility, so it was set up for me to be promoted in his office. There was another LDO Ensign, John Yeager, in the squadron who was two months junior to me. I had learned that I was the "Bull Ensign" of the squadron. The most senior Ensign in a unit or squadron is considered to be the "Bull Ensign." I asked the Skipper if I could pass the "Bull" to John. He agreed, so I bought a small water buffalo statue and put ensign bars on it to pass to John upon my promotion. John was the Assistant Aircraft Line Division Officer. Due to the

Vietnam War, my promotion to LTJG occurred at eighteen months of commission service instead of the normal twenty-four months. I didn't complain about being promoted six months early.

Promotion to LTJG, 1 April 1966
LCDR Fred West   LTJG C. E. Hudson

Lieutenant Junior Grade Charles E. Hudson, 1 April 1966

Orders were issued from NAVAIRPAC in May 1966, for the squadron to send a detachment to Da Nang, Vietnam, for missile exercises involving drone flights. The HAWK missiles were set up around Da Nang Air Base for protection from Soviet MIG aircraft attacks. The drones were used to simulate the MIGs. I had not completed my training at this time, so I remained in Naha. I really didn't mind because it gave me more time to be with my family. I heard from some of the men who went, that it was a rough assignment. It was the first of many such deployments.

After I had approval for my family's entry into Okinawa, I could apply for base housing. The awaiting housing list was published monthly and I made a habit of checking it. I also checked the list for those being transferred out of Okinawa. That way I knew approximately the house we would be moving into. In May, my name was second from the top. I knew then that I should be getting the house that Lt. Art Nash would be vacating. On June 1, my name was not on the list and some others had been assigned to all upcoming available housing, but I was not assigned to any. I wanted to know what had happened to my name. The housing manager tried to claim that I had called his office in May to have my name removed from the list. I couldn't prove it, but I was sure he had taken a bribe from someone wanting to move in early. I started action to get reinstated. The manager said that I would have to go to the bottom of the list. It was then that I requested a mast with the Base Commander to argue my case. I won my case and my family moved on base to 7313 C Navy Housing, Naha Air Base, Okinawa, in June 1966. It was, in fact, the quarters that the Nash family had vacated. It was a four apartment unit. B. J. and Hiro Ko Littlefield lived in apartment "A"; Bud and Barbra Benningson in apartment "B"; our family in apartment "C"; and Herb and Marilyn Jacobson lived in apartment "D." Later Dick and Margaret Norris moved into apartment "D." The Hodges—Bob, Shirley, and four kids—lived in a single house just down the street.

I don't remember the date, but Herb received transfer orders and he and Marilyn vacated the apartment next door. We shared the utility room. Dick and Margaret Norris moved in. He was a LT assigned to the Naval Air Station. They liked to hike in the outlying areas and explore the various caves along the cliffs. All service members were warned not to pick up objects that could be Japanese hand grenades left from WWII. One evening Diann and I were visiting with them in their apartment and I noticed a little blue round vase on an end table by the chair I was in. I asked about it and Margaret told me they had found it in one of the caves. I was looking inside and saw white crystals around the mouth and made a comment about maybe it was a grenade. They had not heard the warning. They called the Bomb Squad to report the vase. Sure enough, it was a grenade and had become unstable. It exploded just as the squad put the vase in the bomb cage. No one was hurt, but any one of us could have been injured or killed. They thanked me for the heads up on the warning.

SAYONARA Party for Herb (Jake) and Marilyn Jacobson

Each time an officer received transfer orders, the squadron would give him and his family a farewell party. It always boosted their morale and everyone had a good time. The parties helped make life bearable in foreign countries.

In the summer of 1966, there was a major airlines strike throughout the United States. In September that same year my brother, Lloyd Herman, had a massive hemorrhage in the cerebellum and was not expected to survive the surgery on his brain. The doctors in Orlando, Florida, asked that all next of kin be at the hospital during the surgery. The Red Cross sent word to the squadron and I was granted emergency leave to attend the surgery. I packed a few clothes, donned my summer white uniform, kissed Diann goodbye, and headed for Kadena Air Force Base for transportation across the Pacific Ocean. After checking in at the passenger desk, I settled down to await the boarding call. I heard over the PA system, "LTJG C. E. Hudson report to the passenger desk immediately." I could not imagine why. An Air Force Captain was in front of the desk and asked me my name. When I told him, he said, "You are hereby assigned Courier for some classified material that will be going on the plane to Travis." I had heard of things like this happening, but I didn't know what to say except, "Yes, Sir." After some men had loaded the things that I was to be responsible for, I asked him if he knew that I was going home on emergency leave. He got a little angry at that time and said that I should have told him up front, that I didn't have to take the assignment if I didn't want to. I told him that the people at the passenger desk knew of my status. Then he agreed that he should have checked; however, this assignment would guarantee me a seat and that no one could bump me off the flight. I accepted the assignment. The flight was on a Boeing 707 aircraft with a stop at Midway Island and Hawaii before arriving at Travis about noon the next day. The flight time was about eighteen hours.

After off loading and transferring the classified material, I reported in at the passenger desk and asked about transportation to Florida. I had already been informed about the airlines strike and didn't even bother to check with a commercial airline. The time was about 1300 hours and I hadn't picked up my luggage as of then. I was told there was a C-130 leaving at 1330 and if I wanted on that flight, I should sign on now. I signed my name to the flight list and ordered a meal box. I think the meals cost $1.00. I learned that we had to carry our own baggage onboard with us. I was sure glad that I didn't have very much. So, I picked up my luggage and headed for the aircraft. All the seats, called "bucket seats," were made of canvas strapped to bars along the outer walls. They're okay for short hauls, but become very uncomfortable within a few hours.

When I boarded the plane, I didn't know that we would be taking the "scenic route." Due to the airlines strike the air force was ferrying military personnel both ways across the United States. The first stop was some place in Montana. The plane taxied to a hangar and lowered the aft cargo hatch. The engines were kept running. Some men got off, others got on, the hatch was raised, and the plane taxied to the runway and took off. The next stop was Omaha, Nebraska. The same thing occurred. The hatch lowered, men got off, men got on, the hatch was raised, and off we went to the next stop, which was St. Louis, Missouri. The last stop for the day was Nashville, Tennessee. It was about one in the morning. My meal that I had purchased in Travis was long gone, every last crumb. The plane terminated at this stop, so everyone had to disembark. By the time we arrived at the passenger desk, it was about 0200. I decided to check about a flight to Mac Dill Air Force Base in Tampa, Florida, then find the BOQ and get some sleep. I had not been in a bed since leaving home in Naha. I was informed that a plane was leaving a 0600 and show time was at 0400. I put my name on the passenger list and called my brother in St. Petersburg to let him know where I was and asked if he could pick me up at Mac Dill. Then I found a couch to stretch out on. I didn't dare go to the BOQ, for fear that once I lay down in a bed I wouldn't wake up for days.

Sure enough, the plane departed on schedule at 1800 hours. Again, I didn't know about the scenic route. The first stop was New Orleans, Louisiana. People jumped off, people jumped on, and off we went to Robins Air Force Base in Georgia. The next two stops were Shaw Air Force Base in South Carolina and Naval Air Station, Jacksonville, Florida. At each stop, people got off and on and away we went. The plane arrived at Mac Dill about 1400 hours. George and Jean were there. They took me to their house for the night. I was too tired to go see Herman, anyway.

The next day, we all went to Orlando to the hospital. My mother and sisters Ruby and Elsie, were there. They had driven down from Dallas the day before. Herman was in ICU, lying on a bed of ice. The doctors were trying to keep his temperature as low as possible to reduce the blood flow to the brain. Only one person was allowed to see him at a time and then for only a few minutes. He recognized me right off and seemed happy that I had come. He wanted to talk, but couldn't. I guess the doctors were waiting for my arrival because they performed the brain surgery that afternoon. We stayed in Orlando about four days after the surgery to insure Herman's survival, and then I helped Ruby drive to Dallas.

After spending a couple of days with Mama, I had to start trying to get back to Okinawa. The airlines were still on strike, so I had to try to get a military flight. My brother-in-law Howard drove me to Carswell Air Force Base in Fort Worth. The man at the passenger desk told me that a flight was scheduled to leave at midnight, but there were only five seats available. He said to put my name on the list and await my turn. I looked around the terminal area and there must have been three hundred men awaiting their turn. I asked to use the phone to call NAS Dallas. I learned there was an aircraft, with plenty of seats available, going to North Island in San Diego, California. I had to get to Travis Air Force Base near Sacramento. However, after looking at all the people trying to get somewhere, I was willing to take any flight going west. A young seaman came up to me and asked if I could help him? He said that he had been there a week trying to get a flight and he was now three days AWOL. Men going into the combat zone in Vietnam had priority on the list. I asked him to go with me over to the Naval Air Station in Dallas, but he refused. He said he would take his chances there.

I checked into NAS Dallas a 0600 the next morning and could see an R6-D sitting on the tarmac in front of the passenger terminal. I soon learned that there were two other R6-D aircraft with several seats available going to San Diego that morning. I thought of all those men awaiting transportation over at Carswell, but there was no way for me to contact them. I checked in and booked one of the flights and ordered a flight ration box. The plane departed about 0900 with roughly ten men onboard and fifteen empty seats. The plane landed at North Island about 1400 hours. I grabbed my luggage and headed for the passenger desk. I asked about a flight to Travis and was told to go hop on a C-141 that would be departing in thirty minutes. Man! I couldn't believe my luck. I made it to Travis at about 1600 hours. I was booked on a flight back to Okinawa the next day. I was happy to be home with my family again, even if it was on foreign soil. That was the longest and most tiring trip I had even taken.

There are so many tales that can be told about my assignment as Ground Launch Officer. I can still remember the preparations and the countdown on launch day for missile exercises. The day usually started early in the morning. Some days, the exercise lasted just a few hours and others were all day affairs. AO1 McGraw and the ground launch crew would have the BQM-34 drone at the launch site by the time I arrived. There were two launch pads that allowed for two launches within minutes of each other. A launch pad consisted of a pair of rails on which the drone could be launched, an umbilical cable for control, an air intake scoop for the engine air intake, and a heat shield to protect the JATO (Jet Assisted Take Off) from the engine exhaust heat.

When I was first assigned as Launch Officer, the crew followed a poorly written list for preparing the drone for launch. There was no check-off list to ensure all tasks had been completed. McGraw and I made a complete check-off list that included a time and initial space for each item as it was completed. The crew and I followed the check-list to the letter when preparing the drone for launch. The day of operation, the JATO would be attached to the drone. Then the drone would be delivered to the launch site and mounted on the rails, the umbilical cable attached to the drone, and electrically operated to ensure proper function. In order to get sufficient air for engine run up, the air scoop and the heat shield were raised into position. From there, all the crew would report to the Blockhouse to await the launch signal. The drone could be seen from the Blockhouse window. It could be controlled from there as long as the umbilical cable was attached. Once the cable was extracted, the drone could be controlled only by remote radio signals from the Aerial Target Control Center van.

The launch countdown went as follows. Set the minus four! This was four minutes prior to the drone leaving the rails. At this point, the engine was started and the drone was checked for proper operation. A chase plane would set the minus thirty, thirty seconds to launch. At this mark, the engine was advanced to 100 percent, the air scoop and the heat shield were lowered, and the umbilical cable was extracted, at which time the Blockhouse lost control. The drone was operationally controlled by remote radio from the Aerial Target Control Center. When the chase plane gave the command, "FIRE, FIRE, FIRE," I pushed the Fire Button for the JATO and the drone left the launch rails. Those were exciting times for all the crew to see the drone flying off into the sky.

During my year and a half, there was never a failure on the rails. Sometimes there would be a fire started in the grass by a hunk of hot metal from the JATO, which a fire crew quickly extinguished. After the JATO burned out, it would drop into the ocean just off shore. Although it was unsafe, there was usually a local Japanese boat waiting there to salvage it. During my first launch without supervision, I was as nervous as a kitten. My hand was shaking terribly when I pushed the launch button. Plus, the Skipper was standing there observing and asking why I was shaking. The only failure I witnessed was a parachute deploying just after launch. The second drone was launched that day.

Ryan BQM-34 Fire Bee on the Ground Launch Pad

After I had been OinC of the White Beach site for a year, I decided that it was time for me to get back into the aircraft maintenance field. I had a designation as Aircraft Maintenance Officer and was missing out on all the changes that were occurring at that time. I had received wind of the 3M system, but had no knowledge of what 3M was about. The 3 Ms stood for "Maintenance, Material, and Manpower." It took some talking with the Skipper about my need to get back into my specialty of aircraft maintenance. Finally on 5 August 1966, I was assigned as the Aircraft Division Officer in charge of both Airframes and Power Plants Branches of the squadron. The branches were responsible for maintaining F8 aircraft with J-57 engines, P2V-5 aircraft with Pratt & Whitney 3350 engines, S2-E aircraft with Pratt & Whitney 1820 engines, and H34 helicopters also with the 1820 engines. LCDR John Snee, also an LDO Mustang, was the Aircraft Maintenance Officer. Although I had a lot to catch up on, it was good to get away from White Beach and back into aircraft maintenance. Plus, I only had to drive one mile to work instead of 40 miles. LTJG John Yeager relieved me and took over the responsibility of the ATCC at White Beach. I always thought that the Skipper had done John a disservice. The ATCC was changed from designated facility with an Officer in Charge (OinC) title to a division under the Targets Department. The Division Officer title on a fitness report was not nearly as impressive as an Officer in Charge title. So, I was the last OinC of the Aerial Target Control Center.

At the same time that I was relieved as ATCC OinC, I was relieved of the Drone Ground Launch Officer and commenced training to be the Ship Onboard Representative during missile operations. Those duties involved briefing the ships' Commanding Officer and crew of the drone configuration and capabilities, as well as to their expected efforts in assisting with the recovery of the drone at the end of the exercise.

The military had strict rules governing military personnel marrying foreign nationals. Several of the men would submit a request through me for approval to marry an Okinawan woman. I established a list of about twenty questions that I would ask them and tell them to consider the answers to those questions before I would forward their request. Some of them would bring the request back to me in a day to a week. But, some would destroy the request and never bring up the subject again. One of the men complained that I would not forward his request to the Skipper. The Skipper called me in and asked why I hadn't forwarded the request. I told him that it didn't matter to me whether or not he married a local woman, but that I felt obligated to ensure that the man really did want to marry the woman and that the woman was not trying to take advantage of him. The Skipper liked my approach and sort of made it a standard practice. The questions were simple, such as: "Can they each eat the kinds of food that the other is accustomed to?", "What kind of house do you want?", "Will both your families accept the other?" Simple, common sense-type questions. Due to my strict adherence to rules and regulations, I soon gained the reputation as a real "horse's butt." I guess I was living up to the expectations as a Navy Mustang. They didn't call me Mr. ED for no reason!

In addition to my assignment as the Aircraft Division Officer, I was also assigned as the Corrosion Control Officer, Typhoon Warden, and the Detachment Duty Officer (DDO). As the Corrosion Control Officer, I had to ensure that a sufficient number of men were properly trained to eradicate any corrosion that might develop on the squadron aircraft.

As the Typhoon Warden, I had to keep track of all the storms in the Western Pacific and inform the Skipper in the event that any would hinder squadron operations. I remember one bad typhoon that caught everyone off guard. The weathermen at the typhoon center kept stating that it was a tropical storm with predicted maximum winds at 45 knots when it passed over Okinawa. I informed the Skipper of such and gave advice on the proper securing of the aircraft into the predicted wind direction. The aircraft was secured with the nose pointing into the wind. Tropical Storm condition one was set and everyone adjourned to their place of safety to wait out the storm. I was at home when the winds hit. I told Diann that the winds were greater than 45 knots and from a different direction than that predicted. I went to the squadron area to check on the planes and equipment. I had on a T-shirt and shorts. The wind was blowing sand so hard that it was stinging my legs. The P2V looked as if it was about to blow over. Although it was tied down, it was parked in a position where the wind was hitting it broadside. I felt that more lines were needed to keep it upright. I had just put two lines on when Lt.

Enriquez (another LDO Mustang), the Maintenance Control Officer, came up. He asked what I was doing to the aircraft. I told him that I thought it needed more tie downs because I thought we were having more than a tropical storm. He agreed and also commenced adding lines. Then LCDR Bastin, the Target Department Officer, came down to check on the area and started helping. We got everything secured to the best of our ability. I told them about the briefing I had received from the weather station on wind direction and velocity. We checked around the spaces and decided to go home. I had driven, but they had walked, so they rode with me. We had just reached the gate when the radio announced that the island was in "Typhoon Condition One" with winds at 98 knots.

LTJG Yeager had told me that he didn't like the typhoon instruction that I had issued when I was at White Beach and that he had canceled it. Things at White Beach didn't get secured properly and there was a lot of damage caused by this typhoon. Also, one man was killed by a downed electrical power line because he was going to a barracks that was having a typhoon party where alcoholic drinks were being served. The Skipper commended me for my actions during the storm, but reprimanded John for his lack of action. I'm sure that affected his fitness report.

I can remember the first time I had to ask several LCDRs to leave the work area. The P2V needed to be weighed in compliance with NavAir Instructions. I didn't know anything about weighing aircraft, but I was responsible to see that the task was accomplished. With the assistance of the Shop Chief, we formed a crew that could perform the job. Second Class Petty Officer Splain had completed the Aircraft Weighing Course, so I put him in charge of the task. The plane was moved into a secured hangar space for the procedure. After I thought all the men in the crew were well informed of their part in getting the aircraft on jacks, I left the area to attend to other things within the division. It wasn't long before I heard that the plane had fallen off the jacks and one jack had punctured a hole in the aircraft fuselage. When I arrived back on the scene, there was complete pandemonium. Petty Officer Splain told me everything was going great until all these people showed up to watch. The Operations Officer, LCDR Stoner, decided he needed to help give orders to the left jack team while LCDR Bastin gave orders to the right jack team. There was someone else giving orders to the nose gear jack team. The PO2 said that no one would let him be in charge. Since I was responsible, I told him to put up a rope around the entire plane. Then I told everyone to step outside of the roped off area and then ordered the jack crews back in. In fact, I told everyone that Petty Officer Splain was in charge of the jack crews and that no one, not even I, was to give any orders to them except PO2 Splain. I asked all those outside the ropes to please leave the area. The weighing of the plane was completed in about an hour after that. Now the hole had to be repaired. That was a job for another crew, which was also my responsibility. The Skipper had witnessed the accident and knew who had caused it. He took no disciplinary action against the crew.

I don't remember when LCDR Tom Stoner reported to VC-5 Det. B, or the date that he departed. He and his wife, Rena, and their family became good friends of my family. After we moved on base, Carla could go to their house to play with Annie, their daughter, but their son, Mike was younger and too young to play with Bruce. Tom was the Air Operations Officer. He completed his tour of thirty months and was transferred to NAS Chase Field, Beeville, Texas.

My tour in VC-5 was a thirty-month tour, meaning that my rotation date was October 1967. My detailer had told me that I would be assigned duty aboard a ship upon the completion of my tour in Okinawa. The duty was so good (being with my family and all), I decided another year would be great. I applied for an extension to my tour on 18 October 1966. I received approval of the extension on 9 November 1966, with a new rotation date of October 1968.

Sometime in 1966, my brother-in-law Harvey Perry had signed on with Air America and was sent to Thailand. My sister Alice and their son Randy joined him in Bangkok. In July, Alice and Randy came to Okinawa for a visit. She asked if they could come back to spend Christmas with us.

That Christmas turned out to be one of the best for them. Their oldest son George Perry had joined the US Marines and was being shipped to Vietnam. It just so happened, and luckily, we learned that the troop transport would dock in Buckner Bay early Christmas morning. I was a LTJG now. I called the Duty Officer of the Day on the ship and asked if it was possible for George to get liberty to come to my house. He told me that the men were only allowed base liberty and he didn't think it would be possible. I then told him that George's mother, father, and brother were at my house from Bangkok and I thought it would be a great Christmas gift for all of them. The Duty Officer got in touch with his CO and it was approved for George to be placed in my custody. However, he had to be back onboard the ship by 1800 hours. I picked George up about 0900 and drove to Naha, which was about forty miles, a good hour's drive. We had planned to have a big feast that day. Diann had placed a turkey in the oven and all was going well. The turkey was about half done then the power went off. She couldn't cook anything. We ended up having cold cuts and beer. We left the house about 1630 hours to take George back to the ship. They had orders to leave earlier than originally planned and he made it aboard just as they were pulling up the gang-plank.

LCDR Fred West was bound and determined to make me a Naval Flight Officer (NFO) as a Technical Observer. Although the Bureau of Naval Personnel had told my LDO class that none of us would be authorized to become an NFO, a request was submitted on 3 December 1966, for approval of orders to duty involving flying. The request was forwarded recommending approval by CDR E. Barrineau, CO of VC-5, Atsugi, Japan. While the request was being processed, LCDR West issued me a set of flight orders and I commenced training as an airborne drone controller in a P2V-5 aircraft.

The duties involved starting and launching the drone from the P2V aircraft for missile exercise. My first launch was a near disaster. The default setting of the drone was in the descend mode to allow the drone to drop clear of the launch aircraft. The normal procedure was to release the drone, count to ten slowly, and issue the command "straight and level" so it would fly just below the launch aircraft. Well! I started the engine and powered up to 80 percent and performed an operational function test. On command from the pilot, I released the drone from the shackle and counted to ten, but not slowly enough, and punched the "straight and level" button. The drone was not far enough below the launch aircraft and there would have been a collision had the pilot not rolled the aircraft in time. He really reamed my butt out about that launch. On the next flight, I made sure the drone was well clear before hitting the "straight and level" button.

On 24 January 1967, I was awarded the Navy Expeditionary Medal (Cuba) for my tour with VP-45 expedition to Guantanamo Bay, Cuba, in May 1961. It was my first medal issued for a hazardous mission. I now had three medals to wear on my uniform. The order of precedence is; the Navy Expeditionary, the Navy Good Conduct, and the National Defense.

I had flown for two months when the response from the Chief of Naval Personnel to the request came back denied on 17 February 1967. Fred was so disappointed. He told me that he wasn't through, that he would resubmit the request at a later date. I really didn't want to be an airborne controller. However, that was the last of my flight duties.

Since I could not be an airborne controller, Fred decided that I would be the "Onboard Rep" for missile exercises. That was an exciting mission. I can remember good enjoyable missions and some not so good. In fact, some were downright scary and hazardous. Although I was the rep onboard several ships, some of the most memorable ships are: the *USS Oklahoma*, the *USS Chicago*, the *USS Reaves*, the *USS Straus*, and the *USS New England*.

Activities for missile exercises started in the squadron the day a message was received from a ship requesting a target. The message would state what kind of configuration the drone had to be and the number of targets desired. Sometimes one drone could be used for another pass after the first exercise was completed and counted as a second target. A briefing was held to discuss the details of the mission the day before the launch. At that point, I would be given specific instructions as to my presentation to the ship's Commanding Officer and the Central Intelligence Center (CIC) crew. As onboard rep, my day started with boarding a helicopter for transportation to the ship that was usually stationed about thirty miles off-shore from Okinawa. After the missile exercise was completed the helicopter would return to pick me up. Once onboard the ship, I would be escorted to the ward room to present the briefing. If it was mealtime, I would be asked to join the Skipper to partake of the meal. After the briefing was completed, all players would report to the CIC to observe the tracking of the drone and the firing of the missile. The ship personnel would be briefed to guide the missile to a close proximity of the drone and prevent a direct contact, which would destroy it. The drones were equipped with a parachute for recovery at sea. Also, the ship's crew was supposed to aid in the tracking and recovery of the drone. I was onboard the *USS Chicago* when one of its missiles made direct contact and destroyed the

equaled one dollar). The truck could haul only 500 bags when filled, so he negotiated for that amount. We made two trips.

On the way to the beach, we passed a refugee camp. That was a sight I'll never forget. We were warned not to slow down, lest we be attacked by groups looking for food. There were people; men, women, and children scooping slop out of barrels and eating it. They were naked and starving. Man! It was a pitiful sight. I really didn't want to have to pass that way again because I had no means with which I could help their situation. I truly felt for them. Once I got the sandbags delivered, I didn't have any trouble getting the bunker built. Everyone who was there during that rocket attack wanted to help. A thousand bags were not enough to build a large bunker, but big enough to give us a false sense of security. However, there was never another attack once we got the bunker built and ready for use.

As a junior officer, I usually didn't get a chance to talk to Commanders, but one afternoon while working on the bunker, CDR Barrineau came to the area and started talking to me. He asked how long I had been in the navy and my age, etc. I answered all his questions as best I could. After a while he said, "You know that you will most probably be Commander one day." Man! I hadn't even dreamed that such a thing could happen. He said that so far I had done everything right and I definitely had the potential. I was a lowly LTJG, but CDR Barrineau gave me a lot of encouragement that day.

The marines really like to unwind after a day in the field. The club at First MAW was a small one-room hut about twenty by thirty feet. One-half of it didn't have a ceiling. The only time I was in it, I noticed all the marines were crowded among the tables located under the part with the ceiling. There were plenty of tables in the other section. Frank Krisman, the XO said, "Why don't we sit at one of those tables?" I don't remember the other two gents who were in our party. We got our drinks and sat down. Later, there were other marines who came in and sat at the tables next to us because all the tables under the ceiling were taken. When they sat their drinks on the table, they covered them with their hands. We wondered about that. One sat his drink on the table which left a ring from the condensation when lifted. I heard him say, "Ten dollars right there." One of the others, "You're on," and made a ring on the table in another area and said, "It's here." About that time I heard a noise up in the rafters. There were birds roosting in the overhead and they were betting where the next bird dropping would hit. We got under the part with the ceiling.

We had almost finished our drinks when there were loud gun shots, BAM! BAM! BAM! It was so close it was deafening. A First Lt. was shooting with a .45 gun at a gecko going up the wall. Man! We didn't need that. There were sandbags stacked on the outside of the wall, but we didn't know that at the time. We left that club and never went back.

LCOL Cameron had invited me to the club on their cantonment, so when I wanted to go to a club I would walk the five blocks to the H&MS 11 Club. One night LCDR Frank Krisman, LTJG Tom Smyth, LTJG Bill Tansky, and I went to the club. We were the only navy men among all those marines. All of a sudden, there was a big commotion. Some young marines had snatched a prize trophy from the Subic Bay Officers' Club in the Philippines and brought it to hang in their club. It was a head and shoulders of a water buffalo called Ensign Toro. Then someone turned to us and asked what we were going to do about Ensign Toro being stolen and now hanging in the Marine Club in Vietnam. We didn't have a response to that. Frank started to conceive a plan for the recovery of the buffalo and returning it to the Philippines. Man! I didn't want to have anything to do with that episode. I had been involved with the incident in Meridian, Mississippi; I didn't need any more of that kind of so-called fun. Ensign Toro was still hanging in that club in Da Nang when the squadron returned to Naha, Okinawa.

I mentioned earlier that my nephew had come through Okinawa at Christmas on a troop transport headed for Vietnam. Well! He was stationed in the area of Da Nang. I tried several times to get through to him by land phone. That was all that was available at that time. The phones were little canvas covered boxes connected to wires lying on the ground that were battery powered with a hand crank. Finally, I got a message to George about my location and invited him to come see me. Due to his location, I was restricted from going to see him. We had a couple of visits during my stay in Da Nang.

LTJG Hudson USN with Nephew PFC George Perry USMC
Next to a P2V-5 with a BQM-34 Drone on the Wing

When I returned to Okinawa from Vietnam on 16 May 1967, I was assigned as Maintenance Material Control Officer with collateral duties of Corrosion Control Officer, Duty Officer, and Typhoon Warden. Also, I started training as a drone controller. John Yeager had been the controller for some time, but was due to rotate out of the squadron in November. I was in training to be his relief.

On 14 June 1967, I was awarded the Vietnam Service Medal with one bronze star and the Marine Forces Combat Operations Insignia for the tour in Vietnam, which we had just completed. It was my second medal for hazardous assignment.

It was during the assignment as Maintenance Material Control Officer I began to learn the procedures and problems concerning the field of Aircraft Maintenance. The NavAir 3M system was now in effect, so my first order of learning was from that manual. I took the manual home to study most every night. As a Division Officer, I was used to working with the men in other divisions, but not giving orders to men in the whole department. Now that I was the Aircraft Maintenance Material Control Officer (AMMCO), I had jurisdiction of assignment of men from each division. I was harder on the men from the electric shop than any other division. Because I had been an AE, I knew how to troubleshoot the aircraft electrical system. Due to the type and age of the aircraft, I had encountered most of the problems that were occurring and determined the corrective measures. There were times when, after reading the repair of a discrepancy, I would call the electrician to my office for an explanation. I remember on two specific occasions that I ordered the electricians to go back to the aircraft and make proper repairs. AE2 Moore was one I remember by name. I passed along to him what Chief Weeks had said to me back in VP-45 when I was an AE1. "A good electrician can repair anything on the aircraft." I must have driven Moore really hard. He told me one time that he didn't like me, but would continue to do his assigned task, just don't ask him to volunteer. As the AMMCO, I must have gotten on several men's nerves. I found my name on the "shit house" walls many times. There was a popular TV series on at that time called "Mr. Ed" about a talking mule. Some of the men started referring me as "Mr. Ed." One man, and I don't know who, gave me a tie tack of the rear end (posterior) of a horse. It had the rump, tail, two back legs, and feet. One of the Chiefs told me one day that I must be doing my job right to get mentioned on the shit house walls so many times.

I guess the assignment was the beginning of my success. I began to learn the importance of factory representatives. There was an incident involving an F-8 aircraft that would not go into after burner. The mechanics worked on it for a week, but could not fix the discrepancy. I learned that a Pratt & Whitney factory representative was located at Kadena Air Force Base. I called him and asked for his assistance. He came the next morning and after listening to the mechanics' explanation for a few minutes he said there was a cracked "B" nut located just behind a particular bulkhead. They walked to the plane and he pointed it out to them. He had basically done in five minutes what the mechanics couldn't do in a week. From that day, I began to pay attention to the factory reps.

As a Drone Controller trainee, I began to learn just how chaotic the operations were during missile exercises. The CO would stand behind the controller and scream orders and commands at the most critical time. If the drone drifted the slightest off course, he would yell at the controller. I've even seen him strike John on the back when something seemed to be amiss. By the end of the day, John would be a nervous wreck. As the Ground Launch Officer, I had heard from Lee Webb some wild tales about the antics of Fred West. Now that I was in the control van with Dick Ballew, who had relieved Fred, I could witness some of the chaos. The quietest day was caused by me placing a tape recorder in the van to record all that went on. LCDR Ballew noticed it and made an inquiry as to its presence. I told him it was for my training, that I wanted to listen to the tape later at home. It was never turned on, but he didn't know that.

For some reason, sometimes we would lose track of the drone. While John was the controller, I would try to observe all the displays within the van. There was the ink track, which traced the flight path on paper, and there was the acquisition radar. Sometimes I watched the acquisition radar just to see how the drone would be displayed. It would be just a blip. I soon learned how to recognize the drone by the size of the blip. Well! One day the ink track stopped tracking. We had lost the location of the drone. The crew was working with all the tracking radars to locate it and had forgotten about the acquisition radar. I saw a small blip at the very edge of the scope and asked if that could be the drone. I told John to give a left-hand turn signal for fifteen seconds. The blip changed direction. I told him to give another left-hand turn for another fifteen seconds. The blip changed toward the center of the scope. It was the drone, but it was beyond the range of the tracking radar. By using the acquisition radar, we were able to get the drone back to within range and the ink track started plotting again. Just a few more minutes and the drone would have been off the acquisition radar. I had saved the day.

One of the smoothest exercises occurred when the Skipper, the Operations Officer, and the Targets Officer were off island in Atsugi, Japan. One Saturday I was in bed when about five in the morning the Administration Officer, LCDR Bob Hodges, called. He wanted to know if I could get a drone ready for launch by 0900 that morning. A ship was passing through the area on its way to Vietnam and had requested a drone for missile exercise. He said if I started organizing things at White Beach, he would get things rolling at Naha. I told him I would and called Petty Officer McGraw and told him to start getting things organized, that I would get there as soon as possible. Then I called Chief Bishop and told him about the exercise. By the time I arrived at White Beach, the drone was ready for launch and the radar control center was up and running. To me, this proved that if an Officer would give the orders to the men and then clear the area, the job would be done expeditiously. The exercise operation went without a hitch and everything was completed by noon, including drone recovery and decontamination.

The restricted area where missile exercises and gunnery practice were held was located about thirty miles off shore. The area measured about 100 miles wide and 300 miles deep. The drones had to be flown to this area before the exercise could begin. There was a drone recovery zone about 15 miles long and 10 miles wide in the corner of the range nearest to White Beach. The drone had only enough fuel for a 90-minute flight. Therefore, time became a critical factor once the drone was airborne. My training had consisted of classroom lectures and book studies and observing John during actual exercises. After many such observances, John finally let me have hands-on experience of controlling the drone. From that day on, if there was any flight time remaining on the drone after an exercise. I was given the controller's seat. That is, until it came time to return it to the recovery zone. The Skipper didn't trust me with that job. One day I asked the Skipper, how was I ever to learn if I was not allowed to perform the whole task while I had the supervision? I wanted him to think about the time when John would be transferred out of the squadron. He finally agreed to allow me to control the drone during the complete exercise from launch to recovery, depending on the name of the ship. If it was the Command Ship with an Admiral onboard, then John was the controller.

John received his orders for transfer. He was extremely elated to be leaving Okinawa. However, the day he was to leave, the *USS Oklahoma*, a Flag Ship, requested a drone for a missile exercise. LCDR Ballew told John that he had to operate the drone controls for the exercise. John's flight was to leave at 1400 hours, so he asked the Skipper why, because I was qualified to control the drone. The Skipper's comment was, "There's an Admiral onboard that ship." John was to send Thelma and kids to catch the flight, but John couldn't go. It was a morning exercise, so there shouldn't be a problem with John arriving at the airport in time to catch the flight. I even begged the Skipper to let John leave and allow me to control the drone. He said, "Nothing doing! And that's final."

Well! There was a problem! The ship was experiencing problems with the shipboard missile guidance and tracking system. So, there were requests for delay after delay. By 1100 hours, John was really beginning to sweat. The Skipper told him not to worry, that he would schedule him on a later flight, but his family could leave as scheduled. Needless to say, that didn't make it easier for John. At 1300 the ship called and canceled, there would be no missile exercise. The Skipper then told John he could go catch his plane to leave Okinawa. It was a half-hour's drive to Kadena Air Base. I guess John made it. I didn't see or hear from him until later in 1975 at Corpus Christi, Texas.

During my tour as Drone Controller, the Skipper continued with the antics that John experienced. LTJG Steve Harrington had started training as a drone controller shortly after John left the island. He, too, could see the chaotic atmosphere within the control center. One day one of the ships wanted two drones; the first one to fly for a long range missile shot, and the other for a close in missile shot. The ship was not to destroy the drone with a direct hit.

It had instruments that would indicate a kill or a miss. After the first exercise was completed, I flew the drone into the recovery zone as close to White Beach as possible. The Skipper was behind me yelling, "Punch it out! Punch it out!" He would get a letter of reprimand if the drone landed outside of the recovery zone. I was depending on the ink track for the exact location. I put the drone in the parachute near what appeared to be a mile from the border. When the second exercise was over, I also flew it into the recovery zone keeping the ink tract slightly below, but parallel to the first track. I told the Skipper that I wanted to land both drones near to each other. He told me that was not possible due to the winds and the running of the sea. Well! When the helicopter went to retrieve the first drone, the pilot called to say that the second drone was about 100 yards from the first one. I was just lucky, but I told the Skipper that I had planned it that way by calculating the wind speed and direction and the sea currents.

I don't know how it was decided that I attend an Aircraft Maintenance Management Course at NAS North Island, San Diego, California. I departed VC-5, Naha, Okinawa, on 11 January 1968 to attend the Fleet Airborne Electronics Training Unit School for two weeks, which commenced on 13 January. I completed the course on 24 January 1968, and was credited with 72 hours of formal classroom instruction. It was the most boring course I had ever taken. The instructor was a civilian who did nothing but talk about himself and his accomplishments and asked us questions like, "What did you learn from today's discussion?" Man! I didn't learn anything that would help me in my daily task. The completion certificate was passed out on Friday morning and I hopped on a plane to Travis Air Force Base where I boarded a plane for Okinawa. It was a happy reunion to be with my family again.

I was promoted to Lieutenant United States Navy temporary appointment on 8 February 1968, with an effective date of 1 January 1968. This was three years and three months from the date of my commissioning, which I considered early. The other LDO, John Yeager, must have had a problem that I wasn't aware of because he was passed over. It was at that time I learned how the evaluations of officers were reported on the "fitness report." There is one space where the Commanding Officer ranks the officers according to their standing. The LDOs are ranked separately from the regular line officers. John and I were the only two LTJG LDOs in the squadron. I was ranked number one of two and he was ranked number two of two. I don't know why the CO had ranked me ahead of John.

Promoted to Navy Lieutenant on 8 February 1968

NAME *(Print)* Charles   Edward   HUDSON   Lieutenant
              (First)   *(Middle)*   *(Last)*   *(Rank)*

DATE PHOTOGRAPH TAKEN: 8 February 1968   685956   6852
                                    (File Number)   *(Designator)*

7165

6354

INSTRUCTIONS FOR SUBMISSION OF PHOTOGRAPH IN ACCORDANCE WITH ARTICLE B-2210 BUPERS MANUAL

OFFICER PHOTOGRAPH SUBMISSION SHEET

Complying with Permanent Change of Duty Station orders without a change in work site, on 1 June 1968, Fleet Composite Squadron Five Detachment Naha was decommissioned and Fleet Composite Squadron Five was relocated from Atsugi, Japan, to Naha, Okinawa. All the men who were stationed in Fleet Composite Squadron Five Detachment Naha were transferred into Fleet Composite Squadron Five. Therefore, I was now in a new squadron, but the same location. Commander J. R. Foster was the Commanding Officer and the former OinC of VC-5B, LCDR R. F. Ballew, was the Executive Officer.

I was not only responsible for the upkeep and scheduled maintenance of the aircraft I was also responsible for the accounting of the squadron operating funds. I was familiar with the BPN-01 funds, which were issued by CNO for operating purposes, but I had not had to keep track of expenditures. As the Reports CPO in Meridian, I had to post the expenditure of the funds for the Maintenance Officer as they were reported to me, but it was a lump sum every fifteen days. Now, I had to know what items were purchased and how much each item cost. All this I had to report to the Commanding Officer. Reports then were submitted every fifteen days to CNO. One day the CO, Commander Foster, called me to his office to ask about a new COMNAVAIR Instruction concerning new reporting procedures for the BPN-01 funds. I had not been aware of the instruction, so he told me to look into it. I read it over thoroughly and could not find any statement about this instruction superseding the OPNAV Instruction. On the fifteenth of the month, I made out the report as usual under the OPNAV Instruction. Of course! The CO wanted to know why I had not made it out according to the new instruction. I told him that it did not cancel or supersede the OPNAV Instruction. It took some time before I could convince him to forward the report as written. Later, he read reports from other squadrons that had been submitted in accordance with the new instruction. Again, he called me to his office and said that I had done it wrong and to submit a late report using the format of the new instruction. I couldn't talk him out of it. I told him that it would take a day to compile all the data. He said get it done. By the next morning there was a message from CNO directing all the squadrons that had used the new format to resubmit using the guidelines of the OPNAV Instruction. The new report that I had prepared the day before was torn up and thrown into the trash can. CDR Foster apologized and said, "You were right, the new instruction was just some whim of an enthusiastic officer at AIRPAC and it did not, in fact, supersede the OPNAV instruction." He never questioned me after that incident concerning reports.

Life on Okinawa was mostly a good life. We made a lot of friends and had a lot of fun. After we moved on base, with Bruce and Carla in school, Diann became active in the Officers' Wives' Club. She took Chinese cooking classes, Japanese doll making classes, and became proficient in both, while I continued to struggle with my golf game. I used the two months combat pay I had received from the Vietnam tour to purchase a new set of Spalding Executive clubs. Carla started the first grade and completed all the way through the third grade. Bruce was in the third grade and went through the sixth grade. Diann had always enjoyed going to the Officers' Wives' Gift Shop. They were having trouble getting ladies to work in the shop, so one day Diann was asked if she would care to work there part time. She agreed. Anyone who worked there would get a discount on all of their purchases. I never knew what she would have when she came home. Sometime later, she became one of their purchasing agents, buying Okinawa pottery and glassware.

VC-5 Officers' Wives' Club

We enjoyed vacationing whenever I could take leave. One of the places we liked to go for a week was a military officers' rest center at Okuma. It was located about sixty plus miles from Naha. It took all day to drive there by car. The drive was an adventure by itself. The road was unpaved and had many potholes. From Naha we passed Kadena Air force Base and then Nago. We would get a cabin on the beach and just relax or swim, or go to the club house and play games. Both Bruce and Carla seemed to have really enjoyed their time at Okuma. The food at the restaurant was excellent, especially the lobster. A three lobster tail dinner cost about a buck fifty. That's what we ate most every night. The restaurant was the only place to eat, which served meals for breakfast, lunch, and dinner. There was a so-called golf course that had sand putting surfaces instead of grass. The fairways had grass, but not the putting surfaces. I enjoyed it, nonetheless. We could hike along trails that led to scenic areas and other beaches, but swimming was only allowed at the one beach by the cabins, due to the abundance of poisonous water snakes. As I had said earlier, there were huge snails in Okinawa, about two to three inches in diameter. One day while walking along one of the trails, we noticed a big snail running ahead of us. We were amazed by its speed. I chased it down to find that a hermit crab had taken up residence in an old snail shell.

Bruce, Front Right Desk, in Fifth Grade of the Military Grade School, Naha, Okinawa

The Hodges, Front Row: Vicky, Robert, and Bobby; Back Row: Shirley, Bob, and Charlie

LCDR Bob Hodges and family lived just down the street from us. They wanted to go to Taiwan, but needed someone to watch after their four children. Diann and I agreed to take care of them, provided they would watch our children at a later date. They were gone a week. On 6 February 1967, we got our chance to go. It was Chinese New Year's week. We left Naha early in the morning on the Naval Air Facility aircraft. LCDR Al Schafer and wife, Patty, were also on the plane. We all had reservations for a week's stay in the President Hotel near the US Embassy.

Upon arriving, we were advised not to drink the water except from designated containers. We could take a shower, but warned not to get the water in our mouths. After receiving that information, we decided that we would eat all of our meals at the Embassy restaurant. That night was uneventful. All we did was locate the Embassy and had dinner there, then went back to the hotel to rest up for sightseeing the next day.

The next morning, Diann and I were up early and raring to go. We knocked on the Schafer's door, but they were newlyweds and didn't want to leave their room. So, Diann and I went to breakfast by ourselves. The restaurant was crowded, every table was occupied. One couple was seated at a table with four chairs. Upon seeing us they invited us to join them. We gladly accepted. The man, whom I don't remember his name, was an air force major from Clark Air Base in the Philippines. After breakfast Diann and I went back to the hotel to find the Schafers still locked in their room. So, we decided to go to Hagglers' Alley. It was a lot of little shops in an apartment complex, which had most anything in the way of trinkets. As we were waiting for a taxi, the couple we had met at breakfast strolled near. They spoke, so we asked if they would like to go to Hagglers' Alley with us. On the way, I tried to explain how to haggle with the venders, but the lady said that she couldn't haggle. That was not her nature, she would pay whatever was asked and would most likely be swindled.

The taxi ride was an experience in itself. There were only three controls on the cab; the steering wheel, the accelerator, and the horn. We just knew we would be in a crash at every intersection. Luckily, we arrived without incident and were happy to get out of that taxi. We had browsed several shops when Diann spotted a ring that struck her fancy. She asked what the stone was and the man told her it was a "wane stone." We didn't understand what he meant. He kept saying wane stone. Finally he pointed to his arm and said, "wane, wane, you know? Bud wane, bud wane." He meant "vein stone" like the blood veins in his arm. He quoted a price, which I thought was way too much, so I offered a bid of about one third the asking price. He said okay. I had overbid, but it was too late now, so I paid him for the ring. Then the lady asked if he would sell her one for the same price. After we left, I explained that I had bid too much because he had accepted my first offer, there had not been any haggling. From that point, she began to haggle for everything. The haggling had really gotten into her blood.

Of all the sites in Taiwan we visited, there are two worth mentioning. One was a trip to the Aborigine village up in the mountains near a waterfall. Al and Patty Schafer were with us this time. Al had checked out a Ford Bronco from the Embassy Compound for transportation. To get from the Aborigine village to the waterfalls we took a rickshaw, which was pulled by a man who was sickly. We didn't have a choice of which one we could ride in. The man huffed and puffed all the way up the incline. Once he had to stop to catch his breath, so we decided to get out, but were told to stay put. After a few moments, we were on our way again. At the waterfall, were several Aborigine women dressed in very colorful native attire. I thought it would be good to have them in a picture with Diann. I was soon to learn that if you took their picture you had to pay them. It didn't matter that you were using your own private camera. They would try to get in your picture whether you wanted them or not. But, if you accidentally took their picture, they wanted their money. It was very hard to get away from them.

There was a flight of stairs that ascended up the side of the mountain for some distance, but there wasn't a structure of any kind at the top. However, I decided that it would give a good view of the waterfall and of the canyon below. I climbed almost to the top and turned to look back at the falls. Low and behold! A billy goat had come out of the bushes onto the steps below me. Now! What do I do? I climbed a few more steps and the goat came after me. Not charging, just curious, like what are you and why are you here? So, I decided to go back down the steps, but the goat stopped and blocked the way. It wouldn't let me pass. I put my hand out and touched his horns to push him away. BIG MISTAKE! The goat lowered his head and charged to ram me. Luckily, I sidestepped the charge and began looking for an escape route before the second charge. I didn't run, though, so the goat walked toward me shaking its head as though getting ready to charge. At this time, there was a noise below me and some people were climbing the stairs. The goat looked toward them and as it did, I stepped behind a bush. The goat looked my way, but didn't see me, so it became interested in the other people and started toward them. By now, they were above me. I descended those stairs as quickly as possible. I don't know if all those people escaped the goat without incident, because we left the waterfalls as soon as I met up with Diann, Al, and Patty. We descended the mountain on foot. Not so much to avoid the ride with the sickly man, but to get a better view of the river on the way down.

From the village, we went through a pass over a mountain from which, on a clear day, one could see the Mainland China. Since it was Chinese New Year, we decided to go to see the Buddhist Temple, which was some distance from Taipei; and because it was Chinese New Year, we got caught in a traffic jam on the road to the Temple. We didn't know the procedures, so we just tried to follow the crowd. The first place we encountered was a complex of vendor stands. This was a place where one could buy incense for burning at the altar, fireworks to scare off the evil spirits, and trinkets to offer to Buddha. The place was so crowded with both people trying to get to the Temple and people trying to sell their wares. We had a hard time passing through. Diann got concerned about purse snatchers and said, "Let's get out of here." We finally got past the vendors only to find ourselves in a line to another structure where people were shooting off their fireworks. It sounded like the Fourth of July. Although we were quite some distance from the structure, it was still extremely noisy and loud. Still, there was no sign of any Buddhist Temple.

We could see another line of people leaving the place where the fireworks were being set off. We decided the Temple had to be behind a hill over which we couldn't see. I climbed the hill to peer over and, sure enough, there was the Temple. The Buddha appeared to be about twenty feet high and thirty feet wide. It took up the whole inside of the Temple. It was solid gold in color and the Temple building itself was highly decorated with red and gold and with dragons. It was beautiful from that distance. Diann and the rest would not climb the hill to take a look. They were ready to leave, so we left and toured the city of Taipei.

The next day Diann and I went shopping by ourselves. We didn't want anything in particular, just wanted to look. Diann spotted a batik painting of chrysanthemums. She wanted it very much, but it was in a gaudy frame, which she didn't want. It was so big that we couldn't carry it on the airplane for the trip home. We asked the shop owner if there were some that weren't in a frame that maybe we could roll up and carry. We searched and searched, but there were none in the store. There were hundreds and hundreds of the same design, but of gaudy colors. The shop owner called the batik factory to inquire about one like the one in the frame. The factory was closed, but agreed to let us in to look. We all took a taxi to the factory to look through piles and piles of batiks. There were plenty with the chrysanthemums, but none in the same colors as the one in the frame. Finally, the owner agreed to remove it from the frame and sell it to us. I think we paid about six dollars for the painting. What a trip! Getting to go into a batik factory on a holiday in a taxi paid for by the owner of a little shop. We were even served hot tea while we looked through all those batiks. Although we were told not to drink any of the water except at designated places, we considered that the water had been boiled to make the hot tea. Then the taxi ride back to the shop was paid by the shop owner. The day we spent shopping was probably our most inexpensive day. We left Taiwan to return to Okinawa the next day.

In late July, I received permanent change of duty station orders, dated 24 July 1968, to report to NAS Chase Field, Beeville, Texas. Both Diann and I were surprised, because the detailer had said that I would definitely be going aboard a ship upon transfer from VC-5. We didn't complain though, because Beeville is about 350 miles from Waco, where Diann's mother lived. We started making preparations for the move. The first thing that needed to be done was to arrange for shipment of the car. The Maintenance Chief gave me some sound advice. The car had been on Okinawa for three-and-one-half years and never driven faster than 30 miles per hour. The wheel bearings had not been properly lubricated at that speed. He suggested that I have new bearings installed. They were in bad shape. I put the car in the shop and thought everything was well taken care of.

We notified the Base Housing Office of our departure and made arrangements for the shipment of the household goods. Again, we found out how corrupt the Base Housing staff was. They said you must hire a cleaning service to clean the apartment before the transfer date. Diann is a good housekeeper, so the apartment didn't look that dirty. We thought we would be able to clean it well enough to pass the inspection. The inspector would not look at the apartment until the week of departure. Sure enough, the inspector found fault. Said there was too much wax buildup. Diann had never used wax on the floor, so how could that be? He said to give him fifty dollars and he would get a cleaning crew in and we could leave. That's what the Nash's had done and the apartment was still dirty when we moved in. It took three full days of cleaning and arguing before we got permission to move. The household effects and the car were shipped and we were ready to depart Okinawa. As was custom, the Squadron Officers gave us a "Farewell" party and presented Diann and I with our Sayonara Plaque.

Sayonara Plaque, Presented October 1968

We had an early morning flight out of Kadena Air Force Base, so we spent the night in the Navy Transit Quarters and departed Fleet Composite Squadron Five at 0200 hours, 24 October 1968. A man from the VC-5 duty office drove us to Kadena. We left Kadena in a Boeing 707 aircraft headed to Travis Air

Force Base in California. En route the plane made stopped at Midway Island and Hawaii. In fact, we had to go through customs in Hawaii. It was a long, tiring flight. We arrived at Travis early in the morning of 25 October 1968.

When I made arrangements to ship the auto, I had also made arrangements with a company in California to pick it up at the docks and delivery it to Fairfield, California, just outside of Travis. That way we wouldn't have to go all the way into Oakland to get the car. I took it to a garage to have their mechanics perform an inspection and make repairs as necessary to pass State safety requirements. There were some problems, which required all morning to correct. We were tired, especially Diann, Bruce, and Carla. We got a motel nearby and they went to bed while I took care of the car. Although I had new bearings put in at a shop in Okinawa, the rear seals were leaking. Apparently, they put in new bearings, but not new seals. The brakes needed to have the drums turned and new shoes. I was able to pick the car up at about 1300.

We could finally get on our way to Texas. I woke the family; we packed the car, and headed out about 1400. We departed Fairfield due east on California Highway 12. This road went through the mountains, but I thought that if we were traveling east toward Texas we were fine. The travel turned out to be slower than I expected. We had gone only about eighty miles before nightfall. I could not see any big towns listed on the road map, so we decided to spend the night in Valley Springs. The only lodging was a Bed & Breakfast type cottage with the bathroom down the hall. Diann and I were concerned about safety, so she and Carla slept in one bedroom and Bruce and I in another.

The next morning we were up at sun up and departed soon after breakfast. We traveled on Highway 12 about fifty miles to Highway CA 49 and headed south to Highway CA 10 near Sonora, California. This road would take us just north of Yosemite National Park (but not into the park) to US 395. Somehow we missed a turn and ended up dead smack in the campgrounds of Yosemite. We saw deer, elk, a coyote, and a black bear while traveling into the park. We asked for directions and had to backtrack about twenty miles to get back on Highway 10 headed now in the right direction for Highway 395 about 70 miles away.

The scenery through the mountains was so much different from anything we had seen in the last three-and-one-half years. There was some snow in the higher elevations and we stopped by the side of the road to let Bruce and Carla play a while. We traveled on Highway 395 for about 100 miles to US Highway 6 at Bishop, California. This would take us over the border into Nevada to US Highway 95, which was about 75 miles somewhere between Hawthorne and Tonopah, in the middle of nowhere. There were so few towns I was somewhat concerned about getting gas for the car. Las Vegas was about 250 miles from where we entered Highway 95. That was the longest and most desolate road I have ever been on. We saw only about four cars along that whole section until we entered Las Vegas. Diann had wanted to see some of the night life in Las Vegas, but we were so tired we decided to just get something to eat and find a place to spend the night. Bruce and Carla were also glad to get out of the car by this time. We spent the night somewhere in south Las Vegas and headed out the next morning without spending one dime in the slot machines.

At Boulder, Nevada, we changed highways to US 93 bound for Kingman, Arizona. As we started over Hoover Dam we saw that it was open to the public, so we decided to stop and take a tour. The attendant took us down an elevator deep inside to the turbines that were run by the water flowing from Lake Mead. It was a worthwhile tour and I've never regretted the time spent.

At Kingman, we picked up Route 66. Although the interstate highways were under construction at various points across the United States, we had to travel the older highways. It was a long grueling trek from Kingman to Texas. The speed limit was 60 mph in the daytime and 55 mph at night. We had to pass through every little town where the speed limit was 30 mph or less. Most all had stop lights and I think we caught every one of them. I was sure glad that we had the 1962 Ford in good shape for this trip. After spending a few days with Diann's mother and father-in-law, Lois and Carl Wilkerson, at 3636 North 26th St. in Waco, Texas, we decided to go see Diann's sister Creba in Vincennes, Indiana, and then down to St. Petersburg, Florida, to see my brothers, George and Herman, and their families. It was a long trip, but we hadn't seen them in a very long time. After the visit in Florida, we headed for Waco again before going south to Beeville, Texas.

NAVAL AIR STATION CHASE FIELD, BEEVILLE, TEXAS

November 1968 to November 1972

NAS Chase Field Logo

W e headed for Beeville early in the morning, not knowing how long it would take to get there. We left Waco on US 81 South, went through Austin, and took Texas 123 South from San Marcos, through Seguin and Stockdale to Karnes City, where we picked up US 181 South to Beeville. We stopped at Barth's Restaurant in Kennedy for lunch. Barth's became a favorite place to stop, each time we passed through. About five miles south of Kennedy, a coyote crossed the road in front of us. I pointed it out to Bruce and Carla. It was the first coyote any of us had ever seen. We got so excited in seeing it. We started looking for wild game. We saw plenty of roadrunners and a few deer.

We arrived in Beeville in the afternoon on 19 November 1968. Diann and I wanted time to find a place to live before I had to check in to NAS Chase Field. We stopped at Drummer's Inn, on the north side of town, not knowing that this was about the only place in town to stay. There was a nice restaurant attached to the motel, so that's where we ate most of our meals. We bought a local newspaper called *The Beeville Picayune*. It had a few places listed in the rent section. Diann and I started looking the next day and found a house at 1115 Widhelm Street on the corner of Widhelm and Hackberry. It was a three-bedroom yellow house with a carport. There were four large palm trees in the front yard by the street.

The first order of moving in was to buy a kitchen stove and refrigerator. Those were not furnished with the house. Thanksgiving Day was the next week. Lack's Furniture store had a promotion on stoves and refrigerators. Buy one and get a free turkey. We made our purchases at Lack's, but the manager of the store would give us only one turkey even though we had bought two items. We didn't really need two turkeys anyway. However, the next week the manager had a change of heart and gave us a second turkey.

Bruce and Carla were registered in the local school, Bruce in the sixth grade and Carla in the third. Diann was the typical housewife who handled all the usual chores of household management. She paid the bills, did the grocery shopping, took care of the laundry, and sundry of other things. The school bus came by the house to pick up the kids, so Diann didn't have to take them to school.

The town of Beeville was relatively small at that time in history, maybe 20,000 residents. I think there was one grocery store, but no supermarkets or big department stores. So, we did some of our shopping in Corpus Christi, which was about sixty miles from Beeville. The first time we went was a sight to see. We drove by the place where we had lived on Ayers Street in 1958 to show Bruce and Carla. We also went by the base and viewed the place where we had lived. Some of the old base housing had been demolished, but the one where we had lived was still there. We just wanted Bruce and Carla to see them. During the three years I was stationed in Beeville, we made several trips to Corpus Christi.

I reported to Naval Air Auxiliary Station, Chase Field, Beeville, Texas, at 1000 hours 22 November 1968. MMCPO Campbell was the Assistant Officer of the Day on duty. Captain Hal B. Stewart was the Commanding Officer of the Air Station. Captain McKinney was the XO. I was assigned to the Aircraft Intermediate Maintenance Department as the Ground Support Equipment (GSE) Division Officer. Commander Hughes was the Department Head. LCDR Bob Graves was the Assistant AIMD Officer and Master Chief AFCM Vargas was the Maintenance Chief. The offices of the Department Head and all the Division Officers were located in a World War II type building, which was remotely located from the actual division spaces.

The Ground Support Division was located in a WWII Butler Hut, near squadron VT-27 and the base Air Operation Department aircraft hangars. There were five civilian personnel plus fifteen sailors assigned to work on the equipment. I had never been associated so closely with Civil Service people before. They were under a whole different set of regulations than those with which I was acquainted. I had to start studying the Civilian Personnel Manual to learn how to deal with them. Senior Chief Lamb, an E8, was the Chief Petty Officer in Charge. The civilians were Charlie Bridges, Mr. Chapa, Mr. Richard Goram, Mr. Bill Moody, and Mr. Charlie Renfro. Charlie Bridges was responsible for ordering and receiving all the parts needed for repairs and maintenance of the equipment. The other men performed the repairs and maintenance of the equipment, relative to their field of expertise.

The division was responsible for the maintenance of all aircraft ground support equipment on the base except the aircraft tow tractors. The equipment included DC generator power units, both diesel and AC powered; hydraulic test units; all work stands; and other various equipment used around aircraft. The aircraft tow tractors were maintained by the station Public Works Department.

The distance from our house to the base was about six miles. At that time, we owned two automobiles, the 1962 Ford Fairlane and a 1969 Ford Station Wagon. I used the Fairlane, leaving Diann with the station wagon for her transportation. However, due to the limited parking space near the office, it wasn't long before I joined a carpool with Lt. Jim Campbell and Lt. Marv Edgett. Jim was the Airframes Division Officer and Marv was the Survival Equipment Division Officer. They both lived just a few blocks from us. Lt. Jim Campbell was also a LDO Mustang. There were two other Mustangs also in the department: LT Cliff Blank, the Power Plants Division Officer; and CWO Robert (Bob) Mueller, the Avionics Division Officer.

After I had been there about a week, Commander Hughes came in with a folder and said, "Ed, look this over and see what you think of it." It was a set of architectural plans for a new Support Equipment module that would be built in a new aircraft hangar. I did not know how to read the plans, but I would do my best to learn. There were all sorts of lines on the plans. Some were solid lines, some made of dashes, some made of dots, and some dashes and dots. Each represented a type of system. I just had to learn what type of system. After about a month of consulting with an architect, I was getting to know what I was looking at. Then one day Commander Hughes came in and said forget all about the plans because the funding had not been approved and it would not be built. So, I put the plans in a drawer and forgot about them.

The next day, Commander Hughes gave me another packet. It was a folder on a Mr. Green, a civilian black man. He had been fired from GSE about a year before I had arrived and had won his appeal in higher courts. He was to be reinstated with pay. Commander Hughes was furious about having Mr. Green back on the job and told me to keep very accurate records on his performance. If at all possible, get him fired for good from the job. I had been studying the Civilian Personnel Manual and learned that it would almost take an act of Congress to get a civilian fired. I didn't know Mr. Green and decided to be up front with him from day one. I told him what I expected from him in the way of performance and of quality of workmanship. He worked for me for two years without incident. Commander Hughes could not understand the improvement in his performance. It's all in diplomacy and tact in dealing with a crew of men on a job. In naval history, John Paul Jones had stated, "If you take care of your men, they will take care of you." I believe that and did my best to treat them with respect. I demanded the same.

The Ground Support Division was a fairly new division within the aircraft maintenance system. Prior to this time, all the equipment had been maintained by the Public Works Department. Now all the aircraft tow tractors, the power generators, hydraulic test units, and anything dealing with the servicing of aircraft was being turned over to the Ground Support Equipment Division of the Intermediate Aircraft Maintenance Department for maintenance upkeep and repair. Manpower to maintain the equipment had been provided by men of various ratings TAD from other divisions. Now a new specialty had been established for personnel working on ground support equipment. Their new designation was GS. There were even schools established, whereby they could be trained to work on specific types of equipment. There was a vast amount of educating to be done in order to get the men qualified to work on all the units. The two years I served as GSE Officer was an enlightening experience.

THE HUNTING LEASE: One of the expected things to do in Beeville, or any place in South Texas, was to be a hunter of deer and birds (quail and doves). As a kid, I had hunted some with a 22 rifle, hunting rabbits and squirrels, but no big game or birds. It wasn't long after arriving that I was invited to go quail hunting by one of the vendors with whom we were doing business. I didn't know it at the time, but accepting such an invitation from a vendor was considered bribery or a kickback, which could result in a conviction by a court-martial. Clarence Weaver, owner of an auto parts store, had a hunting lease where he treated those who made large purchases from his store. I went on two separate hunting excursions to his lease. Mr. Charlie Bridges knew many people around the Beeville area who owned property where we could go hunting. One weekend, I was invited to go on a two-day hunt. We arrived on Friday night and returned on Sunday. It was the first time I witnessed quail hunting from the back of a pickup truck.

Later, five other men and I leased five hundred and fifty acres on the San Antonio River near Charco, Texas, for our own hunting purposes. For fishing purposes, the property had a twenty-acre slough, which contained a variety of fish, in addition to the San Antonio River. I took the boat that I had built in Mississippi to the fishing hole and left it there for anyone's use. It was a year-round lease to hunt whatever was in season, plus fishing and camping. We kept the lease for two years. I bought a 1953 Chevrolet pickup for the sole purpose of using at the hunting lease. Bruce was in the seventh grade and big enough to handle driving the truck. Each time we went, I would let him drive the truck all over the lease property. He became quite proficient in handling it. Carla was too small to drive. I also built a deer blind and positioned it at the lease. Of the five men who leased the property, I think I was the only one who enjoyed it and spent so much time there.

There were several stories I can remember very well, like the first time I saw a deer and had it in the sights of my rifle, but didn't shoot it. Don Roberts and I had gone to the lease that day. We were both in the deer blind, when several deer walked into the field close to us. I could not see any horns on any of the deer. We were only allowed to shoot the bucks, not the doe. Don told me later, that he was wondering why I didn't shoot the buck that was only a few yards from us. I just flat out couldn't see any horns and I didn't know it was a buck. I never killed a deer on that lease.

One day, I decided to get to the lease early, to ensure that I wouldn't cause any disturbance when animals were leaving their dens. I arrived there about four-thirty in the morning and parked the car under a large tree. When I got out of the car, I noticed a strange odor. It smelled as though I was in a chicken coop. I thought it odd, but dismissed the thought and went to the deer blind. About seven-thirty, I heard turkeys leaving their roost. I had parked the car under the tree where the turkeys were roosting. I could have kicked myself for not recognizing that odor. Anyway, the turkeys went down the river, away from my position. About eight-thirty, I saw a dark cloud emerging onto the field. It was a huge flock of turkeys. I convinced myself not to panic, get "trigger happy," and shoot too early. I waited until they were within one hundred and fifty yards, then they turned away from me. I decided to take a shot and killed one at 163 paces. It was my first and only turkey to kill. I tried to shoot another one, but was unable. I did not know a turkey could fly so fast. It looked as though they went straight up to treetop level and then flew over the trees. We cooked the one I had killed on our Japanese Hibachi for Sunday dinner.

There were a lot of bull frogs on the slough. One night, Mr. Chapa and I decided to go frog gigging. We took our 22 rifles and gigs. We could not get close enough to gig any, so we started shooting them on the bank and rowing in to get them before they had time to jump in the water. We had gotten several and wanted just a few more to have enough to provide a meal for each of our families. I shot a big one and started rowing. I could hardly move the boat. I finally got the frog and looked at Mr. Chapa. He was as white as a ghost. He said, "Didn't you see that big snake in the tree next to the boat?" I had not seen any snakes before that moment, but there were snakes in every tree and on the banks. We ended our frog hunting for the season.

Navy Facility Landing Field Goliad was about thirty miles northeast of Beeville. Student pilots made practice "touch and go" landings to simulate carrier landings. The field did not have lighting, so only daylight operations were conducted. The command allowed quail and deer hunting when no flight operations were being conducted. One day I had reserved a deer blind. I got up early and arrived at the field about four-thirty in the morning. The Duty Petty Officer asked if I would like to be taken to the blind. I told him that I could walk to the area. I didn't think about the fact the blind was at the end of the runway and the runway was 10,000 feet long, almost two miles. On the way I heard and passed a windmill turning at the edge of the field. Just after I had reached the halfway point, I heard a cougar roar over by the windmill. WHAT TO DO! It was between me and the operations center. I was in the middle of the runway on a moonless night. My hair was standing up and my spine was tingling. I loaded my 30-30 rifle, put one in the chamber and kept walking toward the blind. The cougar did not change positions and I finally reached the blind. I was sure glad when daylight arrived and I could see further than a hundred feet. I knew I would not see a deer that morning. When a man from the operations center picked me up, he asked if I had heard the cougar. I never went back to NFL Goliad for hunting.

After about six months, Commander Hughes asked how I was doing on the plans for the new GSE workshop. I had not been doing anything with them. He said the funds had now been approved and to start looking them over again. By now, I had learned what all the various lines represented and had found numerous discrepancies. I was over in the engineer's office most every day with changes that had to be made. It got to the point where the Officer in Charge (OinC) of the construction hated to see me coming. He knew that I had found another major discrepancy that would require a change. As long as the work had not been started, there wasn't much of a cost factor involved, so I didn't have any qualms about the changes. Some of the major problems I discovered were with the hydraulic lifts, a grease pit and in the electrical power supply system. The navy had outlawed the grease pit years ago because it was a fire hazard, yet here one was being put in the new facility. There were two 8,000-pound hydraulic lifts being installed and the equipment to be lifted weighed 12,500 pounds. It just wouldn't work! They were changed to 16,000-pound lifts and the grease pit was deleted and replaced with a third 16,000-pound lift. Next was the electrical system. The whole new hangar was being wired for 440 volts. I asked the OinC if a 220-volt outlet was being put in the new GSE module. He told me, "NO!" The GSE Division had to maintain equipment used in the other hangars that ran on 220 volts. I asked him how they were to do that. He swore and started making the necessary changes.

In addition to the assignment as GSE Officer, I was also assigned as Power Plants Officer. In July 1969, Lt. Cliff Blank, who had been the Power Plants Officer, was transferred prior to his relief reporting onboard. Lt. Don Roberts, another LDO Mustang, was designated as Cliff's replacement. Commander Hughes assigned me to the job in the interim. The Division was responsible for repairs of all aircraft engines for all the different types of aircraft on the base. There were J-48 engines used in F-9 aircraft, J-85 engines used in T-2J aircraft, J-52 engines for the TA-4 aircraft, and R-1820 engines used in TUS-2C aircraft. There were some UH-1N helicopters with T400 engines, but those were maintained out of Corpus Christi. Chief Franks was the Chief in Charge. The distance between the two division sites was about a half mile. I had to manage my time so that I was effective in both divisions. Luckily for me, Chief Lamb was a proficient and effective supervisor. He could manage very well without my presence.

When I first arrived at Chase Field, I noticed the new hangar under construction. It was completed by December 1969 and the Aircraft Intermediate Maintenance Department moved into the new office spaces in the new hangar in January 1970. By this time, CDR Hughes had been relieved by CDR G. G. Buc. LCDR Don Roberts, who had just been promoted, had relieved LCDR Graves, who had retired. Lt. Jimmy McKnight, another LDO Mustang, had relieved CWO Mueller. The Power Plants Division, also, moved into new work spaces within the new hangar. I was still wearing two hats, one as the GSE Officer and one as the Power Plants Officer. The GSE Division remained in the old Butler Hut, but my office was much closer to both division spaces.

Besides the assignments as the Division Officer of two divisions, I was also assigned as a member of various boards and committees, plus the Senior Watch Officer. It seemed that I hardly had time to look after my two divisions, because of being in meetings. I was a member of the Base Safety Advisory Committee, the Enlisted Advisory Committee, the CO's Safety Review Board, and the Enlisted Recreation Committee.

I played golf with the XO one Saturday at the Bee County Country Club. He liked the manner in which I assisted him in correcting his golf swing. We both broke ninety that day. He decided to form a Base Golfing Committee and made me the chairman. I tried to tell him I did not know that much about golf. He said he formed the committee primarily to design a golf course for the base. That assignment only increased my workload. I can't remember the other committee members except Warrant Officer Winslette. If I remember correctly, I was assigned to nine of fourteen boards or committees.

Mr. Charlie Bridges was the President of the Civilian Employees Union. I don't know what he did or didn't do at their meetings, but I was always hearing rumblings of disgruntled employees. Like any other situation, some people liked what he accomplished and some didn't. One of the men in particular, who didn't like Charlie, tried to make life miserable for all of his associates. His name was O. J. Hooks. O. J. would rant and rave about Charlie to anyone who would listen. Fact be known, O. J. wanted to be President of the Union.

By the nature of the tasks of the GSE Division, there had to be a strict policy concerning privately owned automobiles (POVs). There were too many components used on the ground support equipment that were compatible for use on private autos. I set a policy disallowing any work on POVs within the GSE spaces. The 1962 Ford auto that I had bought while stationed in Mississippi, shipped to Okinawa, and then brought to Beeville needed a new set of tires. Sears had a sale on tires one weekend, so I bought a new set. I also purchased a "Road Hazard Policy" on them. I had them about a week when the Department Head called me into his office and said that the FBI wanted to see me in their office. I asked as to the nature of their request, but he wouldn't tell me whether he knew or not. The FBI agent said that I had been accused of buying a new set of tires for my car using GSE funds. He said that I was subject to a court-martial, depending on his investigation. I told him that I had a purchase receipt in the glove compartment of my car, showing that I had bought the tires at Sears that weekend. He then told me to go back to work and to forget all about coming to his office. I wanted to know who had reported that I had bought the tires with GSE funds. He said he couldn't tell me. I reminded him that I had the right to confront my accuser, but he still wouldn't tell me. I found out through the grapevine that it was the work of O. J. Hooks.

I don't remember the exact date, but sometime in early 1970 we moved into base housing at 2412 Yorktown. The house was a single dwelling, which normally was reserved for officers of the rank of LCDR or above. I was eligible for government quarters and this house was the only one available. There were no other officers senior to me waiting for government housing, so the house was assigned to me. It was also located on a cul-de-sac (circle). LCDR Don Roberts and family lived next door. The Stoners, who were stationed in Okinawa with us, lived across the street from us. Carla could play with Annie again.

We were living in this place when hurricane Celia hit the South Texas coast near Corpus Christi. It started as a tropical storm in the Gulf of Mexico and lingered for three days just off the coast of Corpus Christi, building up to a Category III or IV. The hurricane hit in the afternoon on 3 August 1970. It caused havoc well inland to Senton, Mathis, and Beeville. There was major damage in the area around Corpus Christi, Portland, Port Aransas, Aransas Pass, and Engleside. We lost electricity at our house, but we were lucky. A wire had been knocked loose at the transformer on a pole behind our house. The Area Disaster Relief Coordinator was asking for volunteers to help in providing aid to all the people affected by the storm. Bill Moody suggested that the Ground Support Division volunteer to assist the people in the Lake Mathis area. Several of us froze water in milk cartons for a week, then on

Saturday we loaded up and took the ice to Mathis. We also took axes and chain saws to cut the brush away from the houses. While the men cleared the brush, Bill and I delivered the ice to the surrounding area. To show the nature of the people in a disaster area, when we asked someone if they needed ice, they would say only if you will also deliver something for them. We ended up delivering candles and canned goods to others in need.

One of the people we encountered called herself "the Cactus Lady." When asked, she told her story. At the height of the storm she stepped outside of her house trailer without her shoes. A small pear cactus flew through the air and hit her in the mouth. The stickers stuck in her lips. Using her hands she pulled the cactus from her mouth only to get the stickers in her fingers on one hand. Shaking it loose, the cactus fell on the ground, whereby she stepped on it and got the stickers in her foot. Using her free hand, she managed to get the cactus off her foot, whereby it landed on the ground again. Having the stickers in her mouth, her hand, and her foot, she was hobbling around, tripped, and fell. She landed on her butt on top of the cactus. Now! She had the stickers in her buttocks also. SO! Just call me, "The Cactus Lady." Later that afternoon, she brought all the men a big pitcher of Kool-Aid made with the ice we had delivered to her.

Although I was a Navy Lieutenant, I still held permanent enlisted status and was eligible for promotion in my enlisted electrician field. I was promoted to Senior Aviation Chief Electrician's Mate, AECS (E8), on 16 August 1969, and to Master Aviation Avionics Chief, AVCM (E9), on 1 September 1971, although in order for me to do that, I had to take and pass the enlisted advancement exams. The men in the shop thought it strange that I could pass their exams. The day the E9 results were posted Master Chief Vargas, the Maintenance Chief, came into the Maintenance Officer's office where a briefing was being held and announced that the department had a new E9 onboard. We all wanted to meet him. Then he looked at me and said, "Congratulations! You're the new E9." LCDR Roberts, Lt. McKnight, and Lt. Campbell had also taken the exam, but I was the only who had made the grade. It was also about this time the people in Washington decided that all service numbers would be replaced with the SSNs. Therefore, my service number changed from 685956/6852 to my Social Security Number.

I was ordered to a two-week Aviation Maintenance Course at Wright Patterson Air Force Base, Dayton, Ohio, in September 1970. I don't know why the Maintenance Officer chose me over the other officers in the department, but I was happy to get any schooling available. The orders allowed one day travel to and one day back. I really wanted to drive my auto, but there was no travel time allotted to drive. I drove anyway. The class consisted of air force, navy, and marine officers. The primary instructions were of data analysis. I did fairly well in the course overall, but in one area I aced the assignment. When I checked into a new assignment I always reviewed the conditions and prioritized the actions to take. On this particular lesson, called "Operation Inbox," we pretended we were the relief of a departing

Maintenance Officer who had already left the area. The inbox was full of papers that had to be reviewed and actions initiated, if needed. We were told that it didn't matter which papers we took action on first or in what order that action was taken. Just start and complete as many papers as possible in the time allocated.

My first action was to look through all the papers and prioritize them as to their importance. Low and behold! There was a classified document buried in the middle of the stack. That was my first order of business. I notified the CO and Security that there was a possible compromise of classified information. From there, I took action on other papers as I saw fit. I only completed about eight or ten of the thirty or so papers, but I must have done it right. I ACED the assignment, probably because I had taken action on the classified document first.

The Public Works Department had always maintained the aircraft tow tractors. But, there was always low availability due to the PWD's lack in considering the tow tractor as a priority item on their schedule. One day, CDR Buc asked me to determine how many men and how much money would be required for the GSE Division to take over the maintenance of the tow tractors. He said the Squadron Commanding Officers were complaining daily to the base Commanding Officer about PWC's low availability, which was normally about 10 to 15 percent daily. I took Senior Chief Lamb and Charlie Bridges with me to see the PWC Officer to discuss the necessary funds and manpower required. He told his Maintenance Forman, Mr. Mills, to give us the information we requested. After the PWC Officer left, Mr. Mills said he had no intentions of complying with that order. His position and pay was determined by the number of pieces of equipment the division maintained. If he turned the sixteen tow tractors over to the GSE Division, he would get a decrease in salary. I informed him that he did not have a choice. This order came from the Commanding Officer and he had to comply. I told him to give us the worst tow tractor in need of repair and a maintenance manual for the tractors. The tractor he turned over had no engine or transmission, but he claimed that all the manuals had been destroyed over the years and that there were none available. I submitted my findings to CDR Buc, that I would need fourteen men initially, eight permanently assigned and six temporarily, and that I would need $20,000 to get the tow tractor repairs up to date and $12,000 per year for upkeep. A few days later, he told me that I would get the $20,000 and the six men TAD, but not the permanent men assignments.

Aircraft Tow Tractor with T-2C Buckeye Aircraft in Background
LT Hudson, AN Shumaker, Charlie Renfro, PO2 Bass, Mr. Green,
Mr. Chapa, Bill Moody, Charlie Bridges

The division took the one tow tractor and completely disassembled it for training purposes. It was completed and reassembled within a week. In order for this to be accomplished, the engine had to be located and turned in to the Supply Department and a new one received. A transmission was ordered and installed. But, while it was completely disassembled, the tractor was newly painted. It looked brand new. The men were proud of their accomplishment. The decision to turn the tow tractor maintenance over to the GSE Division caused some major animosity between the PWC Vehicle Maintenance Division and the GSE Division. All sixteen tractors were under the GSE responsibility within two weeks. I informed CDR Buc about Mr. Mills' attitude toward the turnover of the tow tractor maintenance to the GSE Division and about complaints I had heard about him. I mentioned that he should be investigated concerning his ability to be in a management position. I suggested that maybe it was time for him to retire. However, my suggestion went without action.

CDR Buc was relieved by CDR Calhoun. He was also very easy going and all the men liked him. He had a boat and occasionally took some of us deep sea fishing.

The new GSE Workshop was completed in January 1971 and the men were being transferred out of the old Butler building into the new spaces. They were excited and I was excited about the move. The "BIG DAY" had arrived for the move. The Maintenance Officer, CDR Calhoun, called me to his office and broke some news to me that made me feel like Moses. He said, "This is LTJG Skaberia, he is relieving you as the GSE Division Officer and your new job is the Power Plants Division Officer." You talk about a "low blow!" I sure felt like Moses when GOD told him he could not go into the Promise Land. After all the work I had done to ensure that everything was correct and complete within the new workshop. Now, I could not be the manager. But, that is life and the way within the military. You do what you're ordered to do and go when told to go. I had enjoyed the assignment as the GSE Division Officer, now I would try the best I could as the Power Plants Officer.

Although I had previous experience as the Power Plants Division Officer, I knew this was going to be a challenge. The division was responsible for repairing J-48 jet engines for F-9 jet aircraft, which were very old; and J-85 engines for the T-2C jet aircraft. There were no longer any TUS-2C aircraft with R-1820 engines to repair. One squadron had transitioned to TA-4 aircraft with J-52 engines. The shop made minor repairs, but for anything major the engine was shipped to an overhaul facility. Chief of Naval Air Training was responsible for assigning certain engines to the various Squadrons. However, as the major overhaul facility completed the repairs, the engine was sent back to the Power Plants Division for storage. This procedure created some sort of a dilemma due to a shortage of space. Only CNATRA could authorize the issuance of engines from the storage area. The Squadron Maintenance Officers could see the engines in the storage area and complain that an aircraft needed an engine and my division would not give them one.

Chief Goin was the Power Plants Division Chief. He and I got along generally well, but one day I had to take action to remove him from the Division Chief position and have him reassigned. Several squadron aircraft were without engines and there was much work to be accomplished. I knew that the men had been working hard to get the jobs done, but we could not relax just yet. The normal daily routine for me started at 0700 each morning with morning quarters, followed with a briefing with the Maintenance Officer, then checking if I had any collateral duties to attend to, and then check with the Division Chief. He was supposed to check the workload and get the men started with the work. I usually arrived in the shop area about 0830.

On this particular day, I did have collateral duties, to which I had to attend. I notified the Chief that it would be about 1000 hours before I could get to the Power Plants shop. I asked how things were and he said, "Fine." When I arrived in the workshop, no one was in the shop working. I went to the office where the Chief and two other men were. I asked about the shop personnel and the Chief said, "The men have been working extra hard, so I gave them the day off." I was flabbergasted! I could not believe what I had heard. I asked how he could have thought of such a thing with all those engines to repair and squadron planes needing engines. His response was,

"Hey, this is shore duty! We don't have to work all the time. Besides, I want to go fishing." I did not answer him.

I went immediately to the Maintenance Officer and requested that Chief Goin be removed from the division and reassigned out of the department. I told CDR Calhoun what had transpired that morning. He said that he would have to get the Captain's okay on my request. He asked who I would recommend to replace Chief Goin. I told him that I would assign Petty Officer First Class Conner. The Captain agreed and Chief Goin was reassigned as the base Assistant Duty Officer from 0800 to 1600 hours. He let me know how unhappy he was about the new assignment, but it made my job easier.

The men in the shop knew I would not tolerate slothfulness. I told Petty Officer Conner that he was in charge and gave him a goal. The morning of the third day he reported that the goal had been attained. Now I could give the men a day off, which I did with the approval of the Maintenance Officer.

Petty Officer Conner was also the engine test cell operator. All the engines that were repaired in the Power Plants shop had to be tested and PO1 Conner was the MAN. One day he came to my office all excited! He said that someone had sabotaged the engine mounting. I went with him to the test site and saw that someone had unbolted the holdback chains and wired them in place with wire. Had Petty Officer Conner started, the engine it would have done a lot of damage. It could have also caused injury to the crew. We called base Security and reported our findings to the Commanding Officer. It was never learned who had committed the sabotage.

I mentioned that I was assigned to various boards and committees. One of the boards was the "Enlisted Recreation Council." I was on the board about three months. At first, I did not know the mission or the function of the board. After the first meeting, I wanted to learn the mission and just what I was supposed to do. The mission was to control the funds of the various recreation facilities and programs for the enlisted men. I learned that monies were made available for the enlisted recreation from numerous sources. As I looked at the amount of money coming in versus the amount spent for enlisted entertainment, I questioned how much money was available and why was there such a disparity from that which was received. I never learned the truth behind that situation. I was off the board the next month.

Captain Boston had relieved Captain McKinney as XO and was considered a member of all councils. Sometimes he attended the meeting, and sometimes he didn't; his choice.

Another board I was assigned was the Base Safety Committee and the Base Safety Council. The differences were that the committee inspected the base for safety hazards or problems, determined solutions, and made them known to the Safety Council. The council set the priorities and allocated the funds for correction of the problems. Captain Boston assigned me as the Chairman of the Safety Committee and a Mr. Woodard as Chairman of the Council. Mr. Woodard had difficulty dealing with me. He was a member of my committee and I was a member of his council. He felt that he should be chairman of both boards. At one of the Safety Council meetings a bad scene occurred. Mr. Woodard had laid out a stack of papers at each seating of agenda items to be discussed. Although Mr. Woodard was the Chairperson, we all knew that Captain Boston was the man in charge. Because the Captain was present, it made Mr. Woodard nervous. It would have me, too.

Everyone opened their folders to the first item for discussion. Due to his nervousness, Mr. Woodard started shuffling his stack of papers. After the first item was discussed and set aside, Mr. Woodard picked up the first paper on his stack and stated as the next item to be discussed. Captain Boston and the rest of us picked up the next item in our stack. As he started reading, Captain interrupted and said that his paper did not have the item Mr. Woodard was reading. Then the Captain asked those beside him what their next item was? They were not the same as Mr. Woodard's or each others. The Captain said, "Meeting Adjourned! Mr. Woodard, when you get all the agenda items in order at each member's position, you call the meeting to order again. This will be the only time that I will allow this to happen." We were all asked to leave so Mr. Woodard could get the papers in order. BOY! Mr. Woodard was mad. No one had ever treated him in this manner. He was CIVILIAN and he shouldn't have to take this. But, he put the papers in order and called the meeting an hour later.

Being Chairman of the Golf Committee was quite challenging. The base had a nine-hole golf course, but it was not in very good condition. The Commanding Office decided to have a small lake in the area of the course and the committee's task was to design the golf course to fit the area around the new lake. The CBs came onboard and started digging a big hole and destroyed most of the course. Man! I didn't know what it took to build a golf course. But, working with the CBs, it was completed just before my tour at Beeville was up.

In addition to the various boards, I was also assigned the duties of the Senior Watch Officer. The Base Duty Office and all the men who stood duty as the Officer of the Day (OOD) were under my jurisdiction. However, I had my directions straight from the XO. I had to report directly to him. I had to make sure all the instructions were available to the OOD. I also had to make sure the men who stood as the OOD were properly briefed as per the instructions of the XO. I had made an Instruction Guide and placed it in the Duty Office, so I did not have to brief them each and every day. Generally, everything went smoothly. However, there were a few occasions where things happened that required extra time and effort.

One of those times, I received a call from the OOD at 0100 hours in the morning, stating that there was an Officers' Call, to report at the "O" Club at 0300. We reported as directed and were divided into various teams. We were not told the nature of our mission until we were in position at the enlisted quarters. At 0400 all the enlisted men were roused from their bunks, allowed one pair of trousers, and herded outside. Then, each team was assigned search areas to look for drugs and weapons of any sort. The search took about one and a half hours to complete. I felt lucky about the area I was assigned. All the men were clean. Nothing incriminating was found. However, I did feel for them, knowing that they had been falsely accused of a crime and were paying for the inappropriate actions of others. But, they were relieved that they had been found innocent.

Another time occurred when I was on leave and out of the area. But, I still was somewhat involved. One of the duties as OOD was to inspect all the clubs on the base to ensure they closed at the prescribed time each night. There were three clubs on base—the Enlisted Men's "EM" Club; the Chiefs' "CPO" Club; and the Officers' "O" Club. On this particular night, the OOD had made his rounds and found all the clubs were locked and everything was in order. However, it appeared that the CPO Club attendants had turned out the lights and locked the doors, then posted a lookout to watch for the OOD. When the OOD had departed the party started. They had brought in some "GO GO" dancers and had a wild show. The OOD made another round about the station about 0200 before retiring for the night. He discovered lights on in the CPO Club and investigated. He then reported his findings to the Base Commanding Officer, Captain Hal Stewart who, in turn, called Chief of Naval Training. All hell broke loose after that. Several men were charged with violation of rules and regulations resulting in court-martial. One man was charged with failure to take control of the situation being the Senior Officer present. He had just reported onboard to become the Executive Officer of one of the squadrons. His court-martial resulted in a Letter of Reprimand and reassignment to an administrative position. His career had come to an end. I was called as a witness at Captain Stewart's court-martial to verify that proper instructions were available in the duty office and that the OOD on duty that day had been properly instructed. When first called, I thought people were trying to implicate me in some way. I didn't know how, because I was on leave and out of the area at the time.

Most all navy and air force bases around the US have a unique gate entry to the base, but not NAS Chase Field. It was decided that a TA-4 aircraft would be mounted on a pedestal. A team was formed to locate an aircraft and draft the plans. It took about six months for the pedestal to be completed and the aircraft to be ready for mounting. AIMD was tasked with the mounting. Although I was not directly connected with the mounting of the aircraft, I was still considered a part of the crew. The task was completed about 1100 hours and a big luncheon and party was scheduled afterwards. Everyone was enjoying themselves at the party at about 1400 hours when a young sailor came running shouting, "THE AIRCRAFT IS FALLING!" We all ran to see. Sure enough, two bolts had sheared and the aircraft was shifting on the pedestal. A crane had to be positioned to lift the aircraft back into the proper position. New bolts had to be manufactured, which took about six months. The crane holding the aircraft became a joke. It was the talk of the town and other bases. "Did you see the entry sight that Chase Field put up, the crane holding an aircraft in the air?"

One of the tasks of a Division Officer is to try to help keep the men out of trouble. When trouble occurs, try to help the men or women as much as possible. A Petty Officer Second Class checked into the Power Plants Division from another base. He was a nice enough fellow, but didn't know how to manage his paycheck. He wasn't in the shop long before the Command started receiving "Letters of Indebtedness." I was tasked with counseling him about his responsibility of paying his debtors. When asked why he wasn't paying his bills, he said that he owed more people than his paycheck would cover and still allow him and his family to live. Before transfer he was okay, he had drawn a "dead horse" to help in the move to Beeville. A dead horse is three months advance pay. He had twelve creditors, which together he owed about $4,000. His pay was about $200 every two weeks. His wife also received her monthly allotment. I helped him draw up a budget whereby he could pay off a creditor each month. When I transferred from Beeville, he owed only three creditors.

While in Beeville, I knew that my career was pretty much at an end unless I did something to boost my chance for promotion. I had not had any shipboard assignments or any arduous duties. I decided to volunteer for duty in Vietnam. I had been to Da Nang Air Base in 1968 when in VC-5 and considered it to be safe enough, so I submitted my letter requesting assignment to Fleet Air Support Unit (FASU) Da Nang. We were living in government housing at 2412 Yorktown. Admiral Zumwalt had issued a Z-gram stating that dependants of anyone going to Vietnam could remain in government quarters, if they so desired. So, I requested that my family be allowed to stay put while I was serving in Da Nang. I received my orders in October 1971, to report in November to Survival Training at Coronado Base, San Diego, California, and an approval for Diann and the children to stay put. Also, I had follow-up orders to Hawaii upon completion of my tour of duty in Vietnam. I departed Naval Air Station, Chase Field, Beeville, Texas, on 8 November 1971.

I checked into Coronado on a Thursday afternoon for my survival training and was told to report at 0700 the next morning, Friday. The monitor gave a few words of instructions and then said, "As your name is called, go get on the bus that's parked outside for further instructions." None of us had bothered to bring anything with us. In fact, they didn't want us to have anything, not even a toothbrush. There must have been about two or three hundred people in that auditorium that morning. I waited and waited for my name to be called. About midmorning, the monitor said, "That is all that will be getting on the bus. The rest of you report in each morning by 0900 for the next two weeks, so that we will know you are alive and still in the area." Basically, I had two weeks with nothing to do. I hadn't brought enough money to entertain myself, so I had to watch what I did very carefully.

One of the things that helped me get through this period is that Rena Stoner was living in the area. Tom was in HAL 3, a helicopter squadron, in Vietnam. Rena's parents lived in San Diego, so she wanted to be near them while Tom was overseas. Rena and her parents had me over to their house for

Thanksgiving Dinner. Rena had found all of her dad's medals from his service career and had wanted to have them mounted in a shadowbox frame. I told her that I thought I could do that for her. It took me about a week to complete the task, but this gave me something to do. It kept me off the streets and out of the bars, so to speak.

After completion of two weeks in San Diego, I took thirty days leave before departing for McCord Air Base, Seattle, Washington, for transportation to Da Nang. Just before Christmas 1971, I was lying in bed when the phone rang. It was Jim Janes, the person I was relieving in FASU. He said, "Ed, I'm in California and I just wanted to give you a turnover before your arrival at FASU." I was still half asleep and didn't get all in my mind that he had told me. I never heard from him again. Diann would not accompany me to the airport to see me off. LCDR Don Roberts took me to Corpus Christi Airport for my departure for Seattle, Washington.

FLEET AIR SUPPORT UNIT
DA NANG AIR BASE, VIETNAM

January 1972 to December 1972

Fleet Air Support Unit Logo

This is about my year in the Vietnam War. On 6 January 1972, Diann asked a friend, LCDR Don Roberts, to drive me to the airport in Corpus Christi, Texas. I boarded the plane at 0700 for Seattle, Washington, and then a bus to McCord Air Force Base.

I stayed about four nights at McCord before boarding another plane for Vietnam via Anchorage, Alaska, and Tokyo, Japan. The weather was lousy. It would rain a while, snow a while, and occasionally the sun would shine. Since I came from a warm climate and was going to a place of warm climate, I only had warm weather clothing, like short sleeve khaki shirts, and a light jacket. Needless to say, I didn't go out of doors except when necessary. When I left Corpus Christi, the temperature was 85 degrees. The temperature at McCord was fluctuating in the low forties to upper twenties. Where I was going, the temperature was in the nineties. The temperature at Anchorage was 35 degrees below zero. We were warned not to step outside due to the extreme low temperature. I have no idea what the wind chill factor was.

I met Lieutenant Dan Rumbley, who was also on his way to FASU. He told me that he was going to be assigned as the Unit's Assistant Officer in Charge. Since he was a pilot and I was a "ground pounder," we didn't have much in common to talk about. However, we did manage to get along with each other. He, too, was in short sleeve shirts and warm weather clothing.

I arrived at Fleet Air Support Unit, Da Nang, Vietnam, on 11 January 1972. Commander J. J. Higgins was the Officer in Charge (OinC). I was assigned the title of the Aircraft Maintenance Officer, Head of the Maintenance Department, Ground Support Equipment Division, the Line Division, and the Fuel Farm. Dan didn't get the assignment as Assistant OinC, as he thought he would. Bill Rossley was already assigned and spot promoted to Lt. Commander (LCDR) by CDR Higgins. CDR Higgins was not going to replace him. Needless to say, Dan was extremely unhappy about that deal. He was temporarily assigned under me as the Ground Support Equipment Division Officer. Later Dan became the Head of the Security Department.

Fleet Air Support Unit Aircraft Maintenance Office

Maintenance Officer Lt. Hudson   *Line Division Office CWO 2 Crawford*

The place had changed a lot since I was there in 1968. FASU had only one aircraft, a C-1, but the unit was tasked to service all the Naval Fleet aircraft that taxied into the area. The mission was the support of the Seventh Fleet within the Tonkin Gulf. The Line Division downloaded all bombs and other ordnance with which the planes could not land aboard ship. The Division also refueled the aircraft that BINGO into FASU. Sometimes this was done with the aircraft engines still running, called "hot" refueling. There were two officers under me in the department. Lt. Burt Graham had replaced Lt. Rumbley and was in charge of the Ground Support Equipment Division and Chief Warrant Officer (CWO2) Bob Crawford was in charge of the Line Division and Fuel Farm. The last time I saw Bob, he was a Chief Electricians Mate performing the duties as the Squadron Leading Chief in VC-5 in Naha, Okinawa, in 1967. Lt. Graham was also a Limited Duty Officer (LDO) Mustang who was commissioned two months after me.

Most of the buildings were Quonset huts or Butler buildings. The maintenance office was in a Quonset hut. The living quarters were two-story wooden buildings. The Maintenance Office and the BOQ had fifty-five gallon barrels filled with concrete positioned around them for shrapnel protection. The BOQ where I was berthed had an Officers' lounge called the "Red Dog Saloon." The lounge was located on the first floor, as was my room. This is generally where we gathered after work to relax before the evening meal. Sometimes the Skipper would join us to give the briefings for the next day's events. The head (bathroom) and showers were between my room and the lounge. Anyone going to the lounge usually came into the building, passed by my room, down the hallway, and through the head into the lounge.

The USO girls lived in the BOQ next to ours. In order for them to get to the lounge, they had to pass through the head. Sometimes the other men and I would be taking a shower or shaving at the sink buck naked when USO girls would walk by on their way to the lounge. It finally got to where we paid no attention to each other.

Each Department Head was issued a portable radio, which they had to carry around with them at all times. This was so they could be readily in contact with the CO. We also had our own transportation, which was a Ford Bronco. Each officer was issued a .45 pistol to wear on our side, but we were never allowed to keep it loaded or to use it unless it was a life and death situation. Can you imagine confronting the enemy with an unloaded weapon and telling him he had to wait until you loaded your gun before engaging in a battle? It became the joke of the Unit. Anyone having the weapon taken away from them or losing it could be court-martialed. Well! I turned mine in after two months because I didn't want to be held liable for it.

Living Quarters

My Room Doorway

My Bunk and Table

My Closet with Helmet and Flak Jacket

Da Nang was noted for the USO and the shows that they held for the men stationed there. Shortly after I had arrived, I was informed the USO had planned a fishing trip. I asked the Skipper if I could sign up for the trip; he had no objection. We left the pier from Da Nang Harbor early the next morning. We were supposed to go into the China Sea. Everything was going well until halfway across the bay. A gunboat started shooting at us. They were firing across the bow of our boat. The Captain of the boat stopped and the gunboat came alongside. They checked for the permit and our ID. After being satisfied that we were on a pleasure tour, they let us continue. A short time later, another gunboat started firing at us. They did the same as the first boat. By this time, I was ready to turn around and head for the base. Needless to say, I didn't do much fishing. We went into a small cove, cooked a meal of hamburgers, and then started for home base. Two gunboats fired on us during the trip back to the harbor. I did not ask to go on any more fishing trips in Da Nang.

#1   #2

The "Red Dog Saloon" Bar
Lt. Dan Rumbley, LTJG Mike Tyler, and Lt. Sam Houston at the Bar Relaxing

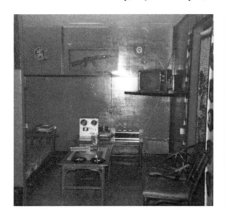 

#3   #4

"Red Dog Saloon" Lounge "Graffiti" Wall Where Anyone Could Write Words of Wit

I got acquainted with the perils of war on my first tour of the area. There were two aircraft in the hangar with damage from SAMs (Surface to Air Missiles). One was an F4 Fighter that had shrapnel penetration all over it. One of the engines had been damaged, but the pilot was able to get the aircraft to Da Nang. I don't know if he had been wounded or not. The other was an A6 Intruder Attack aircraft, which had been hit in the copilot's area and had killed him, but the pilot was able to make it to Da Nang. Since neither aircraft could be repaired on site, our job was to tow the aircraft twelve miles through Da Nang across the river to the Deep Water Pier to be shipped to the Philippines. This feat could only be accomplished after curfew when there were no vehicles allowed on the roads except by special permit. This meant towing the aircraft after midnight. Although there was an armed escort, I felt vulnerable. As we moved along the roads, we could hear gunfire off in the distance all around us. It definitely gave me an eerie feeling.

There were some things that I was warned to watch for. Like when traveling in a vehicle, always ride with the window most of the way closed, but if the window was down, always keep your arms inside, never resting on the sill. There had been reports of acid being thrown in the window causing severe skin burns to a person's face. People have had their watch snatched off their arm while riding with their arm resting on the door. It seemed that kids would catch a person looking in front and then sneak up beside the vehicle and grab for the watch. They didn't worry about scratching and tearing the flesh.

One day, CWO2 Al Nelson came into the office raving. His watch had been snatched off his arm by a young boy while he was driving through Da Nang. He had scratches from his elbow to his hand. I was able to see firsthand the results of not obeying the warning. I made sure that I observed all safety rules after the incident with Al. Al had relieved Lt. Graham as the GSE Division Officer. Lt. Graham transferred to the Security Department.

After getting settled into my BOQ room and the Maintenance Department office, the Senior Watch Officer, Lt. Tommy Mauldin, told me that he would give me one month to become familiar with the area and command procedures and then I would be assigned to Command Duty Officer Watch. That meant that I would have duty on 9 February. All during the time between 11 January and 09 February, there were no enemy attacks on the Da Nang Air Base. I kept telling myself that there would be a rocket attack on my first duty night. Sure enough, the rockets started coming at us at 0205 hours in the morning. Although I had always thought this would happen, I still was not prepared for an attack such as this. I jumped out of bed, donned my flak vest and helmet, and went to my duty station at the secondary Command Center, which was also the Maintenance Office. During the attack, twenty-eight rockets impacted the Air Base, six of which hit the FASU cantonment. Seven men were wounded in action (WIA), two seriously and five with minor burns. An aircraft was damaged and a fire started by a severed fuel line. After the attack, it was my responsibility to gather all the data from the Damage Control Teams and fill out and submit reports to Seventh Fleet Commanders. The Skipper and I worked on those for the rest of the night. By midmorning, all reports were completed, the fuel line repaired, the two seriously wounded were in the Field Hospital, and the five men with burns treated at the local infirmary.

Both of the wounded were just passing through from one of the ships. One was on his way home for discharge. He only had nine days left in the navy. He'd had a close call with a piece of shrapnel that cut his neck and almost hit his jugular vein, causing him to nearly bleed to death before being found. After a few days in the hospital, he was fully recovered and sent on his way to be discharged. The other WIA, Seaman Booker, was much more serious. A piece of shrapnel entered his body just below the waistline, went up through his back between the muscles, and chipped his shoulder blade. He was in the hospital several weeks before he was in condition to be sent out of country to another hospital. I visited him on a regular basis. I was sure glad when he started showing signs of recovery.

During my stay in Vietnam from 11 January 1972 to 26 December 1972, Da Nang Air Base was attacked by the NVA/VC Rocket Units thirty-five times, many of which were within minutes of each other. During those attacks, 367 122mm rockets impacted within the confines of the base, of which twenty-eight rockets impacted within the FASU area causing personnel injury and property damage. Fourteen men were killed and 168 men were wounded by fragmentation and burns. Twenty-two of the wounded were within the FASU cantonment. High power lines were downed and fires started over pipelines supplying JP-4 fuel to the flight line area. Several dud rockets had struck both working and living spaces. The 122mm rockets are capable of penetrating all buildings and bunkers within the FASU cantonment rendering the entire area unsafe. The most severe attacks, besides the 9 February, were 3, 18, and 19 August, 23 September, 28 November, and 26 December. There were two attacks on 3 August within minutes of each other with a total of fifty-two rockets hitting Da Nang Air Base. The second attack caught many men out in the open assessing the damage caused by the first attack. There were four impacts in the FASU area causing moderate structural damage, but no injuries. On 18 August, forty-five rockets hit the air base in two separate attacks. On 19 August, only two rockets were launched against Da Nang Air Base, both impacting the FASU area, one causing extensive damage to four vehicles and moderate damage to two buildings, a C-1A aircraft, and a power transformer. The other hit a mobile gas storage tank, causing a fire which threatened two garage buildings. There were three of twenty-seven rockets impacting FASU area on 23 September. Two of the rockets impacted on the aircraft parking ramp, causing minor damage to the ramp. The other one hit the living spaces with shrapnel penetrating through the barracks wounding five men. First Class Petty Officer McDonald had both legs severely injured. The sad part was that he was scheduled to leave Vietnam and head home for discharge after completing twenty years of service. The attack on 28 November started at 0200 in the morning and really scared the daylights out of me. There were only seven, but they got my attention. I was lying in bed when the first one hit with a low far away sound (BOOMM!). The second sounded a little closer than the first (BOOMM!). Each impact sounded closer than the last. The VC was walking the rockets toward the fuel storage area. My living quarters were in the line of fire. Each rocket came a little closer to my BOQ and I knew it, BOOMM! BOOMM! BOOMM! BOOMM! BOOMM!

Lying on the floor with my helmet on my head and my flak vest over me I called out, "GOD, protect me, the next one will be on top of me!" There was never another rocket after that prayer. The next morning, I went out and followed the line of impacts the rockets had made. The distance between them indicated that if there had been another rocket it would have landed on my BOQ. Who says that God does not answer prayers? He did mine.

The Mess Hall
OinC LCDR Rossley and ASC Anttila

Chinese Restaurant Attack, 9 February 1972

Here are some highlights of events that occurred during some of the attacks, but I can't remember which attacks. There was a little Chinese Restaurant on base where we had dinners on special occasions, like birthday celebrations, etc. It took a direct hit and was completely destroyed. No more Chinese food. One night a rocket landed in the napalm storage bunker. It torched the bombs, which exploded and burned for a whole week. The fire was too hot and dangerous to extinguish. It just had to burn itself out. Other rockets hit the liquor warehouse on two separate occasions. The exploding cases of the different kinds of liquor burned with the most colorful flames; sometimes red, sometimes blue, or amber, or yellow and green, or purple. It was interesting and amusing to watch. Chief Warrant Officer Al Nelson would always go to the passenger terminal to mail his letters so they would leave Vietnam the day he mailed them. One morning he was at the terminal when the base came under attack. He got out of his truck, leaving the door open, and jumped into a ditch close-by. A rocket hit near him. Dirt from the crater covered him and filled the truck. He came into the maintenance office looking like he had been dragged through a plowed field.

The Liquor Warehouse Destroyed 9 February 1972

Damage from Rocket Attack

I don't know how the officers before me ran things, but I could see many things that needed immediate attention. Everybody was driving a Jeep that they had put together from other wrecked vehicles. Each officer thought that he could task the Ground Support Equipment maintenance crew to keep them serviced and in good repair. That was not their job and since that division was under my control, I would not let them work on Jeeps anymore. I upset a few officers, but I didn't care.

Dan was being transferred to the Security Department and I told Burt Graham to go with him. If he wasn't going to stand up for the men, I didn't need him anymore. Those men had certain equipment to repair, which was being neglected. When I informed the men that they were no longer required to work on Jeeps, their morale improved greatly. It wasn't long until the availability of the support equipment was very high. That made the Skipper happy. Another thing that had been allowed in the past was beer and liquor kept in the line shack and other work spaces. I had that removed. Anyone wanting a drink had to wait until they were off work and could go to the various clubs. The morale decreased somewhat with that decision, but I didn't need any drunken men working on aircraft or handling explosive ordnance.

The area was cluttered with junk and obsolete equipment. I tasked First Class Petty Officer Mullins with the job of inventorying all the equipment and determining whether or not the equipment was of use to the Unit. I sent messages to COMFAIRWESTPAC citing all the excess equipment. It took four months to ship all that stuff out of country. When I was through, the place was beginning to be livable.

The Fuel Farm was not able to keep up with the demand because of the limited storage capacity. There was one metal 40,000-gallon storage tank and one 10,000-gallon fuel bladder, plus four 1,000-gallon fuel trucks. The men were pumping fuel night and day and still couldn't keep up. I had two more 20,000-gallon fuel bladders installed and would have put in a couple more except there was no more room. With the extra fuel the pumps could be at rest some of the time.

My job was to make sure all the divisions were sufficiently manned with properly trained personnel. Due to transfers, the Fuel Farm became shorthanded and the men were being overworked. The Line Division had an abundance of personnel. So, I decided to transfer Airman Brown from the Line Division to the Fuel Farm. Airman Brown said that he didn't want to go and that I couldn't make him. He was right! He told me that he was going to see the Captain. I told him that if he wanted to see the Captain, he had to submit a "Request Mast" chit. Again, he smarted off about Admiral Zumwalt having issued a CO's "Open Door Policy" and with that, he didn't have to request mast to see the Captain. I told him that he had better leave before I put him on report for several offenses that he had already committed. One of the men from the office took him out. In the meantime, I told the Line Division Petty Officer to proceed with the transfer of Airman Brown to the Fuel Farm.

The next day, a "Request Mast" chit crossed my desk to the CO. CDR Higgins called and wanted to know what it was about. After telling him, the CO said, "Send him to my office." I asked if he wanted me there also and he said, "No." So, Airman Brown went to see the Captain. Shortly after he got there, the Skipper called and told me to report to his office on the double! I was asked to explain why I was sending Airman Brown to the Fuel Farm. I told him about the shortage of men in that area and had randomly selected an individual to fill part of the vacancy. The Line Division had a sufficient number of men and could spare someone easier than from other areas. Airman Brown just happened to be my selection. After hearing my explanation, CDR Higgins said it was my department and I had to do what was necessary to ensure the accomplishments of all missions. So, he would not interfere with my decisions. With that statement, Airman Brown jumped up, BANGED his fist on the Skipper's desk, and said, "YOU SON OF A BITCH, you're against me too; I'm going to request Admiral's Mast." CDR Higgins was so taken aback he was speechless for a few minutes. He then composed himself, said, "Ed, you're excused."

I left his office as he was calling for the Admin Officer. The next time I saw Brown, he was wearing Airman Recruit stripes. He had been reduced in pay grade from E3 to E1 and was awaiting transfer orders for a "Dishonorable Discharge." Brown was right, he did not have to go work in the Fuel Farm, and I couldn't make him.

Early in May 1972, I felt a sharp pain in my left side. I reported to the Unit Medical Facility for treatment. The Corpsman told me that I had a hernia, which needed immediate attention at the hospital in Subic Bay, Philippines. I departed Da Nang the morning of 10 May 1972, and checked into the hospital at 1530 hours that same day. I was told to return prior to noon on 14 May for surgery. I stayed in the hospital about ten days after surgery. There were two other men who had surgery on the same day as I. Although I was an officer, because of overcrowding, I was placed in a ward with them instead of a room. One of the men was a clown, always causing us to laugh. Man! It hurt to laugh, but it helped us get through the day of pain. We would go for a stroll each day outside around the grounds. We were not supposed to exert ourselves, though. One day we were strolling along the perimeter fence when a clan of monkeys came along. The clown threw a stone at them. The leader of the clan came charging toward us and started climbing the fence. Although we weren't supposed to run, we had no choice. We just barely made it inside the door before the old monkey could attack. We made sure there were no monkeys about on our next walks.

Three days after surgery, I was moved to a semi-private room. At first I was the only person in the room, but that night a Lieutenant Commander was brought in. His feet were tied to the foot of the bed and his head was in a brace with weights attached. His spine was being stretched. He was looked after day and night for two days. Finally, he was allowed to move somewhat and to talk to other people. I asked him about the cause and nature of his problem. He said it was just a dumb thing brought on by his own pride in showmanship. It appears that he and a group of men had taken the Admiral's barge to go on an outing. They decided to stop at a beach and have a party. As they approached the beach, a coxswain was taking soundings to make sure they didn't beach the barge before setting the anchor. They were about one hundred yards offshore when he decided to dive into the water and swim ashore. There was coral reef about two feet beneath the water that he did not see. He had dove head first into the reef. It jammed his neck and spine. He swore that if he ever recovered from that dumb trick, he would be more careful of going into the water. I learned a lesson from his mistake. I was released to the BOQ Cubi Point for convalescence. The convalescence was supposed to be for thirty days. But, after seven days, I couldn't sit there doing nothing any longer. I convinced the doctor to release me so I could return to FASU in Da Nang. That decision was a mistake. I had not healed sufficiently to perform my duties as I should.

An A-4 Fighter aircraft had landed and the pilot wanted to "Hot" refuel and be on his way back to the carrier. While refueling, the pilot was checking various systems on the aircraft and, for some reason, decided to check the fuel tank pressurization. When he hit the switch, rivets started popping from all over the wing panels. In one split second, he damaged the aircraft so badly that it was not flyable. We had to tow the aircraft to the Deep Water Pier, located on the far side of Da Nang Harbor, for shipment to the Philippines. CWO Bob Crawford had made all the arrangements and was planning to act as Officer in Charge when towing the aircraft the twelve miles to the pier. The Line Division had a going away party for one of the men and Bob got skunk drunk. He was in no condition to do anything except go to bed. So, although I was not completely physically fit due to my surgery, I had no alternative except to be the OinC that night. During the trip, we encountered all sorts of hurdles that had to be dealt with. We left the air base at midnight and finally completed the task at four in the morning. I finally got back on the base about 0530, just in time to eat breakfast. I was unable to do but very little the whole day.

Instead of celebrating and relaxing on the Fourth of July, it was one of our busiest work days. The Fuel Farm pumped more aviation fuel on that day than any other while I was assigned as Maintenance Officer. A big air strike was being conducted up north with many aircraft involved. Fuel tankers would taxi in to FASU area and load up so they could replenish the fighters and boomers in the strike zone. The department pumped almost a million gallons of fuel that day.

There were several things that should not become routine, like going to the office on a regular schedule or by a certain path. The officers were a primary sniper target. Therefore, all officers were to keep from doing anything on a routine basis. But, one thing I did on my lunch hour was to lie in an area to get a suntan. The location of my sunbathing spot varied each day. By July, I was as brown as I could ever possibly be. In July I got to go home to Beeville for two week's Rest and Relaxation (R&R).

The Red Dog Beach

CDR Jack Higgins

For entertainment, I did several things. Sometimes I would engage in a Pinochle game in the Red Dog or go sightseeing. Sometimes I would go to the China Beach Club and sunbathe on the white sand beach. China Beach was a rest area where a person could get rest and relaxation. It seemed odd to lie on the beach and hear gunshots in the distance. For some unexplained reason, I never felt threatened or in any danger there. I always thought that the area would make for a great resort center. One could always find some interesting sights along the way to China Beach, like the Vietnamese women in their local attire and the local service stations. I often wondered how many men went to go somewhere only to find their fuel tanks nearly empty. Where else could these vendors get their supply of fuel? Other times, I would visit with the officers in the Red Dog playing a friendly game of Klondike or just go down to the Flight Line and visit with the crew.

Sunbathing on China Beach

Local Citizens

Local Service Station   *Local Supermarket*

When I first went to Vietnam, all the Armed Forces Exchange stores were going full blast. There were many great bargains on all sorts of items, especially electronic items. But, having just arrived in the country, I didn't need to buy anything, because I couldn't ship it home. One could ship things only if he or she was rotating out of country. This was necessary to reduce the black market and cut out the graft. All the USO shows were going great. Freedom Hill was one of the biggest facilities outside of Saigon. Bob Hope always put on a show there. He scheduled to appear in March 1972, and I was looking forward to seeing him. Then on 6 March, I believe, the North Vietnamese started their TET Offensive Drive toward Da Nang. Naturally, Bob Hope canceled the show in Da Nang because of the danger, and went to see the troops stationed in Thailand instead. I didn't get to see Bob Hope. The NVA came within fifteen miles of Da Nang before retreating. FASU was getting ready to BUG OUT.

Around mid-year, about August, the US forces started a retreat, turning all outlying posts that guarded Da Nang over to the South Vietnamese Forces. The 173 Armored Division started withdrawing. The Exchange at Freedom Hill closed and the USO personnel started to leave. Not knowing all that was happening, I drove to Freedom Hill one day and was astonished to find myself among the Vietnamese troops with no American troops around. I felt as unsafe that day as I ever had been. I didn't panic though; I calmly drove into a parking lot, stopped, looked around, and calmly drove out of the area and back through the gate to the American control site. By September, a lot of the units on Da Nang Air Base itself had begun turning sections of the base over to the Vietnamese control.

One of those areas was the oxygen plant that produced the oxygen for the aviators. One day the person that always kept the unit's supply tanks full, came to me and said that the oxygen plant was down and that there was very little oxygen available. I had to send a message to the Seventh Fleet Commander letting everyone know that FASU could no longer service the fleet's aircraft with oxygen. From that time until the close of the unit, a 500-gallon tank of oxygen was delivered every week to FASU from Cubi Point, Philippines, by C-130 aircraft.

Shortly after the oxygen problem, up jumped another problem. A Petty Officer who took care of the vehicles used by FASU came into the office and reported that all the vehicles had to be returned to the parent command, NAV VI V Da Nang. I contacted the Officer in Charge to find out the reason for those orders. He said they were being pulled out of the area and all the vehicles had to be shipped out of country. I asked where we were to get the vehicles needed by FASU. He didn't know and didn't care, he was leaving. I told the Skipper and sent a message to COMNAVAIRPAC stating the situation and requesting advice. They responded by reassigning the vehicles to FASU. The OinC of the previous unit wanted to know how we would be submitting the required reports for the vehicles. I let him know that there had not been any mention of a report until this time. I told him that we now had custody of said vehicles and not to worry about reports. One day a large package appeared on my desk. It was in a plain envelope with no markings except my name. I opened it to reveal another envelope with "TOP SECRET" stamped on it. Inside was a set of instructions about the vehicles and a requirement for a monthly report. The reports were to be sent to an individual in Saigon. I called for the man only to learn that he was no longer in country. I asked his relief what he knew about a certain instruction, but he had never heard of it. I didn't bother to ever make that report. I kept that TS instruction for three months and then burned it. I never heard anymore about reports on vehicles.

A party was always given for the person celebrating their birthday. I turned FORTY on 26 September 1972. The officers threw a party for me at a newly opened Chinese Restaurant. I consumed too much wine and too many drinks that night. The next morning, I really didn't want to go to work, but knew I had to. I did sleep in until 0800. When I got to the office, there was all kinds of commotion. There had been a plane crash and it had involved a navy aircraft. Man! I didn't need that kind of news. My head was not feeling too good right then and I knew that since I was the Maintenance Officer, it would be my job to supervise the salvage and clean up.

That had to be one of the most senseless crashes that I have ever known. The pilot was one of those "show offs." He was going to demonstrate what a "hot" pilot he was. We discovered his second mistake first and his first mistake last. At the end of the runway, he had pushed the "override" button and raised the landing gear handle before he started his "take-off" roll. As explained by other pilots who had either done that or thought about doing that, he had in mind that after lighting the afterburner and gaining enough speed, he would lift the aircraft off the runway just enough to get the landing gear to retract. Then he would be able to fly down the runway at about four feet from the pavement. Then, when he had enough airspeed he would pull back on the yoke and ZOOM! Straight up and disappear out of sight. Well, he hadn't taken into account the fact that the runway was not level. He had enough airspeed to stay level, but not enough to get the aircraft up. He passed over a low spot in the runway and the gear extended then retracted, then he was back level on the pavement. His plane could not rotate to become airborne. He knew that the aircraft was going to crash at the end of the runway. He had no other choice than to eject himself from the aircraft. Well! That was when his first mistake was discovered. He had failed to buckle himself in the parachute. He was killed when he hit the ground. Now that the canopy had been blown off, there was a pressure point that lifted the aircraft causing it to take off as it normally would. The plane flew out about ten miles and dropped a wing just enough to get it turning back toward the base. The Airbase Commander thought it would have to be shot down before it reached the base. Luckily, it crashed into a rice paddy about a mile from the end of the runway; lucky for the base, but unlucky for me.

CDR Higgins told me that I was designated the Salvage Officer, which meant I had to go into that paddy to supervise the recovery of the wreckage. The first order of business was to locate and recover the two Side Winder missiles that had been installed on the aircraft. There were about thirty men assigned to my charge. I had them spread out about an arm's length from each other and wade through the rice paddy in a grid pattern. One of the missiles was found almost immediately, but the war head was missing. It took most of the rest of the day to find the other missile. By dark time, a lot of the bits and pieces of the aircraft were pulled from the rice paddy and loaded on trucks to be carted to the salvage yard, but the war head from the one missile still had not been located. We secured the search site in order to return to the base before it would be unsafe to be in the open area with Charlie.

When I walked into my BOQ the maid looked at me and said, "You shit can; me no wash." She was talking about the clothes that I was wearing. I know they smelled something awful, like I had been in a cesspool. I went into the shower stall completely clothed and washed my clothes while I was still wearing them. After they were somewhat clean I pulled them off and threw them to the maid. She accepted them then without further complaint. After changing into a fresh uniform, I went looking for the Skipper to give my brief about the day's activities. He told me to take fifteen men to the rice paddy at daybreak to continue the search for the missing war head. He said that if we didn't get it now, Charlie would send it back to us some night in the form of a bomb. So, the fifteen men and I had breakfast at 0500 and headed for the rice paddy. I had to leave a crew to guard the vehicles to keep the Vietnamese kids from field stripping them. Luckily, one of the men could speak Vietnamese. Again, I started the men searching in a grid pattern on the far side of the paddy and work toward the trucks. After about an hour, I saw the men at the trucks waving for me to come to them. The man that spoke Vietnamese had been talking to some kids that came along and one of them said that he knew where the war head was located. I told him that I would pay him a 100 Posadas (Vietnamese currency) if he would lead us to the war head.

I called some of the other men and we went in search of the war head. The young boy took us to two rice paddies down from where we had been searching and dug the war head out from under a dyke where Charlie had buried it. Had it not been for that boy leading us to the war head, we would have never found it until Charlie launched it at us.

There were about four other boys with the one who knew where the missile head was, so I had to come up with some money to pay each of them also. I had to borrow the money from the whole crew to have enough to give each of them fifty Posadas.

Some parts of the fuselage and the wing sections were too large for the men to retrieve from the paddy. I located an army salvage unit and had to call upon them to recover the larger pieces and deliver them to the salvage yard. They used a CH-54 Ski Crane for the task. An Army Captain piloted the helicopter with a Warrant Officer as copilot. I was the only other person onboard. We had attached a large triple hook on a cable and drug it through the paddy as though we were trolling for fish. The fuselage was snagged and flown to the salvage yard. Next, we tried to snag the wing section, but could not latch on to it. Finally, the Captain told me that if I wanted it, I was the one that would have to go into the paddy and secure the cable to the wing. Man! That would make three days in a row that I would have to go into that paddy. I was reluctant, but knew there was no other way. After securing the cable, they carried it to dry land nearby, landed, and waited for me to wade out of the paddy and get aboard the helicopter. When we arrived at the salvage yard the Captain cut the cable and let it fall, not even stopping to recover the hook. He was tired of the operation and so was I. I never wanted to see a rice paddy after that day. Each time I came into the BOQ in wet clothes the maid would say, "You shit can; me no wash."

The Time I Endangered Myself to Save Two Aircraft, Pilots, and Crew - A Navy Captain from COMFAIRWESTPAC came into the area on an inspection tour. The Skipper asked me to escort him around the area to let him see what kind of jobs FASU was assigned to do. There were two F-4 Phantom aircraft hot refueling at the time. Four marines were handling the task of refueling the aircraft with the engines running and the pilots and copilots sitting in the cockpits. When the tanks were filled, the marines would disconnect the fuel lines and the aircraft would taxi out of the area for takeoff. As the Captain and I were walking across the ramp, I noticed fuel running out of a revetment and flowing under the aircraft. The hot engine exhaust was blowing the fuel into swirls, creating a vapor that could ignite at any time. The marines had not noticed the fuel on the ground and were in danger, as well as the aircraft, if the fuel ignited. I broke into a run through the fuel, which was by now about two or three inches deep, to warn the marines to secure the fueling operation, get the hoses disconnected and taxi the aircraft out of danger. After I got their attention, I would turn off the valves of the fuel lines. As I was about halfway to the marines, Bob Crawford was driving by. He stopped and told me that he would go into the revetment and secure a valve to stop the leak. He placed himself in great danger also. Had the fuel ignited, he would have had no way out of the revetment. When all was over and the fuel had not ignited, I went back to where the Captain was watching. He asked if that was routine procedure. I told him that I sure hope not, but when things like that occur we cannot hesitate in doing what becomes necessary to make things safe again. I thought he would have said something to the Skipper, but he never said a word. I regret now that I didn't say something to the Skipper and at least recommend Bob for a Bronze Star.

The Time I Walked in the Clouds - That was an awesome, yet eerie feeling. This was another time when some men of higher rank came into the area wanting to be taken somewhere. This time two men needed to go to the LINKS site, which was on Monkey Mountain, about twenty miles from FASU. The Skipper told me to drive them up there. I could see Monkey Mountain from the base and I could also see the clouds that always covered the top of the mountain. I really didn't think too much about the clouds at the time. We made it known by radio that we were coming and left the base about 0900 hours. We drove through the gate, through the city of Da Nang, across the Da Nang River, and through the smaller Vietnamese villages. Finally, we started the climb up the mountain. There were a few monkeys in the trees that watched us go by. The drive consisted of switchback curves, which were sometimes pretty sharp turns. I hoped that if we met an oncoming vehicle, that it would be on its side of the road. About four-fifths of the way we entered the clouds. That's when the driving became difficult. The visibility was reduced to about one-tenth of a mile. Now, I was really concerned about meeting a vehicle coming down the road. We made it at about 1100 hours. Although I had secret classification clearance, I did not have a need to know, so I was stuck with being on the outside. I walked around in the clouds for about an hour with nothing to do. It was like walking in a fog. I got somewhat damp, but not soaking wet. About noontime, someone came and took me to lunch. Then I was back in the clouds again until the men had the information they needed and were ready to return to FASU. The drive down through the clouds was worse than the drive up. Now I had to watch the speed to keep from running off the road and down a cliff. We got back to the unit at about 1700 hours.

The hazards of war were not always enemy initiated. Sometimes our own forces were the cause of our jeopardy situations. I was awakened about midnight one time by the sound of exploding ordnance. I rolled out of my bunk onto the floor and put on my flak vest and helmet. There would be loud BOOMS! Then there would be sounds like small arms fire. Then the loud BOOMS would go again. I kept listening for the sirens, warning of an enemy attack, but there were none. From my window, I could see a red glow with all sorts of flashes. Finally I went outside to see about the ruckus. It turned out that a man who was supposed to be guarding the ammunition bunker had popped a flare sideways instead of straight up and it had landed in the bunker and started a fire. With all the shells exploding, it was too dangerous for the firemen to try to put out the fire. Although the bunker was divided into sections, which separated the different types of ordnance, as they exploded it would send a shower of molten material into the next section and start a fire among the ordnance stored there. Those explosions went on for about four days.

Another time that we were endangered by our own came from the army unit next to FASU. It was a helicopter HOT rearming unit. A man was removing live rockets from the packing crates and accidentally pulled a safety pin from one of the rockets. Instead of pitching the rocket into a pit which was provided to absorb the blast and shrapnel, he dropped it back into the box and ran out to a bunker. The rocket exploded sending all the other rockets into the air and over onto the FASU area. Also, the explosion ignited other rockets, which also exploded sending more live ordnance flying through the air. I was sitting in my office when all the action started happening. Luckily, none of the stuff that came into the area exploded and we were able to evacuate to a safe area. An ammo demolition team was dispatched to clear the area and make it safe to return to the office.

Sometime in September, CDR Higgins was relieved as OinC of FASU by CDR Holland. CDR Higgins went to Corpus Christi, Texas, XO of Training Squadron Twenty-Eight (VT-28).

I had heard of some bad things happening to people who were assigned to Consolidated Mess Treasurer duty. I knew that was one job I didn't want. Well, we don't always get to do or not do certain things. On 1 November 1972, CDR Holland assigned me to that position. I relieved CWO2 Alfred Nelson who was being relieved by Lt. Paul John, also an LDO Mustang. It really was a headache. All of the cash receipts and stock on hand had to be inventoried twice each day; once just before opening time and the other after closing at night. Then there were the club personnel who had to be considered each day. Some of the waitresses had friends who had worked at clubs that had been closed and they wanted to come to work in the FASU club. One day I received a special invitation to a luncheon by Snow. Snow, a Vietnamese, was the club secretary/bookkeeper. She had invited the OinC, the Security Officer, and me to the luncheon. It was downtown Da Nang. I asked the others if they were going and both replied that they were. It turned out that I was the only one present. I had been warned not to eat certain foods that had been prepared by the Vietnamese. It turned out that they were buttering me up to hire one of their friends. I had to tell them, "NO." The club did not need any more waitresses. I was on call each night to help corral a ruckus within the club. The secretary/bookkeeper, Snow, had been accused of embezzlement of funds. Although she had been acquitted, the money had never been recovered. So, how much could I depend on her records. It made me work extra hard to make sure everything jived and was accurate. It wasn't long before all the men who patronized the club knew me, but I didn't know them. I guess the prices were reasonable, fifteen cents for a beer and twenty-five cents for mixed drinks. I was relieved of that duty on 20 December 1972, by CWO2 Edward W. Anderson. CWO2 Anderson had relieved CWO4 Crawford as the Line Officer.

I was in the zone for promotion to Lieutenant Commander under US Code 5787. Because of the number of people in the zone, I had no idea that I would be selected. When the list was published on 18 December 1972, my name was on it, along with Dan Rumbley. The effective date was 1 July 1973; however, the CO said that he could and would frock me, which meant that I would get all privileges of a LCDR, but not the pay. He said that if he had a pair of Lieutenant Commander collar devices, he would pin them on me that evening. Lt. Sam Houston spoke up to say that he had a pair in his desk in his office. Since his name was not on the list, he would give them to me. It didn't take me more than five minutes to have them in my hands. I was frocked to the rank of Lieutenant Commander by CDR W. R. Holland at 1900 hours on 19 December 1972. Since I had been the Consolidated Mess Treasurer, I decided to have an open bar for thirty minutes for the men. It was my way of celebrating my promotion to LCDR. I could not believe how many drinks could be consumed in that short period. When the men heard that the drinks were on me, they called all their friends and many of them ordered two drinks at a time, which was the limit. They ordered two more when the waitress came by again, although they had not finished the first ones. I think the tab came to one hundred ninety dollars.

I was due to rotate out of FASU in January 1973. Although I had follow-up orders for an assignment in Hawaii when I left Da Nang, I was not happy. My thoughts were that, although I had twenty years of service and ten years as a commissioned officer and was eligible for retirement, we did not own any place to settle should I decide to retire. I called the Detail Assignment Officer and asked if I could negotiate a new set of orders. He was extremely happy with that request. It would cost a lot of money to ship my family and household goods from Beeville to Hawaii. I asked to be transferred to Corpus Christi, Texas, instead. That move saved the government a bunch of money. I called Diann and told her not to ship Fluffy, the cat, that my orders had been changed from Hawaii to Corpus Christi. Needless to say, she was unhappy about the change. She said that she had screamed so loud that the entire world could hear her. Knowing that we were going to Hawaii is what kept her going while I was in Vietnam.

My relief was Lt. Ed Aberley, another LDO Mustang. He was also on the selectee list for promotion to Lieutenant Commander. On 22 December 1972, Ed came into the office and introduced himself. I was really surprised to see him. I was not expecting him to be there before 11 January. He said that he was divorced and got tired sitting around the house, so he decided to come over early. He was ready to assume the duties and relieve me as the Maintenance Officer just as soon as I gave him a tour of the area. We spent all day 23 December going to the various sites with which he should be acquainted. That evening, we were in the Red Dog having a drink when the Skipper came in. Out of the blue, Ed said to Commander Holland,

"Commander, as far as I'm concerned, I hereby relieve Ed Hudson as Maintenance Officer. He can go home." That statement really took me by surprise. So I said, "In that case, how about tomorrow the twenty-fourth? CDR Holland said that it couldn't be done quite that fast, but he would have Admin start cutting orders and making arrangement for transportation. I could leave the day after Christmas. On the twenty-fourth, I spent the day packing and cleaning out my room. Man! I was ready to leave. I shipped two boxes of personal effects and a refrigerator home so I wouldn't have too much to carry with me on the plane.

Christmas Day was a fun day. LCDR Tom Smith, who had been stationed in Beeville when I was there, flew in from one of the ships on his way home. He saw me and asked what I was doing in Da Nang? I told him that I had been stationed there for almost a year, but was going home the next day. He asked if I could show him and two of his friends around Da Nang; that he would like to see the city and a few sites, if possible. His two friends were both Navy Lieutenants, I didn't get their names. I had not turned in the keys of the truck that was assigned to me, so I said sure. We put two lounge chairs in the bed for his friends and commenced our tour. I wanted to see the area one last time anyway. We drove out the gate and went through a little village headed for Freedom Hill. Bob Hope had put on many of his shows there, but not while I was there. I did not know that Freedom Hill had been turned over to the Vietnamese army and there were no American soldiers guarding the place. When I discovered this, I tried not to panic and acted like we were supposed to be there. We took a few pictures, and then calmly left the area and got back on the base. I can tell you that I was concerned for our safety. Next we went out another gate, crossed the Da Nang River and went to China Beach Club house and had lunch. That place, too, was almost deserted. We went to Deep Water Pier and then drove through the town of Da Nang. I showed Tom and his friends a lot more than they expected. We must have presented an odd scene with Tom's friends seated in the bed of the truck in civilian clothes in lawn chairs.

I knew on Christmas night that there would be a rocket attack on the morning of the 26th. I just didn't know the time. In the evening after dinner, I watched the "Magic Dragon," flying over Happy Valley aiming his stinger at something. The "Magic Dragon" was a C-130 aircraft armed with a Gatling gun, used to fire at the Viet Cong (VC) setting up rocket launchers. I watched it fly around for about an hour and then decided to go to bed. I was going home the day after Christmas and sure didn't want to sleep late and miss my flight. Sure enough, the rockets started hitting the base at 0605 hours. One of the rockets landed about eighty feet from my room. Lucky for me, it had a delayed action fuse and was buried about six feet in the ground before exploding. I said that Charlie had held reveille and gave me a going away present, a piece of shrapnel to take home. I left Da Nang without getting the statistics of the attack.

I departed Da Nang at about 1000 hours headed for Saigon. I just knew that things would not be pleasant there. I had been through there on several occasions and the living conditions had not been good. The army treated the enlisted men and officers 03 and below with very little respect. Beds were given on a first come first serve basis. I was really surprised when I got there. I was now 04 and was assigned to a separate berthing area with head of the line privileges. When it came time to board the plane for home, I was told to go aboard first. It was a 747 and all passengers had the run of the whole plane until we got to Manila, PI. In Manila, several civilians came onboard and then we were assigned to the coach instead of the first class section. The plane made a stop in Agana, Guam. There was a two-hour layover, so I called a friend, Ralph Nadeau, whom I knew was stationed there. He picked me up and took me to his house for about an hour. It was good to see him again. I had not seen him since Okinawa in 1968. I landed at L.A. Airport about 1600 and only had about a forty-five minute wait to board another plane for Dallas, Texas. I took time to call Diann at my mother-in-law's house to let her know that I was on my way home, would be in Dallas about 0600 the next day, and asked if she wanted to pick me up at the airport. It was 27 December and all I had on was a short sleeve khaki shirt. I felt out of place walking around the airport in that dress and everyone else wearing coats. It sure was good to see my family again and to be back in the good ol' USA. After checking for my luggage, I learned that it was not on the plane with me. We drove to Waco to my mother-in-law's house. The first thing she said was, "Pull down your pants; I want to see the scar of your hernia operation." She just knew that I had been in the hospital for wounds rather than for a hernia. We spent a few days in Waco before heading for Beeville. Remember, Diann, Bruce, and Carla had remained in government quarters while I was in Vietnam.

NAVAL AIR STATION, CORPUS CHRISTI, TEXAS

January 1973 to February 1976

NAS Corpus Christi Logo

After spending a few more days just relaxing and getting myself orientated to the local time zone, Diann and I went looking for a place to live in Corpus Christi. Corpus Christi is only about sixty-five miles from Beeville.

Since I had orders to NAS Corpus Christi, we had to start making arrangements to move out of the Beeville government housing very soon. We bought a local paper and screened it for Realtors. We settled on Manard Kowns Realty. I was not sure what we could afford or what we needed or even wanted. We had never been looking for a house to buy before. An agent named Phil was assigned to show us around. We had looked at several, when Phil told us that he thought he had the place we were looking for. He took us by and we thought it was nice, but would cost way more than we could afford. So, we kept looking. One place I thought I would really like was out in the country along the Nueces River. I could just see myself fishing in the Nueces River from my own backyard. Upon arriving, we could see that the house was built on stilts. When I saw watermarks about six feet high on the walls, I knew this was not the house for us. My dreams of fishing in the Nueces River were dashed.

The next day the Realtor took us back to the house we looked at before. We liked the house, but still didn't think we could afford it. The address was 906 Carmel Parkway, Corpus Christi, Texas. Then we learned that we could get the house for $27,000 if we put $6,000 down and took out a conventional loan. I had saved $6,000 while in Vietnam. We took the house and moved in on 19 January 1973. I learned years later that, while we were negotiating the purchase of the house, the property owners who lived on Carmel Parkway were having us investigated to determine our suitability for their neighborhood. I guess we passed their approval.

After completing the transaction to buy the house and having closed the deal, I went to the base and requested shipment of our household goods from Beeville. Our effects and furniture were packed and loaded one day, but would not be delivered until three days. We stayed in the house in Corpus Christi, but had to sleep on pallets.

Upon checking into the Naval Air Station, I was assigned to the Aircraft Intermediate Maintenance Department. Captain Zeisel was the Commanding Officer, Commander Hackney was the XO, and Commander M. R. Rumelhart was the Department Head. I was assigned as the Maintenance Material Control Officer, replacing LCDR John Lyde, another LDO Mustang. LCDR Cal Bright, another LDO Mustang, was the Assistant Department Head. During the time I was in Vietnam, I saw that John Lyde had been the FASU Maintenance Officer in 1970. John and I had something in common. He wanted to hear all the news about Da Nang. Shortly after I had checked in, another LDO Mustang, Lt. Walt Carlyon, was assigned to AIMD. That made four LDOs in the department. Walt and I became good friends and did all sorts of things together, like golfing, fishing, and hunting.

Cal Bright, John Lyde, and I were all Lieutenant Commanders with Cal being the senior. In fact, I had only been frocked to the rank, awaiting my promotion date of 1 July. Every piece of correspondence submitted by our section had to be screened and approved by Cal. It seemed that neither John nor I could write worth a hoot. Our messages and letters would be returned to us with all sorts of corrections. One day John got the idea to see what Cal would do to a letter that had already been sent by his office. John hand copied the original and forwarded to Cal's office. The next day it came back to John's desk all marked up with corrections. We knew then it was Cal's nature. He could not accept another person's correspondence.

There were other men of interest in AIMD. Chief Flores (AEC) was in charge of the Electric Shop. Since I had been an electrician, he and I had a lot in which we could converse. Chief Parkas (ADC) was in charge of the Power Plants Division. Since I had been the Power Plants Officer in Beeville, I knew some of the problems associated with engine maintenance. Ensign Purdy was a young officer who had dropped out of flight training. He was assigned to AIMD temporally awaiting transfer orders.

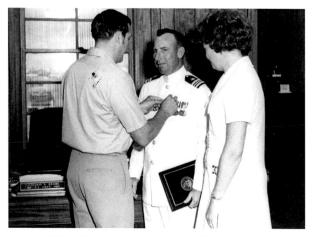

Awarded the "Navy Commendation Medal" (with Combat "V")

The reading of the Citation

On 8 March 1973, I was told by CDR Rumelhart to report to the CO's office at 0900 the next day, 9 March, and to bring Diann with me. I did not know what to expect. I was also told to be in my full dress whites. Naturally, Diann dressed appropriately for the occasion also. I was being awarded the Navy Commendation Medal with (Combat "V") for service in FASU Da Nang, Vietnam.

There were four Training Squadrons, VT-27, VT-28, VT-29, and VT-31, located on NAS Corpus Christi. I learned that CDR J. J. Higgins was the XO of VT-28. He was my CO in FASU Da Nang. I looked him up to let him know I was at AIMD. We had a lot to talk about concerning Vietnam. A bad thing happened to him and his career. He took over as CO of the squadron after serving as XO for one year. The second week after he had assumed command, there was an aircraft accident involving student pilots. Some of the students were killed in the accident. Of course, there was an accident investigation to determine the cause and to place blame. It was determined that there were some discrepancies in the training instructions being taught to the student pilots. These instructions had been taught for many years, long before CDR Higgins had reported in to the squadron. But, it didn't matter, CDR Higgins was the Commanding Officer, so he was to blame. He was relieved of command and his career; as far as promotions were concerned, was over. He was transferred to Training Wing Four under Captain Wynn. I really felt sorry for Jack. He was such a nice Officer, Man, and Person. He didn't deserve that kind of a raw deal. He left Corpus Christi sometime in the spring of 1976 and I never heard about him again.

Walt and I heard about a Rattlesnake Roundup in Freer, Texas, about eighty miles west of Corpus Christi. We thought that might be fun to participate in, so we submitted a request chit to the Department Head on 9 April 1973, for approval, stating that all proceeds from prizes won would be donated to the Navy Relief Charity. We did enter the contest and hunted on the Los Lomas Ranch without having any luck. Walt and I went again in April 1974, and this time we captured two rattlesnakes. One was five feet eight inches long. I held the snake up in the air (my bare hand was just behind the head where it couldn't bite me) and Walt took a picture. I did not know that he intended to have it published in the base paper, *The Beam*. Walt and I had a total of four snakes to turn in for the Round-up contest, two of which I had caught earlier. We netted a sum of eight dollars for our efforts, which we donated to the Navy Relief Charity Fund

Freer Rattlesnake Roundup

That same month, 13 April 1973, I was appointed Summary Court-Martial Officer. NAS Corpus Christi was designated the processing center for all AWOL sailors in the Eighth Naval District. The wayward sailors would be tried by Summary Court-Martial when apprehended within the jurisdiction. I was one of several officers designated as Summary Court-Martial to try their cases. I held at least one trial and sometimes two or three days per week for two years. Sometimes I would have as many as four people to be tried in one day. I asked to be scheduled on Tuesday and that other officers be scheduled on the other days. That way, we would be able to tend to our regular tasks more effectively. The XO, CDR Hackney, liked my idea, so I was now scheduled every Tuesday. It got to where I dreaded going to work on Tuesdays because some young man or woman would be in trouble and I would be the Presiding Officer of their Summary Court. I didn't mind convicting the truly guilty, but hated to sentence a person who just happened to be in the wrong place at the wrong time and enticed to get involved. I later learned that I was the only officer holding Summary Court Duty. I protested to the Legal Officer and he said that I was always there so he chose me. After that day, I had fewer court-martial duties.

I was promoted to the appointment of Lieutenant Commander United States Navy under the US Code 5787, effective 1 July 1973. This was an early promotion program designed to bring the LDOs in line with the regular officers' promotion cycle. I had been commissioned nine years nine months. Normally, it would have taken eleven years to make Lieutenant Commander. Although I had been promoted under US Code 5787, I still had to be selected under the regular promotion program in order to retain the rank. There were other officers in the command who were promoted under the same program who would not be promoted under the regular promotion program and would have to either retire or be demoted back to Lieutenant. Luckily I did get selected at the regular cycle.

Promoted to Lieutenant Commander USN 1 July 1973

The navy had a policy requiring all officers to have an annual medical physical during their birthday month. I was due in September since my birthday is on the twenty-sixth. I checked into the Base Dispensary on 11 September 1973, for my physical. I had all sorts of tests run on me—blood tests, EKG, hearing exam, feet examined—and others I can't remember. Then the doctor started his examination. He checked my ears, nose, and throat plus running his finger up my anus, which didn't feel too good. He also poked around my groin area, which really didn't feel good. He would shove a finger way up under the skin of my lower right stomach and tell me to cough. Then he would do it on the left side and tell me to cough. When he was finished, he told me that he would not declare me physically fit for duty until I had my inguinal hernia repaired. I told him that I had it repaired in May 1972. He said yes, he knew that because it was in my record, but that was the right side and now you have one on your left side. Man! I didn't need to hear that kind of news. I couldn't believe that could be possible.

When I was in Vietnam I started jogging each day with the Skipper and the XO. About one month later is when I experienced the pain in my left side. I don't know how long I had this hernia. After we moved to Corpus Christi I started jogging again in July. It was a little over one month from that time that I had my annual physical. Although it possibly caused the hernia to develop, I wasn't experiencing any pain. I had just had a hernia operation the year before and it took almost a month and a half to recover. I didn't want to go through that pain again so soon. Well, the doctor told me that jogging was probably the cause, but that I had thirty days to check into the hospital for the operation or I would be discharged from the navy for medical reasons.

I didn't hesitate any longer. The hospital was a WWII vintage; all wooden structures scattered over several blocks. I had the operation 28 September 1973. I was in the hospital ten days, and then put on thirty days convalescent leave. One night, while I was in the hospital, a black man was brought in with a gunshot wound and placed in the bed next to me. We were both near the nurses' station so they could keep a close watch over us. The next day we were both awake enough that we could carry on a conversation. I learned that he had been shot while in a bar in Houston. His name was Hall. That's about all I was able to learn from him. We didn't have anything in common, but I tried to be friendly. I was released about two days later to go on thirty-day convalescent leave. That meant that I had to stay home for thirty days and do absolutely nothing. I forgot all about Seaman Hall. The timing could not have been better. Since I couldn't do anything, I watched all the baseball playoffs and the World Series. To this day, I can't remember who played, much less who won.

Sometime while I was stationed in Corpus Christi, I learned that our nephew Fred Vieck was at NAS Kingsville, Texas, undergoing flight training. Kingsville was not all that far from Corpus. It was nice to have relatives close-by, where we could visit now and then. We had Thanksgiving Dinner at their house in 1973. Fred is Diann's nephew who was in the marines. His wife, Jenny, and their young son Craig were accompanying him on this assignment. I'm not sure how long he was in Kingsville.

The Operations Maintenance Department (OMD) was responsible for the maintenance, repair, and upkeep of the Naval Air Station aircraft and the aircraft used by Chief of Naval Air Training Command. The aircraft were three UH-1N helicopters, two C-117 transports, and one C-131. The C-131 was considered the Admiral's plane. LCDR Martin was the OMD Officer. Sometimes Walt and I would go to the Fleet Reserve Club for lunch. On our way we went by the golf course and LCDR Martin would be on the number four hole. It was a nine-hole course and we didn't know if he was on his first round or second round. We said to each other, "I sure would like to have his job where I could play golf every day." He retired on 1 October 1973, and was relieved by LCDR Jenkins.

LCDR Jenkins followed LCDR Martin's manner of management. He let the Maintenance Chief oversee the maintenance of the aircraft while he prepared for his retirement. His retirement date was 1 October 1974. On 26 September 1974, I was assigned as Operations Maintenance Department (OMD) Officer, relieving LCDR Jenkins. Commander Sid R. Graham was the Air Operations Officer. I went over on Monday to have a week of indoctrination and turn over.

On Friday morning at quarters and after muster, LCDR Jenkins bid his farewell in a speech to the men. He told them what an excellent job they had performed while serving under him and how much he had enjoyed the assignment. Then he said that effective this date, LCDR Hudson is the Operations Maintenance Department (OMD) Officer. He had been relieved. He asked if I had anything to say.

YOU BET I HAD SOMETHING TO SAY! I addressed LCDR Jenkins and the men. I accepted the assignment by telling him, "I hereby relieve you." To the men, now…"I have been in the area for a week and don't like what I have seen!" For one thing, the aircraft availability was very low. A lot of the time the flight schedule had not been met due to the lack of a ready aircraft. Then there were the work spaces! They were extremely filthy and in great need of a good old fashioned "Navy Field Day." Next, there was the absenteeism. Come 1400 that afternoon, no one was around and no work was being performed. "Therefore, I have no recourse except to declare tomorrow, Saturday, a normal working day. We will all muster at the regular time tomorrow morning, 0730 hours." The "we" meant me included. I did not believe in ordering men to do something that I myself would not do.

A Chief standing in the rear ranks yelled out, "I knew when I saw his picture in the *Beam* he was a mean SOB; he uses rattlesnakes for whips."

Then I said there would be a Chiefs' meeting in my office at 0900. LCDR Jenkins couldn't believe I meant those words. He and I went to the Air Boss's office to report that I had relieved LCDR Jenkins. I told him that I had declared a normal work day for the men on Saturday. He just said, "Do whatever you think best."

At the Chiefs' meeting, I dropped another bombshell. I told all the Chiefs who were on the flight crew that I was taking away their flight pay. There was protest, but I explained that the Chiefs were supposed to be managing the workshops and they could not do so if they were off to Timbuktu. I needed them in the shops. I also told them that if they worked with me, I could get them promoted in pay grade. However, if they worked against me, I could more easily get them demoted. At that, I dismissed them to go to work. The Maintenance Chief, an E8 named Jaynes, asked if he could speak to me after the meeting.

After the door was closed, he said, "Welcome aboard, Sir. I have been trying to get that done ever since I arrived, but could not get the backing. We are going to get along just great."

There were two officers under me, Lt. Acuff and LTJG Fonteneau. Both were helicopter pilots and on SAR (Search and Rescue) flight duty most of the time. That's why I had to rely on the Chiefs to be in their work spaces. The Chiefs did work with me. That first afternoon by 1400 the shops were completely cleaned, everyone was still there working, and the aircraft availability had jumped to 80 percent. However, it's hard to break old habits. After about a month, the men started sloughing off. The aircraft availability was steadily declining and the men started leaving earlier. The day before Thanksgiving Day, we couldn't meet the flight schedule. Therefore, I declared Thanksgiving Day a normal working day. That really caused a stir, not only from the men, but also their wives. Some of the wives even called Diann, chewing her out for my actions. I hadn't told her yet, but her comeback was that if the men had completed their work instead of leaving early every afternoon, they wouldn't be working on holidays. She also told them that if I declared a normal work day that I would also be there with them. My action let them know that the consequence of their infractions did not come cheap. I had fewer problems after that day.

The old adage, "Be careful what you ask for because you may just get it," really proved to be true. Now that I had gotten what I thought wanted, getting the job that LCDR Martin had, I found that I didn't have time to play golf like he did. In fact, by him playing golf so much, he had let the OMD get into a bad state, requiring a lot of overtime to correct.

The Quality Assurance Branch and Technical Library were almost non-existent. I put AMC Fred Titmas in charge and told him what I expected. Within three months, he had it well organized. I gave him a "well done" on his efforts and he was promoted to E8 on the February exam. The Maintenance Chief was promoted to E9. Chief Parsons was the Chief in Charge of the Airframe/Power Plant shop. His performance was satisfactory, but he held the rating as AMSC, which was a closed rating. No matter how great of a grading I would give him, he would not get promoted to E8. ATC Bishop was in charge of the Avionics shop and continued to resent me for taking away his flight pay. He was not recommended for promotion.

The Operation's Officer was a hard man for whom to work, not that he was around telling you what to do or how to do your job, but for his lack of guidance during times of need and backing when needed. I soon learned to just do the tasks as best possible and keep him informed. I did not want him hearing about a situation within the division from some other source. A problem arose concerning availability of parts to maintain the C-117 aircraft. I wanted to inform the Operation's Officer of the situation. On the way to his office, I met LCDR Eldon Armstrong. He was in charge of the airfield maintenance. He also had a problem, which involved student pilot safety and needed advice from the Commander. Eldon said that since his was a safety problem, I should let him be the first to talk to the Commander.

When Eldon said that there was a problem, the Operation's Officer said, "Do not bring me problems, I have enough problems! You bring me solutions!" Eldon was taken aback and said, "But...." Commander said, "No buts; go take care of your problem." Then he asked me what I wanted? I told him, "Nothing, I just came to give Eldon support." I did not go to him for advice after that date. I know this is disrespectful, but I phrased a statement about him, "He was Nixon trained; 'Yes, I'm responsible, but you're to blame.'"

A "Gooney Bird" Retirement

The C-117s (called "Gooney Birds"), were so old that there were no more spare parts available to maintain them. The parts were not available within the Supply Department warehouses and new parts were not being manufactured. I was getting some parts from scrap yards throughout the US—Miami, Tucson, etc. Finally, we had to start cannibalizing one of the two assigned aircraft to keep the other one flying. On 1 December 1974, we retired one of the Gooney's with Side Boy Honors. I turned over the log books and the aircraft airframe to Lt. Walter E Carlyon of AIMD for destruction. It was a sad day for us, but that helped to relieve the workload.

Shortly after being assigned to OMD there was a RIF (Reduction in Force) in manpower allocation. The division lost several billets at this time, which put a strain on those men who were left. They had to work harder and longer to meet the flight schedule. I, too, stayed with them. The men knew that if they had to work late, so did I. I gained their respect by my actions. The billets lost included engine and structural mechanics. Also, the Data Analyst billet was cut. I now had to rely on the Logs and Records Yeoman to do the job. The XO knew of the shortage of men. He and the OPS Officer decided to assign people awaiting medical discharge to my department. They were all limited in their ability to perform the various tasks needed to maintain the aircraft. I thought they were there on temporary duty, so I did not concern myself with them. As the regularly assigned personnel transferred out, no replacement was ordered. The Personnel Department was considering the billet filled by the people with the medical disabilities. It took a while to convince the OPS Officer not to accept any more people awaiting medical discharge.

One day, the Operations Officer told me there was to be a change in the number of helicopters that would be assigned to the division. We would have six instead of three to maintain. I told him that we didn't have enough manpower to maintain that many. He said that he didn't want to hear it, that I had to make do with what I already had assigned. We argued a bit then he asked me how many more I needed and he would see what he could do. I told him that it was not that simple. A new Manpower Authorization Request, Form (E-4), had to be submitted to Chief of Naval Personnel listing all the required billets to maintain all the assigned aircraft. It would be just as if we were starting anew. It would be time consuming. He told me just don't worry about that form and come up with the number of additional men that I needed to do the job.

I ignored that request and filled out four sets of the E-4 forms as per NavPers and CNATRA Instructions. The billet for the Data Analyst had been deleted earlier, so I put it back in for the division. CNATRA Personnel Manager called to set up a meeting to discuss the upcoming changes in manpower allocations. I had given Sid the numbers he had requested, but I had not given him a copy of the E-4 form. Captain Maddox called the meeting to order and asked for a copy the Manpower Authorization Request, Form (E-4). CDR Graham gave him a list stating the additional number of men, which I had given to him at his request. The Captain looked at Sid and wanted to know what that was supposed to be. Sid told him that it was the number of additional men above the number already assigned that were needed to perform the maintenance of the additional aircraft being assigned. I thought Captain Maddox was going to come unglued. I thought about letting him lower the boom on Sid, but decided not to. I retrieved the copies of the E-4 forms from a briefcase and asked, "Is this what you're looking for, Captain?" That cooled the Captain. He looked it over and asked how those figure cited on the form had been derived. I cited the formulas used to determine the number of men of each rating required in maintaining a certain number of aircraft listed in the NavPers instruction, the number I can't remember. He had a copy of the NavPers instruction in front of him, so he went over the form I had given him in great detail. Sid couldn't believe that I had ignored his order not to fill out the forms, but glad that I had and saved him and the command an embarrassment. The Captain then started referring all his questions to me for the answers. He knew that Sid didn't have a clue as to any of the answers. The command was granted all the billets that had been requested with an 80 percent approval of the manpower. If a division was 80 percent manned, it could do the assigned tasks. CDR Graham never once thanked me.

Each month an "officer's party" was held at someone's house. It was a social gathering when we could get better acquainted with one another. We would visit, play games, and tell sea stories. One evening I was telling the story about riding around Da Nang on Christmas Eve with two Lieutenants in the back of a pick-up truck. Lt. Knudgen spoke up and said, "Hey! I was one of those guys. Man! That was the neatest thing I have ever done!" I had no idea that I would ever run into any of those Lieutenants again. He was one of the helicopter pilots in the department.

The Vanderhules lived across Carmel Parkway from us. Juanita worked for CNATRA. One day I asked her if she would consider being in a carpool with me and she thought that was a great idea. At first her husband, George, didn't like the idea, but Diann thought it was great. It sure would save on gas expense. Finally, George agreed. She would drive one week and I would drive the next. Everything was going smoothly, I thought, until one day someone in the Admin Office asked me about my girlfriend. They said that the women in the office watched me pick her up every day after work. I had to explain that we were in a carpool and that our spouses approved. It just goes to prove that gossip can be started over very innocent activities. Even years later, people still believed we were having an affair.

Each division within any organization has its share of problem people. I sure had mine; partly because of CNO Admiral Zumwalt's relaxation of a lot of the restrictions. One of them was about having an alcoholic drink with the noon meal. Knowing the situation of alcoholism with some of the men, I made a standing order that there would be no beer lunches. However, that order didn't deter some of the men. AT3 Kelley was picked up several times and brought to the base for being drunk in public, even at lunchtime. Each time he came to work in a drunken state, I would have him placed on report and sent to "Captain's Mast." He was placed in Rehab for alcoholism and finally was discharged from the navy. AD2 Foster was another one who had been sent to Rehab. However, he benefited from it. He came to my office one day with two cokes and asked me to have a drink with him in celebration; it was one year ago that day since he had an alcoholic drink. I gladly accepted his offer. I had the most problems with AD1 Kovalt, until one day his wife called the office at noon asking for him. The Petty Officer answering the phone told her he had already gone to lunch. He said that he would have Kovalt call her when he returned from lunch. She responded with, "Don't bother because he won't find me alive when he gets home." The Petty Office repeated what she had said. My immediate thought was a suicide threat. I found their address and called the local police department and, after telling who I was, relayed the message to them. I told them that I would find Kovalt and deliver him home ASAP. I found him at the Base Exchange Restaurant and, sure enough, with a beer in his hand. I ordered him to come with Chief Titmas and I, but didn't tell him why. His wife denied that she meant to commit suicide, but I left Kovalt at home anyway. The next day he came to my office stating that he wanted to turn himself in to the Rehab Center. The word got out and I had no more problems with alcoholism in the department.

As Division Officer, I had to handle all sorts of requests. However, I didn't dream that I would be called to act as a marriage counselor. During the time that AD2 Foster was into partying, his wife was enjoying the nightlife with him. After he had gone through Rehab and was no longer drinking, he quit the partying, but he was having problems adjusting to a life without alcohol. His wife didn't care for their new lifestyle. She wanted to continue with the old style. He came to me one day and asked me to go talk to his wife and to try to get her to reconcile with him. To me, this was for a marriage counselor, not me. However, I went to see her and I guess I said the right things. A few weeks later, he came in and thanked me for saving their marriage.

Another problem I had to deal with was financial indebtedness of people assigned to my division. I had to deal with this problem in every duty station since I had received my commission—in Okinawa, Beeville, and now here at OMD. One day, I received a notice from the XO about a "Letter of Indebtedness" of one of the men in the division. I called him into my office to discuss the letter and try to help him find a solution. I asked him why he didn't pay his debts. He asked how much he had to pay them. He had been paying thirty-five dollars a month for over six months on a one hundred dollar loan. I didn't believe him and told him to bring in a copy of the contract the next day. Sure enough! He had been paying that amount according to the receipts. I reviewed the contract and could not believe what I was reading. It was made out to him stating that the loan shark would lend him one hundred dollars at 116 percent interest. I wanted to know why he had signed such agreement. He said that he needed the money at the time. He had paid thirty-five dollars for five months and missed the sixth month. When he went in to pay the sixth payment the loan shark told him that since he had missed that one month, the loan was reinstated and that he owed the entire amount of one hundred dollars. He refused to pay it. I told him that I would see what I could do to help him clear up this matter.

The local TV station, Channel Six, was noted for getting involved with the local city management and businesses. I called the station and talked to one of the reporters, a Mr. Caldwell. I asked him if he knew of any laws that would allow the loan companies to charge high interest rates. I then told him about this one charging 116 percent. He asked if he could come out to the base and have an interview with me. I said okay and we set a time. I did not think about clearing this meeting with the XO, CDR Hackney. He arrived on time and set up the camera and a tape recorder. We called several local loan companies and he called a lawyer friend of his. We learned about class "B" loan companies. Texas law allows a class "B" company to charge any interest that is agreed upon by the individual borrowing the money, as long as it does not exceed one hundred dollars. We talked about how the local loan sharks were taking advantage of the young sailors. We also decided that all the people in the area of city of Corpus Christi should be aware of the high interest being charged by the area loan companies. When Mr. Caldwell and the cameraman left the base, they took pictures of the loan offices just outside the base. That night the interview aired on both the 6 o'clock and 10 o'clock news.

The next morning the XO called me and said, "Good job, Ed! We sure need someone to be looking out for the men." It's the XO's job as well as the Division Officer's to look out for the welfare of the men. A woman from one of the local loan facilities just outside the base called me. She thanked me for getting her place on TV. She said, "Do you know how much it would cost to get that kind of advertisement?" She had missed the whole point I was trying to get across to the public about the loan sharks in the Corpus Christi area. The loan shark agreed to clear the debt of the man and we dismissed his letter of indebtedness,

The Reenlistment of Petty Office Beach
LCDR Hudson,   AM1 Sandy Beach, His   Wife, Virginia,   and Son, Stormy

When a person decides to reenlist, the reenlistment ceremony is usually held in the Commanding Officer's office. The CO also does the swearing in. One day, Petty Officer First Class Beach came into the office and said that he wanted to re-up in the navy and asked if I would do the honor of swearing him in for the reenlistment. I called the XO and explained the situation and was given the green light to perform the honors. A date was set so that his wife and child could be present during the ceremony. It was held in my office. The fact that he thought enough of me as his Department Head, I felt honored to perform the ceremony.

A few weeks after I had sworn in Petty Officer Beach, Petty Officer Jensen asked if I would also perform the swearing in of his reenlistment. I could not refuse and felt just as honored by his request. Not many officers get to perform reenlistment ceremonies during their career. After all the necessary paperwork was completed, a date was set and the swearing in took place.

Petty Officer Jensen's Reenlistment 1975

One of the things that never changed throughout my naval career was the assignment of "Military Watch Duty." From the first tour in boot camp, I was assigned some sort of Military Watch. A Military Watch is a period of time in the performance of a military function. I always tried to get myself promoted to a position whereby I no longer would be assigned a watch. No such luck. As a Lieutenant Commander at NAS Corpus Christi, I was assigned to stand as Command Duty Officer (CDO) about one to three times each month. During the time of the watch period, the CDO was charged with command of the whole base under the directions of the XO. The watch usually commenced at the end of the normal working day or on the weekend. The CDO would report to the XO for instructions prior to the beginning of the watch. There were also written instructions to refer to in dealing with situations when in doubt. The Officer of the Day (OOD) usually took care of most problems or situations; therefore, the CDO was only on call for special occasions.

I received a call around 1900 one evening about a rowdy individual. Security personnel had wanted to put the individual in the brig for safekeeping and the OOD did not have that authority. Only the CDO could make that authorization. So, I reported to the duty office and reviewed the instructions concerning placing a person in the brig. The instructions were fairly restrictive as to my authority. I could place a person in confinement for safekeeping only to prevent him from harming himself or other people, to prevent the person from destroying government property, or if he was a flight risk.

I went to the brig where Security had the person in a straightjacket and inside a patty wagon. Although they had him restrained, I could hear him inside the paddy wagon saying, "When I get loose, I'm going to bust me some heads." I learned from the Security MPs that they had been wrestling with this person since two in the afternoon. No one told me his name. I'm not sure that they had even learned his name at that time. It appears that he had gone to the base library about ten that morning, found a secluded place, and started sniffing dope (don't know what). About two he was high on something and started getting boisterous and rowdy. The Librarian called Security.

When the guards arrived, he spit in their faces and started kicking them. He broke loose and fled. They had spent the afternoon in the chase and capture. I determined that the person inside paddy wagon was a threat to himself, as well as anyone he could get his hands on. So, I agreed with the MPs to commit him to the brig. We all went to see the brig warden. He said that according to his instructions, the person had to be examined by a doctor and be declared physically fit. We called a doctor to the scene, but the man was thrashing around in the patty wagon yelling, "I'm gonna bust me some heads," and kicking the sides of the van. The doctor tried about three times to enter the wagon, but because of the violence, he was afraid of the man. Finally, he said that the man was too violent to examine, he would wait until the drugs wore off and then examine him. The Brig Warden and I got into a confrontation about putting the person in a padded cell to keep him from hurting anyone including himself.

I called the XO, Commander Hachney, and told him the situation. I wanted to commit him, but the warden would not take him into custody. The XO agreed with the warden, so off to the hospital we went. The longer we waited the more calm the man became. The drugs were beginning to wear off. About the time he was calm enough to be examined, which was about midnight; an emergency occurred, which required the doctor's attention.

As we were waiting in the waiting room, the person's girlfriend came in to see if she could take him home. That was a shock! How did she know about this problem? Who called her? I never learned. He looked at me and asked if I knew who he was? No, I didn't recognize him. He said, "Commander, don't you remember in the hospital about a person being brought in with a gunshot wound named Hall?" Then I knew the name. He told me that he was calm now and was sorry for all the trouble he had caused. I told him that may be the case, but he was being charged with several offenses and that he would be turned over to the base Legal Department for prosecution. He asked me why he had to be committed to the brig now that he was sober. I was still mad about the fact that the Commander Hachney wouldn't let me put him in the brig when I felt the need.

Finally, about 0200, the doctor said he was free from the emergency and could now examine the offender. After about thirty minutes, he came out of the examining room and declared the individual sober and physically fit to place in the brig. I told the man to go home and report to the legal office by 0800 the next morning. The security personnel became really angry with me for letting him go. I told them that as far as I could see, he was no longer a threat to anyone or anything and according to the instructions, I could not commit him to the brig. We all left the hospital about 0300. We were all tired, mad, and somewhat confused.

The next morning, Commander Hachney called me to his office and wanted to know why I didn't commit Seaman Hall to the brig after the doctor had declared him physically fit. I told him it was his doing, not mine; that he wouldn't let me when he should have been committed and after he had sobered and was no longer a threat to anything or anyone, according to the instructions, I couldn't commit him.

There were new instructions written shortly after that episode. I was told by the Admin Officer that I had really caused some heated arguments and much discussion on the matter, but because of my action, things would be better for future CDOs.

On 11 July 1974, I was assigned as the Air Operations Aviation Maintenance Safety Officer. I was responsible for investigating all aircraft accidents and mishaps that occurred to the station aircraft. I don't remember anything of significance that occurred during this assignment. There were no accidents involving aircraft or any incidents, which required the need to convene an investigation board.

A Navy Relief Fundraising Drive Festival is held annually for a weekend in May throughout all the naval bases. During that time, all sorts of events are scheduled. There is always a carnival with many booths and rides. An Air Show is also scheduled. Sometimes even the Navy's Blue Angels are there. They always put on quite a show. May 1975 was no different. CDR Holloway was in charge of the festival. He called me at the office one day and said that he wanted my department to play host to a British Wing Commander and the crew of a British Nimrod Squadron. The Commanding Officer was Wing Commander Burton with a crew of ten junior officers and fourteen enlisted men. I asked CDR Holloway what was expected and he said, "Just take care of them so I won't have to worry myself about them."

I asked Chief Fred Titmas to assign some men to help him play host to the enlisted men and I would handle the officers. That turned out to be one of the highlights of my tour in Corpus Christi. I arranged for two autos to be assigned to the squadron—one to Wing Commander Burton and one to the Sergeant Major. The Squadron arrived on Thursday afternoon and the Nimrod was parked at the aircraft display area at the festival site. The Wing Commander was met by CDR Holloway and me. I have no idea where the Naval Air Station Commanding Officer, Navy Captain Edward A. Skube, was at the time. Wing Commander Burton was expecting to meet him and the Admiral of CNATRA. For some reason, Wing Commander Burton was never allowed to meet either of the two during his stay at Corpus Christi.

On Friday morning, I asked Wing Commander Burton if he and the rest of his officers would like to go eat Mexican food that night. He said that they surely would because they wanted to sample the different foods from our cultures. I called Diann and told her we were going to Ponchos' that night with the crew from England. Poncho's is a Mexican food restaurant that served the food buffet style. The food was really good and reasonable. One of the items they specialized in was sopapillas with butter and honey. That evening we went to the BOQ and took as many as we could in our car and the rest went in the car assigned to Wing Commander Burton. It was really funny to watch them taste the food. Some of them could eat the HOT stuff and some couldn't take it. The ones that could would drink everything in sight to wash away the burning sensation. The sopapillas were eaten last, more as a dessert. One of the men had a full beard. He really enjoyed the sopapillas and ate many of them. He hadn't noticed the honey running into his beard until someone told him. He had quite a time cleansing the whiskers. He told me that he still had honey in his beard the next morning. I learned years later that one meal was one of the highlights of their trip to Corpus Christi.

I invited Wing Commander Burton and three officers to breakfast at our house. I wanted to invite all of them, except I didn't have room, plus I didn't want to cause Diann any more troubles. We had sausage, eggs, and biscuits with cream gravy. Mother-in-law, Lois Wilkerson, and father-in-law, Lefty Wilkerson, were there also. That time was most hilarious. Lefty, who was in his seventies, kept calling all of them "Boys." Finally, Commander Burton said that he would accept that from him because they were boys according to the age difference. We made sure they ate all they wanted and Lefty kept trying to get them to eat more. He kept them laughing during the entire meal. The other three officers were James, Peter, and Peter. We called them Pete and RePete.

After breakfast, I asked them what they would like to see. Wing Commander Burton said he would like to see some of the countryside, and maybe some cotton fields and oil wells. I knew just the place to take them. We drove north of Corpus Christi along I-37 toward San Antonio. There we could see both the cotton fields and the oil wells. At one place, we stopped alongside the road and went into the field to get a close look at an operating oil well pump. They were fascinated. Near Robstown we changed to US-77 and headed to Odem. En route, one of them spotted a train and became really excited. It had three or four engines pulling about a hundred rail cars. They had never seen a train with more than one engine. At Odem, a train was sitting on a side rail waiting for another coming from the opposite direction. We had to stop and they got out of the car so they could talk to the engineer. From Odem we drove through many more cotton fields to Portland. At one point, Wing Commander Burton got out and pulled up a few cotton stalks with blooms and green boles. It was too early for the boles to start opening. From Portland, we took US-81 back into Corpus Christi passing over Nueces Bay Bridge. On the way I made the comment, "I hadn't intended to drive 150 miles this morning." They all yelled at once, "We've gone 150 miles already today!" I told them that it would be by the time we reached our house which was at 906 Carmel Parkway. Peter said that he was stationed 100 miles from home and he could only make that trip once a year. I told him that I lived 15 miles from my work. They could not get over the vastness of South Texas.

At breakfast, Wing Commander Burton invited all of us to take a tour of the Nimrod. Everyone was excited about the tour except Lefty. He decided he would stay home and not go to the air show. The Nimrod was to remain secure during the normal opening hours of the Navy Relief Festival, which started at noon, but we were going aboard before the gates were open to the public. So, after we returned from our jaunt through the country, we went to the base to tour the Nimrod. The crew powered up the electronics systems and put on a demonstration for us. Wing Commander Burton even had my mother-in-law sit in the pilot's seat. She got a kick out of that. We spent about an hour on the tour, but had to be out by eleven. By the time we were leaving, people were trying to talk the crew into letting them take a tour. But, that didn't happen.

Wing Commander Burton wanted to fly his aircraft, the Nimrod, in the air show. He asked Commander Holloway why he was not scheduled. The reply was that there was not enough time. The Wing Commander was very disappointed with that reply. Not only was Commander Burton insulted by the shunning by the Commanding Officer and the Admiral, the editor of the base paper referred to him and his crew as "Limies." Commander Burton had asked me to send him several copies of the paper. I tried to get the paper reprinted by asking CDR Holloway to do so, but he and the editor refused saying it was too expensive. I didn't send any copies to England because of that write up referring to them as Limies.

Since the Nimrod was only on display and not participating in the actual air show, I asked Wing Commander Burton if he would like to go play golf. He and I went to the golf course while most everyone else went to see other things going on at the festival and to watch the air show. We played the base course, which was a nine-hole course. Besides us, there were a lot of Texas jackrabbits on the course. He had not seen any of those before and became fascinated with them.

Plaque Awarded to Diann by Wing Commander Burton

Sunday night Commander Burton called and wanted to be sure that I would bring Diann and Carla to the base on Monday morning to see them off. The Nimrod was parked on the Operation Department's aircraft parking ramp, which was by the hangar where my office was located. Since I was the OMD Officer, I didn't have any trouble with security. We were there about nine that morning. We were taken aboard the Nimrod and Diann received an unusual surprise. Commander Burton gave her a very nice plaque for the hospitality she had rendered to him and his officers. He said that it was supposed to have been given to the Corpus Christi Naval Air Station Commanding Officer, but since he never made an effort to invite him to his office, he decided to give it to Diann instead. The plaque hangs on our living room wall now. After that little ceremony, we were asked to go stand in front of the operations tower and watch their takeoff. After takeoff, he flew the Nimrod by the front and tipped the wings to say "Goodbye" as they departed heading back to England.

On several occasions there would be an electrical problem on the C-131 that the electricians could not seem to repair. One time, it was with the G-2 compass system. I allowed them to work for a week without the repair being accomplished then decided to call CNATRA for assistance. Although I had been to school for the system in the 1950s, because it had been so long, I did not feel that I had the expertise to offer any advice about the problem. Mr. Bill Moss came to assist in the repair. He was the expert on the system. He and the shop electrician crew worked on the aircraft for two more weeks and could not find the cause of the problem. CDR Graham was really getting all over me to get the aircraft ready for flight. One Thursday, I told him that I was going to see if I could find the problem. I had taken the aircraft electrical schematic home that Wednesday night and studied it. I found the power source fuse and circled it. I could not leave the office until about ten o'clock. When I arrived at the aircraft, I found it almost completely disassembled and Mr. Moss was scratching his head. He told me he had no idea of what was causing the problem. I had the men reconnect the system so I could take look. By the time they completed the connections it was lunchtime. So, I had them go to chow while I reviewed the schematic. I had bought a sandwich and a cola from the snack bar in the hangar and took them to the plane. Mr. Moss also got a coke and sandwich and stayed with me. When I opened the schematic to the page with the proper bureau number I saw the circled fuse. It was labeled IFF. I told Bill that I had intended to check that fuse earlier, but with all the confusion I had forgotten. He looked at me and said that fuse is for the IFF, not the compass system. I told him to check the bureau number, it was the right fuse. Sure enough, the fuse was no good! I replaced the fuse and applied power to the plane. The compass system came alive and swung around to the proper heading. All this time (three weeks), no one had bothered to check the schematics for the proper bureau number. The fuses were labeled G-2 compass on some schematics and IFF on others. They had been using the wrong schematic. Word got out that LCDR Hudson had solved the problem in half a day by replacing the fuse.

One day I was sitting at my desk when AFCM John Yeager came into the office. He was stationed there on the base in VT-28. John and I had served together in VC-5, Okinawa, from 1965 through 1967. We were both LDO Ensigns (Mustangs). Both of us were promoted to LTJG in 1966. I don't know what John did in his career that prevented him from getting promoted to Lieutenant. By navy rules, upon failure to be promoted, he had to revert to enlisted status. Luckily, he had kept up with the enlisted promotions and was now an E9, which is the highest an enlisted man could obtain. However, I was now a Lieutenant Commander.

He and I had a good visit that day. We talked a lot about our tour in Okinawa, of the White Beach drone control site. John said that he had arrived at Corpus Christi the week before Hurricane Celia. He and his family had moved into a house, bought a freezer, and filled it with a side of beef. When the hurricane hit, it wiped out his house. The freezer ended up in the backyard with the meat still frozen. He said they had a huge barbeque for the whole neighborhood. Diann and I went to see him, his wife, Thelma, and their kids. I only saw him a couple of times after that visit. He was eligible for transfer and retirement. I don't know if he retired or was transferred.

About the end of this tour at NAS Corpus Christi, I had enough time in service I could retire from the naval service with LCDR pay. I asked my wife, Diann, if I could talk the detailer into sending me to Hawaii for another tour would she like to go? She readily agreed. I received orders 23 October 1975, to depart NAS Corpus Christi in April 1976, and report to Patrol Squadron Four based at NAS Barbers Point, Hawaii. The orders also directed me to attend a three-week familiarization course on the P-3C aircraft at Patron Thirty-One, NAS Moffett Field, CA. I got approval to attend the FAM course in California and then return to Corpus Christi for thirty days leave and travel to Hawaii with my family. Bruce would be graduating from high school in late May, and I wanted to be home for his graduation.

Lt. Acuff relieved me as OMD Officer. He knew some of the ordeals I went through under the present Operations Officer. I considered Commander Graham a Nixon trained man. He gave me the impression that, although he was responsible, you were to blame when something went wrong. He would take the credit, but would not accept the blame. Lt. Acuff asked me for advice on how to endure the assignment. I told him, "Never allow your frustrations to overcome your ability to laugh." After coining that phrase, I decided to make it my motto.

PATROL SQUADRON FOUR (VP-4), NAVAL AIR STATION, BARBERS POINT OAHU, HAWAII

June 1976 to September 1978

VP-4 Logo

P3-C Orion

I departed Corpus Christi early 28 April 1976. Driving to Moffett Field, California, I stopped in Plainview, Texas, and saw our cousin Ruth. Then I went to our aunt Elsie's to spend the night. The next night, I stopped at a motel on Route 66 in Flagstaff, Arizona. I checked into VP-31 at 1929 hours on 30 April 1976.

The two weeks went by rather smoothly. I learned a little about the P-3C aircraft, met a few friends, and had a good time. CDR Ted Rogers was also attending a familiarization course, but he was in pilot training and I was in aircraft maintenance. He was ordered to VP-4 as the Executive Officer. He later became the Commanding Officer of VP-4. LCDR Gene Raulston was stationed there at the time. Gene was an LDO classmate of mine. We were commissioned on the same day, 1 October 1964. Gene and I just had a few hours of visitation after work. I also went to the home of Bud and Barbra Benningson. They had lived next to us in Okinawa. He was out of the navy now and working in a law firm. I had dinner at their home one night.

CDR Rogers had a friend (I don't remember his name), who had been a POW in Vietnam. He owned a 35-foot sailboat, an Erickson, and one Saturday they invited me to go sailing with them. It turned out to be a fun day, although neither of them knew how to sail a boat. The boat was harbored at Oakland Yacht Basin. We exited the basin into the Oakland Bay where the pilot proceeded to rig the sails, the main and jib. I think the only reason Ted asked me to come along was to assist in the handling of the boat. I could tell the sails were not set properly because the boat was listing to starboard about fifteen to twenty degrees. Finally, the pilot said that was the best he could do so we sailed along at about five knots. We went under the Oakland Bay Bridge. I thought sure we were going to ram one of the columns, but we made it through without hitting anything. After a while, Ted took the helm and couldn't manage to upright the boat any better. We had to sit on the high side to keep the boat from tipping. After about an hour into the trip, the pilot asked me if I would like to try my hand at maneuvering the boat. I took the helm. I had not been to sailing school, nor had any training instructions in sailing. Common sense told me that the sails should be set in a different manner. There are a few indicators on the boat that give speed, tilt, and direction of the wind relative to the boat. The list angle was very severe. I thought if I moved the jib slightly it should help straighten the boat. It sure couldn't be much worse. So, I turned a wheel that shifted the jib and the boat did, in fact, upright slightly and increased the speed to about seven knots. I moved the wheel again and the boat flattened out even more and increased speed to ten knots. The ride was even smoother. One more time and the boat was nearly level and we were cruising at about twelve knots. That's when the pilot noticed how well we were cruising and asked what I had done to make the boat ride much smoother. I told him how I had calculated the position of the jib and to make the proper adjustments. He said that he had never been able to do that and he took the helm. I did not get to operate the boat anymore. We sailed all around Oakland Bay, over to Deer Island, then back under the Bay Bridge into San Francisco Bay, around Alcatraz, and along Candlestick Park and Treasure Island before heading back to the yacht basin.

I completed my indoctrination in the P-3C maintenance course. I checked out for Corpus Christi on 20 May 1976, at 0400 hours. I had placed an ad on the bulletin board requesting that if anyone would like a ride to Corpus, to let me know. I thought if I could get a rider with a driver's license willing to share expenses, it would help both of us. A Chief, last name Six, answered the ad. We drove straight through. It took us about thirty-six hours.

When I got home, Diann and I made shipping arrangements for the household goods and the auto. Of course, we waited until Bruce had completed high school. He graduated on about 3 June 1976. I asked him what he wanted to do upon graduating and he decided to go to Wyoming with Mr. and Mrs. Wiekel and their three sons and daughter. The older boys were Loran and Shelby, who were friends of Bruce. I let Bruce keep my 1973 Ford pickup to drive while we were in Hawaii. Since I would be paying for the insurance, he was told that it was for his use only and could not be used for commercial contract work. Carla had just finished the tenth grade at Ray High School. We had a flight to Hawaii from Travis Air Force Base on 26 June 1976, but first I had to deliver our automobile, a 1973 Pontiac Grandville, to the Oakland shipyard for shipment to Hawaii.

We decided to make the trip to Oakland, California, a memorable one by taking a ten-day tour through Cody, Wyoming, to see Bruce and then through Yellowstone National Park. We departed Waco on about 15 June 1976, all excited about seeing places we had not been. We traveled via route US 84. Our first stop was in Idalou, Texas, to see Aunt Elsie, then to Plainview where Carla met Cousin Ruth for the first time. The next day we continued on US 84 to Las Vegas, New Mexico, then up Interstate 25. As we neared Colorado Springs, we decided to tour Pike's Peak. It was about noon and we thought we had plenty of time before nightfall. The gas tank was about half-full when we arrived at the entrance to the National Park. The ranger on duty would not let us through. He said our auto did not have enough gas to drive the nineteen miles to the top and back. We had to find a service station to fill up before we could enter the park. After topping off, we went back to the gate. The ranger gave us some literature about Pike's Peak and some instructions with which we had to comply. The drive up the side of the mountain was challenging. It was a very narrow road that had a lot of switchbacks. The last ten miles was dirt and very steep. I had to stay in low gear most of the way up. We arrived about 1400. It was very cold even though it was June. The view was spectacular, except when the clouds rolled in. One could see the mountaintops in the distance. It even snowed some while we were there. We stayed about an hour and decided to head back down the mountain. Coming from Corpus Christi, the weather was extreme to us. One of the requirements on the way down was a stop for a "hot brake check." I had put the car in a low gear to let the engine hold the speed in check rather than rely on the brakes. The Ranger that checked my brakes couldn't believe how cool they were. He complimented me, said I must know how to drive in the mountains. This was my first time ever. We were able to proceed without delay. There were several cars that he wouldn't let pass due to hot brakes. After a stop at Santa Claus Land, we went on up the road to Denver where we spent the night.

The next day we decided to leave early and have breakfast in Cheyenne, Wyoming. The road we wanted to travel turned a long way before we neared Cheyenne. So, we continued to the next town for breakfast. There wasn't any place to eat in the next town, so we had to keep going. We finally stopped in Chug Water about ten o'clock. There was only one restaurant there. We were so hungry that we didn't care what it looked like, as long as they served food. We got tickled at the town signs. All the signs gave both the population and the elevation. Most read similar to this, POPULATION 10, ELEVATION 10,000. **PG.DES.: SMALL CAPS**

We arrived in Cody about 1800. Can't remember the name of the motel we stayed in, but there weren't many. We got in touch with Bruce and the Wiekels. They were sleeping in tents in a campground near a river. Bruce came to the motel that first night. He brought fresh clothing and took a shower. He stayed in the shower a long time, and said it was the first good bath he had since leaving home in Corpus Christi.

We spent three nights in Cody sightseeing with Bruce, and then headed for Yellowstone National Park. We got to see an unusual sight while touring through Yellowstone National Park. We were waiting to see the geyser, "Old Faithful," which usually erupts on a regular schedule; we were witness to another geyser eruption. It shot way up into the air and all the viewers "oohed and aahed." We were ready to leave once the eruption subsided, knowing that it would be several hours before it erupted again. The tour guide said to sit still because we had just witnessed a geyser that erupted about once every fifty to a hundred years. Old Faithful was still to come. Old Faithful was not as impressive as the first one.

We exited Yellowstone by the northwest gate into Montana on US Highway 20. Our plans were to travel to Grants Pass, Oregon, for the night. I had heard on the news when we were in Waco that the Teton Dam had broken and created a lot of damage to the area below the dam. I did not know where the Teton Dam was located. Apparently, the dam had not been rebuilt, because I can't find it on the map today. Anyway, as we traveled on US 20 we came upon the flooded area and had to make a detour. US Highway 20 was completely under water near Chester, Idaho. The flood damage was extensive. There were dead animals, cows, horses, deer, etc., lying everywhere. The highway department had built a makeshift road. It was really narrow. If one was unfortunate enough to slide off the road, they would sink into the muck. We only made it as far as Boise by nightfall, where we had to spend the night.

The next day, we continued along US 20. The scenery was the same as we had been seeing for the last few days. It was becoming boring by this time. About ten o'clock, I decided I would nap in the backseat while Diann drove and Carla could sightsee or read. Diann drove for seventy-five to one hundred miles when she woke me with a startling alarm. She said, "The highway just ran out!" Sure enough, the pavement had been removed as though the road no longer was in use. I asked if she had made a wrong turn, but she said she did not see another road and also had not seen a road sign or any other cars for several miles. I took over the driving and we continued moving forward. About twenty miles later, we came upon a road crew digging up the pavement. After that, there was the US 20 sign, so we knew we were on the right track. Carla went to sleep in the backseat for a while. I saw a huge dust storm on the horizon. I really didn't want to get caught up in it, but didn't see how we could miss it. I had Diann awaken Carla so she could see it. It turned out to be a big cattle drive coming up the highway. There were fences on each side of the road and the cattle were coming right down the road on the pavement and in the ditches. We had to stop as the cows passed on each side of us. There must to have been 500 to 1,000 head of cows.

Somewhere along the route, we changed our plans to go south for the night rather than Grants Pass, Oregon. We were thinking of Crescent City, California. We left US 20 at Riley and took US 395 south into California. Even later, I said we would go further south to Eureka, California, because it would be closer to the entrance to the Valley of the Giants, the big redwood forest. I don't remember the routes we took after that, except California Highway 36. I don't guess we will ever forget that route. After we had traveled a short distance, Carla asked if I had noticed the comment on the map, "Very bad road." I didn't see the note. It was an extremely mountainous curvy road with a lot of switchbacks. The road was used mostly by logging trucks. The only way to pass one was the driver would wave you around when he could see the way was clear. That was only on bends in the road. We were either hugging the cliff or nearly going over the side when passing or meeting another vehicle. Diann was keeping a close watch for the edge of the road to make sure I didn't get too close. It took us almost all day to go 120 miles. To say the least, "It was a hairy ride." Neither Diann nor Carla will let me live that down. We arrived in Fortuna, California, just before sunset, where we had dinner and spent the night.

The next day after breakfast, we entered the Valley of the Giants, Redwood National Forest. The trip was breathtaking with trees taller than we had ever seen. We took a few pictures and tried to reach around the trunks by holding hands. They were too big. We even drove through one of the trees. We took pictures of us sitting on the hood while the car was inside it. After leaving the forest, we drove along highway US 1 by the coastline. That, too, was a beautiful drive. We finally arrived in San Francisco. We got a motel in Palo Alto and had dinner with our friends, Bud and Barbra Benningson. We didn't eat until about eleven o'clock that night.

The next day, Carla went with me to the Oakland shipyard to deliver our auto for shipment to Hawaii. In order to get back to the motel in Palo Alto, we had to take the BART, the train, and then the bus. That was another adventure. I had us get off the bus way too soon and we walked what seemed to be a hundred blocks. Carla complained to me all the time we were walking. Then the following day, we went to Travis Air Force Base to catch our flight to Honolulu. Diann remembers that Carla was upset with me because I couldn't get her curling iron unplugged from the bathroom wall socket. I had to cut the plug off and leave it in the socket. I hope no one got electrocuted.

Diann, Carla, and I arrived in Honolulu early 26 June 1976. The squadron, VP-4, had made arrangements for us to stay in the Iliakai Hotel in Waikiki while awaiting government quarters. We spent two weeks in the hotel and were assigned housing at 5887 Gannet Ave., Ewa Beach, Hawaii. I checked in at the Squadron Duty Office at 1900 hours on 26 June 1976. There were several patrol squadrons stationed at Barber's Point—VP-1, VP-4, VP-6, and VP-22.

The car would not arrive in Honolulu until about two to three weeks after our arrival. Ed Higgins let us use his 1973 Cadillac. We told the Higgins that we didn't want to take their car and cause Betty to be without wheels, but they insisted. It sure was nice. We were staying in the Iliakai Hotel in Waikiki where they filmed the TV series *Hawaii Five-O*. Our daughter, Carla, had a ball while at the Iliakai. She tried her best to get into a scene that was being filmed there. The crew would shoo her away, but she would still try to get in a scene. She never made it. The drive to work at Barber's Point was about thirty miles one way. After about two weeks, we were assigned Base Housing. We moved into 5887 Gannet, Ewa Beach, on 8 July 1976. We were now nine miles from the base.

Hawaii had changed tremendously since we were there in 1955. Where there had been only seven hotels in the Waikiki area, there were about seven hundred now. In fact, one had to go through the lobby of one hotel to get to the Royal Hawaiian Hotel. It could only be seen from the ocean side. Diann called the Waikiki area the "Concrete Jungle."

Waikiki Beach Area as Seen from Diamond Head Lookout 1976

Other changes were at Pearl Harbor and the Punch Bowl National Cemetery. At the Punch Bowl, the trees had matured and a Memorial had been erected depicting the WWII Battles of the Pacific in honor of those who had perished during those wars.

Punch Bowl National Cemetery

Punch Bowl WWII Memorial

Arizona Memorial
At Pearl Harbor, the Arizona Memorial Had Been Erected over the Ship

When we left Corpus Christi, Carla had just finished the tenth grade of high school. She started to school in the eleventh grade August 1976 at Ewa Beach, Hawaii. She had left all her friends in Corpus Christi and really didn't want to go to school at Ewa Beach. But, being the type person she is, it wasn't long before she had many friends. She graduated from there in June 1978.

Commander W. R. Broadwell, Commanding Officer, told the Maintenance Officer, LCDR Ed Higgins, that he would allow me to make a choice of assignment between Assistant Maintenance Officer, Maintenance Material Control Officer, or Quality Assurance Officer. I told Ed that I wanted his job as the Maintenance Officer. That didn't go over too well with Ed. He stormed out of the office and reported to the CO, "That SOB! He wants my job!" The CO thought it funny and said that it demonstrated I had ambition. I chose the Assistant Maintenance Officer slot. LTJG Tom Huggins was the Maintenance Material Control Officer. The navy had a maintenance system known as the 3M for Maintenance, Material, and Manpower. The VP-4 Maintenance Department became known as the 3H system—Higgins, Hudson, and Huggins—for the Maintenance Officer, the Assistant Maintenance Officer, and the Maintenance Material Control Officer.

AECS Flores was there also. He was in Corpus AIMD when I was there. Now, he was in charge of VP-4 electric shop. He had been promoted to Senior Chief Petty Officer after leaving Corpus Christi. Senior Chief Flores told me that Senior Chief Parkas was in VP-1, which was a squadron in the same hangar as VP-4. Also stationed in VP-1, was Master Chief Oberloe, who had been stationed with me in VR-8 at Hickam AFB in 1954. Oberloe was AEAN when I last saw him.

It didn't take me long to find out that Ed Higgins knew very little about the functions and procedures of aircraft maintenance. He told me that he wanted me to teach him everything. I was reluctant to do so, because I wanted his job. There were so many things that were amiss. For one, the department did not have a Corrosion Control Team in place and the aircraft were in bad condition with corrosion. Also, there was a lack of trained personnel to do component repair within AIMD, for which it was the squadron's responsibility. When I attended the weekly AIMD/Supply meetings, the AIMD Officer would complain about the lack of TAD personnel. As AMO, my first task was to contact BUPERS and set up to have people sent to "C" schools in route to the command. It took about three months before the new people started arriving onboard. Once the people started arriving, the AIMD Officer quit complaining.

One day, a First Class Petty Officer, AMS1 Koons, reported onboard. As he came across the hangar deck, he took notice of the aircraft. One of his first statements to me was, "Do you know that the aircraft are eaten up with corrosion?" I told him, "Welcome aboard! You are now the Corrosion Control Petty Officer." I gave him two weeks to get moved in and get acquainted with the men within the squadron, then, he could pick the men he wanted for his team. Within a month he had two of the sixteen aircraft in good shape. Shortly after that the Wing Four Maintenance Office held a surprise corrosion inspection. The squadron failed the inspection, but he told LCDR Higgins and me that he would not report it as a failure at this time. He knew that VP-4 did not have a Corrosion Control Team in the past and was surprised to find one in place upon his arrival. He liked Petty Officer Koons and would give him another two months to get the aircraft in good condition. My action of forming the team when I did saved the CO from being relieved of his command. There is a strict NAVAIR policy about corrosion. Failure of a Corrosion Inspection required the immediate relief of the Commanding Officer's command. Ed Higgins did not know of this policy. I had saved the day!

Each Monday, the NAS Barber's Point Aircraft Intermediate Department (AIMD) Officer held a meeting to discuss the upcoming week's events and what support the squadron could expect from them. Sometimes problems existed, which prevented AIMD from supplying the needed components. The AIMD's main function is to repair the various components that fail. It was the squadron's responsibility to ensure trained personnel were placed in the AIMDs to perform those repairs. I asked Ed Higgins if he ever attended those meetings. His response was that he thought the meetings were a waste of time. He had no idea of the importance of the meetings. So, I made it my responsibility and soon became acquainted with men assigned to the Maintenance Departments of the other squadrons located on the station. Problems always existed, but collectively the people at those meetings could solve most of them. I soon learned that in the past, VP-4 did not have a good repute with the AIMD Officer. The first thing I had to do was establish a relationship with the people. I assured them that I had served in an AIMD at two other duty stations. After about three meetings, I had proved myself, which improved the relations between the AIMD and the squadron.

When I reported aboard, the squadron had a three plane detachment assigned to NAS Agana, Guam. The various Lieutenant Commanders in the squadron were rotated from Hawaii to Guam as the Officer in Charge. At this time a man, AMS3 Robinson, was having trouble complying with rules and regulations. Master Chief Smith would come to LCDR Higgins and ask what to do about Robinson. He was late again or didn't show up for a watch. The MO would say give him extra duty, a slap on his wrist, or something of insignificance. The Master Chief would ask for more strenuous punishment, but the MO would not hear of it. One Day Master Chief Smith came in "hopping mad"! That Robinson had been AWOL for two days, but came in this day as if nothing wrong had occurred. LCDR Higgins said that he wanted to recommend him for promotion, so that he would have enough rank to give him incentive. I spoke up and said, "No! Let's put him on report, send him to Captain's Mast, get him busted in rank, and boot him out of the navy." Ed didn't like my idea, but the Master Chief did. Nothing happened. Well, Ed went to Guam in August for a two-week assignment as OinC. The day after he left, the Master Chief came and said that Robinson was absent again; what to do? I told him to go through with my previous suggestion. Robinson went to Captain's Mast and was dishonorably discharged from the navy. Ed had been back from the Guam assignment about three weeks, when it dawned on him that the Master Chief had not been in complaining about Robinson. He asked me about the reason. I told him that we had Robinson discharged. He couldn't believe it had been that easy.

In Hawaii, Pearl Harbor Day, December 7, is always a big event. A memorial service is always held in remembrance of those who perished on 7 December 1941. The *USS Oriskany* had moored in Pearl Harbor for the dedication December 1976. Chief Parsons was now stationed onboard. He knew that I had never been on an aircraft carrier. He called my office and invited me to be his guest onboard. I readily accepted. He could not take me to certain areas because of the ceremonies that were being held at the time. But, I did get to see the AIMD spaces and his work area. He even took me to the Chiefs' Mess for lunch. That was a fun day. Now I could say that I had been on an Aircraft Carrier, even if it had been only for a day.

My mother passed away on 24 January 1977. The Red Cross called the squadron OOD to inform him about Mom and stated that I should be allowed to take emergency leave. Diann agreed that I should attend the funeral, which was to be held in Duncanville, Texas. I wanted both Diann and Carla to go with me on leave, but we just didn't have the money for all of us to go. Talking to the Skipper, he said that a cross-country flight had been scheduled to Dallas about the time my leave would expire and that he would allow me to take that flight back to Hawaii. That sure would save me a lot of money for airfare. All I had to buy was a one-way ticket to Dallas. I arrived in Dallas with plenty of time to spare before the funeral, which was held 28 January. Luckily, all of Mom's children were there. My four sisters all lived in the Dallas area, but my two brothers lived in Florida and I was now stationed in Hawaii. That day was most unusual. The funeral was held in Duncanville, but the burial was in Elm Grove Cemetery, five miles east of Anna, which is about seventy-five or eighty miles from the funeral home. The funeral was held at 1000. With the pace of the hearse, it took about two hours for the trip to the cemetery. With noon being considered, the ceremony at the cemetery was at 1400.

That morning, the weather was strangely hot for the time of year, about 85 to 90 degrees. I was in my dress blues and really feeling the high temperature. At the cemetery, the weather suddenly changed. At the start of the burial it was still hot and I was sweating, but about halfway through, a "Texas Blue Norther" came howling through. The temperature dropped from the eighties to the forties with wind in excess of thirty miles per hour. Everyone had been sweating, now they were freezing. I remember standing at the head of Mom's grave shivering while surrendering my last farewell salute to her.

The funeral was on Friday. Saturday was very cold and it started snowing that afternoon. I had to meet the VP-4 cross-country flight that Sunday morning at NAS Dallas for the flight back to Hawaii. That was one day that was not good. I arrived at 0600 for a 0700 departure. The flight crew didn't arrive until seven and the pilot didn't show up until eight. When the crew went to pre-flight the aircraft, they discovered the wings covered with about three inches of snow. The snow was cleared and a de-icing truck was ordered. The plane pre-flight for departure was completed, but no fuel was ordered. The pilot asked the Flight Engineer how much fuel was onboard. The engineer gave the amount and stated that he should call for a fuel truck, but the pilot said there was enough onboard to fly to Corpus Christi, our next stop. Cross-country flights were meant to be for training purposes. However, if the training route was to various Naval Air Stations, the Commanding Officer would allow squadron personnel that had family living there to visit them. On this particular flight, the pilot had stopped at the Albuquerque International Airport, NAS Corpus Christi, and NAS Dallas.

The engineer lost the argument about the fuel, so we loaded aboard the aircraft and taxied to the end of the runway to await the okay for takeoff. This is where things started to deteriorate. It was now about 0930 and the weekend warriors were performing their routine training, and practicing takeoff and landing exercises. So, we had to wait our turn for takeoff. The longer we sat at the end of the runway the lower the fuel became. Finally at about 1000 hours, the pilot was cleared for takeoff. When we were over Austin, Texas, the pilot decided that there was not enough fuel onboard to get to Corpus Christi, so he made the decision to land at Lackland Air Force Base in San Antonio to take on fuel. It took about three hours to get that feat completed. We arrived in Corpus Christi about 1500 hours. While at Lackland, I called some of our previous neighbors in Corpus and told them I would be there sometime that afternoon. They met me in the Operations Department and we had a good visit.

The pilot told the crew member to put on enough fuel to get to Albuquerque and we departed Corpus Christi about 1700 local time. We arrived in Albuquerque about 1830. The two men were waiting to board the plane to head for San Diego, CA, to pick up two others and then head for Hawaii. The pilot called for a fuel truck. The station master told him that he hadn't read his NATOPS manual; if he had, he would have known that 1700 hours was the latest that fuel would be available on Sunday. We were already late, but the pilot had to fly back east to Clovis, NM, to get fuel to go to California. I was getting concerned that this pilot was unfit to be in command of a cross-country mission.

It was early the next morning when we finally arrived in Hawaii. I reported all the events to the CO. The pilot was released from the navy shortly after that incident. I don't know if my report had anything to do with his dismissal or if his contract had expired.

In February 1977, the squadron was involved in the Operation RIMPAC exercise. I was to perform the duties as host of the New Zealand maintenance crew. I met the crew aboard their P3 aircraft at the Operations area. I rode with them in the plane to the VP-4 flight line. It was a short distance, but it seemed to be taking a long time to get there. I asked for a reason and was told that there had been a bomb threat called in and that the Bomb Squad was searching the area for the bomb. Finally, the "all clear" was announced and we arrived shortly afterward. We were almost drunk by the time we arrived. The crew had brought about 100 cases of New Zealand Green Label beer on the plane, and it was being passed around while we were waiting for the bomb squad to give the "all clear." What a way to start the RIMPAC exercise. The New Zealanders are a breed of their own.

The bomb scare turned out to be a false alert, but during the investigation, some criminal activity was discovered. Some classified matter was compromised and the compromiser was court-martialed. I was assigned as the senior officer of a Special Court Martial. Although I knew the man was guilty of the offense, only circumstantial evidence could be found. I had to declare the man not guilty for lack of evidence in connecting him to the crime.

Sometime in March, the PGA held its annual Hawaiian Open Golf Tournament at the Wailai Golf Course in Waikiki. They advertised for volunteers to help with crowd control. I asked the Skipper if I could take a week leave so I could attend the tournament. He agreed. I applied to serve as a Marshal and was accepted. That was a most memorable experience. I was selected and assigned to the sixteenth green, a par four hole. There were four of us, but I can't remember the names of the others. I got to visit with J. C. Snead, Lee Travino, and others. On Tuesday, the practice day, a small plane flying over the course developed engine trouble and landed on the eighteenth fairway. I was visiting with J. C. Snead at the time. I heard a tale later about a player putting on the green. Another player told him to look out! There was a plane taxiing up the fairway toward them. He said, "You will say anything to distract me while I'm putting." He turned and looked, "My Gawd, you're not joking!" We all got a big laugh out of that story. Hale Erwin won the tournament.

In May 1977, the squadron deployed from Hawaii to NAS Cubi Point, Philippines. Since LCDR Ed Higgins was primarily a figure head as the Maintenance Officer, the Skipper sent me as the Advance Liaison Officer for the Maintenance Department. I established a good rapport with the Cubi Point AIMD Officer, CDR Corsie. He let the Skipper know that he found me to be the most cooperative Maintenance Officer he had encountered from the various VP squadrons that had deployed to the Philippines. He held weekly meetings to discuss the support and problems with operations going on at the time. We became good friends and often had dinner together at the "O" Club. It seemed that many problems were resolved and decisions made at the "O" Club. Sometimes the Supply Officer, CDR Risenor, and his wife would also join us. One night, I walked into the lounge and Mrs. Risenor yelled at me, "Your socks don't match!" I looked and both were the same color. Then she said they don't match your shirt. I thought, *what difference does it make?* All those present got a big laugh out of that incident.

Commander Broadwell had orders to be reassigned in July 1977. It was a policy that he was required to write a Fitness Report on each officer under his command. He called me to his office to discuss mine. He told me that he knew that he had to grade me as one of one since LDOs were not graded with the Line Officers; he considered me number three of the nine Lieutenant Commanders in the command. To me, that was great news and the best compliment one could ever hope for. He had even placed me above my immediate supervisor plus others. He had graded me in the top one percent. He was relieved by CDR Ted Rogers on 1 July 1977; CDR John Wayne Stark was assigned as Executive Officer. LCDR Higgins also had transfer orders and was relieved by LCDR Jim Gompper. Jim didn't know anything about aircraft maintenance either. I learned that the COs of the VP squadron assigned their aviators to the Maintenance Officer position just so they could get their ticket punched as a Department Head. They didn't have to know anything about aircraft maintenance.

At the Change of Command ceremony, all personnel were required to be in full dress whites. For the officers, that meant wearing the sword. I had left mine at Barber's Point, Hawaii. I really did not know what I was going to do. I had to find someone I could borrow one from. As luck would have it, I met LCDR Bill Hefty. He was an LDO classmate of mine. He loaned me his for the Change of Command ceremony. It was a close call for two reasons. One, because of my negligence and, two, because Bill was in the process of changing duty stations and all his personal effects were being packed the next day. I had to get his sword back to him as soon as the ceremony was over.

On 5 July 1977, the XO invited me to play a round of golf with him, LCDR Spangler, and Lt. Burns. We had completed the first nine holes, but during that time I started experiencing pains in my chest. I didn't really think too much about it at that time. After we had played the next two holes, #11 and 12, the pain was so severe that I had to stop playing. There was a bench nearby, so I sat and waited for them to play the next four holes. By sitting the pain subsided, and by the time they returned, I felt well enough to finish the last three holes with them.

Afterward I went to my room to rest. There was a knock on my door. It was the squadron Flight Surgeon, Lt. Anne Dibala. She told me that the XO had told her about my chest pains and recommended that I go to sick bay to be examined. She could not determine the cause, but said that it could have been a mild heart attack. That incident did get my attention. However, it didn't keep me from playing golf. I really enjoyed the PI Golf Course. It was built on the hill sides. In fact, on one hole the tee box was on a hill that was so steep that one had to be pulled up by rope. Also, the players were required to hire a caddy, I think primarily to help the poor people.

While deployed to the Philippines, VP-4 also had a three plane detachment at Diego Garcia, an island in the middle of the Indian Ocean. The maintenance crew of the detachment sent word that they were experiencing problems and needed help. The Skipper sent me to find out their needs and try to solve their problems. The flight to Diego Garcia was long, requiring an overnight stay en route. I don't remember the pilot of the flight. The overnight stop was Toc Lei, Thailand. When the plane landed, we were met by armed guards and escorted to the mooring site. When we departed the plane, only the pilot and plane captain were allowed to reenter the plane and get it properly secured for the night. Once the plane was secured, we were escorted to our sleeping quarters, which were enclosed with a very high fence, and told that we were allowed to go to three buildings—the dining hall, a small bar, and our room. Then they told us to be careful of the cobras. I had not thought about snakes until then. Of course, it could have been a ploy just to make us afraid to go anywhere in the dark. There were no nightlights to guide the way.

The next morning, we were awakened about 0500 hours to get ready to continue the trip to Diego Garcia. After breakfast, we were escorted by the armed guards to the plane and allowed to leave about 0800 hours. We arrived in Diego Garcia about four in the afternoon. I had heard about Diego Garcia and its primitive conditions, but I did not expect things to be as bad as they were. The living conditions reminded me of the conditions of 1967 Vietnam. There were a few structures on site, but so dilapidated that they were uninhabitable. Everything was temporary. The maintenance crew was working out of a rusted out Butler building and an old adobe shack. The only thing new was the aircraft runway and taxi lanes. The CBs had completed those just a few months earlier. The only help I could offer them was to send a few spare parts on the next available aircraft. As components failed, they could send them to Cubi Point and I would send them replacements.

Since I could do nothing else, I spent the next day touring the island. The island was V-shaped with two long fingers about seven to ten miles long. The island was owned by the British, but the US had leased one finger. The British side had been a coconut plantation. Blight had hit the area many years earlier making the coconut unfit for commerce. The owners had shipped in many donkeys to work the plantation. When they left the island, they turned the donkeys loose to fend for themselves and they became untamed. One tried not to encounter a wild donkey. The CBs had put up a fence to keep the donkeys on the British side of the island and off the runway.

I heard many fish stories from the men, but only about the ones that got away. I didn't get to do any fishing while there. One story was about a huge shark that stayed under the ship dock. No one went swimming because of the big fish. One of the men bought a new rod and reel with 25-lb. test line. The line broke on the first bite. He put 50-lb. test line and, again, the line broke. Then he put on 100-lb. test line and tightened the brake. This time, the line wouldn't break, and the fish stripped the line and burned up his reel. He gave up fishing.

After a total of thirty-six hours on Diego Garcia, I boarded a plane to return to Cubi Point. After another night at Toc Lei with the security guards, we arrived back at Cubi. It was a short time that I was in Diego Garcia, but a memorable one. At least I can say, "I've been there."

The aircraft carrier *Constellation* pulled into port at Subic Bay while I was at Cubi Point. I received a phone call from Master Chief Titmas who was aboard the "Connie." He had been stationed with me in Corpus. In fact, he was one of the Chiefs from whom I had taken away his flight pay. He said he knew I had never been on an aircraft carrier before and wanted to take me aboard for lunch in the Chiefs' Mess. I told him he was too late, Chief Parsons had treated me in Pearl Harbor aboard the USS *Oriskany*. However, Master Chief Titmas did take me aboard and showed me around the AIMD spaces. It was a sight to see, although I can't put that in this writing.

After the tour, we went to the home of a friend of his for dinner. The Master Chief's wife, Martha, was there. She had flown to Subic Bay from the Mainland USA to meet him in port. It was good to see friends from the past. She told me that the best thing that ever happened to her husband was when I had taken away his flight pay and put him in a responsible assignment. She said that he had become stagnant and was not interested in advancing his career. But, by my actions, I gave him incentive to strive for advancement. She said, "You gave him E9." I didn't give him E9. I just gave him the push that he needed. We bid farewell that night and the "Connie" pulled out of port the next morning. I never saw or heard of Master Chief Titmas or Martha again.

Cubi Point was located in a beautiful setting with the forest surrounding the base and nice beaches close-by. One could see families of monkeys most every day near the BOQ. The weather was very rainy during the time VP-4 was there. The VP-4 living quarters were across the street from the main BOQ and general ward room. One rainy morning after breakfast when returning to my BOQ with two others, a monkey family came down the street between the ward room and my BOQ. I had to wait for them to clear my path. I had learned during my stay in Vietnam, "You don't mess with monkeys!" The "old man" of the tribe will attack if you mess with his family. On this particular day, a young monkey was running and climbing everywhere. It climbed an electrical power pole near us. Everything was wet. The young monkey grabbed a hot wire and was electrocuted, but not killed, only stunned. It fell to the ground and didn't move. The old man came charging to attack whatever had stunned his young one. He ran up the pole, but couldn't find anything. Then he came charging at us. We didn't hurt the young monkey, but we went back into the ward room for safety. The pole was close to our BOQ and we had to wait until the old monkey left the area. The little monkey came to after awhile and went into the woods close-by. The old man went with it, so we started to our room. We were almost there, when the old man came charging us, but we made it to safety. That incident was the hot topic for days.

COMFAIRWESTPAC was located in Misawa, Japan. The Admiral called a conference of all the squadrons in the Western Pacific Arena. The CO wanted all of the departments to be represented. The Maintenance Officer, LCDR Gompper, was in Diego Garcia, so I went in his stead. I was allowed to attend the first session that concerned aircraft maintenance and materials. The Admiral asked Commander Rogers why he had such a low number of FMC (Fully Mission Capable) aircraft. If any of the systems were not functioning on an aircraft, then it was not FMC. There were several problems concerning component repair in the AIMDs and most of the squadron aircraft were not fully equipped. All the VP squadrons were experiencing problems. Commander Rogers did not have an answer for the Admiral's question. He squirmed in his seat and looked in his briefcase, but couldn't come up with an answer. After a few seconds, I stood and told the Admiral that I was the maintenance representative and asked if I could field the question. I was told, "By all means, tell him." I mentioned the problems concerning the lack of replacement components within the supply system and cited the components that were considered necessary to make an aircraft fully mission capable. That must have satisfied the Admiral because he never asked Commander Rogers another question. It was never mentioned, nor was there any recognition that I had saved the CO of any embarrassment that day.

At this time in history, the Far East was noted for the good buys in merchandise one could find in the different countries. The Philippines was noted for certain items and Korea was noted for others. For morale purposes, the CO allowed the men in the squadron to go on flights that were going to Korea. The CO, Commander Rogers, wanted all the men, including the officers, who were not on a flight crew to have a chance to go. It was known by the men as a Liberty Run. Even though I could have gone on any one of the flights, I wanted all the men in the Maintenance Department to have their chance before I went. There were just a certain amount of seats available on each flight. I really wanted to go. Finally the day came for the last flight to Korea before the squadron redeployed back to Hawaii. I had a seat. As I was leaving the wardroom after breakfast that morning for the flight, someone said, "Did you see that P3 on its nose this morning?" I stopped them and asked what P3? They said that there was a P3 with the nose gear collapsed. I knew then that I was not going to Korea. LCDR Gompper was still in Diego Garcia and I was in charge of the department.

When I arrived at the aircraft parking ramp a P3, YD-7 was indeed sitting with its nose to the ground and its tail to the sky. Man! What a disappointment! I knew there were reports to be filed, people to be notified, and an investigation to be conducted. Both the CO and XO were there to observe my performance. There was an aircraft rework facility at Cubi Point and I knew some of the people who worked there. I sought their advice and did not like what they were telling me. So far, only minor damage had been inflicted. If the aircraft could be lifted and the nose gear extended, it could be repaired at the rework facility in about seven days. But, no one knew how to raise it without inflicting further damage. It would be damaged to the point as to make it a major accident instead of a minor incident. A Major Report could result in a Commanding Officer being relieved of command. To ensure no one got hurt or further damage was done, I had the Flight Line crew rope off the area around the aircraft. Meanwhile, the rework team was briefing the CO and XO about how much damage would occur when the aircraft was lifted. Aviation Boatswain Mate First Class Johnson came to me and said that he knew a way to raise the aircraft without causing any further damage. I had been considering the possibility that he proposed. I told him that's the way we will do it. I went over to where the rework team and the CO were and told them that my crew would handle the aircraft to return it on three feet. When we could move it, we would deliver it to their facility for the repairs. There was an argument, but I told them that I was not going to let them cause any more damage to the aircraft and that they were dismissed. The CO looked at me really hard then turned and walked off without a word.

I turned the task over to Petty Officer Johnson and he accomplished what he said he could do. I stayed with Johnson and his crew. Every now and then I would catch a glimpse of the CO watching. That afternoon the aircraft was towed to the rework facility for repairs. I regret to this day that I did not recommend Petty Officer Johnson for the Navy Achievement Award. It took several hours to fill out the Incident Report. During the investigation, it was revealed that a plane captain had placed the landing gear handle in the up position before preflight. The intent was to test a student plane captain. He was supposed to check the position of all controls and switches before applying electrical power to the plane. He did not. When power was applied, the hydraulic pump raised the nose gear. Also, the safety feature of the nose gear had failed. I turned that part of the investigation over to the Safety Officer and don't know the outcome. The only damage was to the nose gear doors and hinge area. It took the rework facility three days to repair. I also had the number 2 and 3 engine mount area tested, since those two propellers had contacted the pavement. I could not know if the two engines had sustained any damage, so I had them replaced. Now, I considered the plane safe for flight.

LCDR Gompper returned from Diego Garcia shortly after the incident and told me that he was glad that he had been away during that time and that I was the one who had to deal with it. I flew on this aircraft for the return trip to Barber's Point.

Upon returning to Barber's Point, Jim Gompper was promoted to Commander and received transfer orders. LCDR Bushong assumed the duties as Head of the Maintenance Department. I was still the assistant.

I thought everything was going well until sometime in early 1978. I asked Commander Rogers if I was ever going to get a chance to be assigned as the Department Head of the Maintenance Department. His answer was a flat NO! He reserved that job for his aviators and no LDO would ever get the assignment. I had sensed in the Philippines that he did not really like LDOs in general, but liked me as a person. It wasn't long after I asked about the Maintenance Officer job that I was reassigned as the Maintenance Material Control Officer. It was really a more responsible task, but did not have the prestige that the AMO or MO carried. I already knew the XO did not care very much for LDOs.

Daughter Carla Greeting Me upon Arrival from the Philippines

Being Greeted by Wife, Diann, and Daughter, Carla

I accepted my new assignment without any more fuss. In fact, the men seemed to appreciate the fact I was in that position. They all knew that I had been an enlisted man before and they felt that they could tell me their problems and I would understand and give them advice. It was my job to keep track of the squadron operating fund and to advise the Skipper of the amount remaining for flight operations. He could be relieved of command from over expenditure. I didn't do the day-to-day accounting, Petty Officer Third Class Smith, Smitty, did that task. However, someone had to brief the Skipper on a weekly basis. Since Smitty did the work, I thought it appropriate that he be the one to brief the Skipper. Smitty was overweight by navy standards. He weighed about 350 pounds and was about 5'8" in height. The briefings went well for several weeks, and then one day I saw Smitty with a "down-in-the-dumps" look when he returned from the briefing. He told me that the Skipper and XO had ridiculed him so hard about his weight. The next week the same thing happened. So, after that day I did the weekly briefing. The Skipper asked me the reason Smitty wasn't doing the job. I told him that I had Smitty doing another important task at the time. Because I took over the briefing task, Smitty's disposition and his performance changed for the better. I even got him to take interest in losing weight.

Around June 1978, I became disheartened with my assignment as Maintenance Material Control Officer and asked the CO if he would consider an early transfer for me. I had been assigned a three-year tour. I said surely the navy has greater need of my talents somewhere rather than a Lieutenant's assignment. The Skipper seemed only too happy to approve my request. I called the detailer in Washington, DC, and asked if he had an opening in Corpus Christi. He said that, as a matter of fact, there was a position that needed to be filled, but first I had to submit a request for the assignment. As soon as he received my request, he would send orders. He said that no one wanted to go to Corpus for some reason and I had, in fact, saved him the agony of trying to find the person to send. The orders arrived in July for transfer in September.

Diann and I started immediately preparing for the transfer. The household goods were to be shipped in August. During the process of preparing for shipping, I discovered termites in the wall behind the chest-of-drawers. We decided to have the furniture fumigated before being shipped. Diann and Carla both departed in late August. Carla had cried when we left Corpus, but she really didn't want to leave Hawaii! I could not leave until late September. We had two autos, so I shipped them and moved into the BOQ on base.

It seemed that a tension developed between the XO and me. At first I thought he was happy about my early transfer, but there was such a disposition between us that I was concerned about. I needed to get away. So, I volunteered to be the maintenance representative at NAS Agana, Guam, of the Squadron detachment. I went to Guam on 4 September 1978, for a two-week stay. This allowed time for the XO to get over whatever was bothering him about me.

The time in Guam went smoothly, except for a few occasions. I enjoyed seeing another old shipmate. Gene Raulston was stationed in VQ-1. He and I were in VR-8 in 1954, and then we were LDO School classmates. We had a good time reminiscing. There was one sad incident that occurred that's hard to describe. A retired Marine Colonel had pulled into port on his yacht. He had a small dingy in which he would sail around the bay fishing. One afternoon, for some reason, he decided to go outside the breakwater barrier to fish. The wind came up and his little motor was not strong enough for him to get back to safety. The wind carried him out to sea. The squadron aircraft searched for three days, but did not locate him. He was lost at sea. Sad!

One day, one of the men called me to look at one of the aircraft. The pilot had complained that it drifted during landing. The man assign to check the problem discovered a worn bushing on the nose gear. It allowed the nose gear to shift about one quarter of an inch. I knew that there was not a repair facility at Agana. I also knew that a Planner and Estimator (P&E) request should be submitted. I personally thought this should be done from Barber's Point, not from Guam. So, I conferred with the pilot and OinC of the detachment concerning the severity of the bushing wear and the decision was made to make a one-stop flight to Hawaii. The plane left two days later. I was also on the flight back to Barber's Point because I had one week left in the squadron. The XO wanted to know, by what authority I made the decision for the one-time flight. I told him, "As the Maintenance Officer." I thought he wanted to make an issue of my decision, but he let it go. I guess the reason was that I was short-timer and would be transferred soon. LCDR Al Treadway was my relief. The last time I had seen Al was in Beeville, Texas, in 1972. He was a Warrant Officer at that time.

I departed VP-4 at 0630 on 13 September 1978, for my flight from Honolulu Airport to San Francisco International. Before leaving, I gave Mr. Perry Johnson's address and phone number to the Personnel Officer for emergency purposes. I wanted someone to contact me in case I had left something behind. Upon arrival in San Francisco, I picked up my bags and caught a cab to the Oakland Shipyards to pick up the autos. Before shipping the cars, a Pontiac Grandville and a Chevy Vega, I had prepared both for towing. I had placed the tow bar in the Chevy and the tools for assembly in the Pontiac. When I picked up the cars, everything was there except the tools. Someone had taken my tools. Luckily, I was able to borrow some. It took about an hour and I was on my way. The trip to Waco took two nights en route. I made it to my mother-in-law's house in one piece and was glad to see Diann and Carla. After a few days leave, we headed for Corpus Christi, Texas.

CHIEF of NAVAL AIR TRAINING
NAS CORPUS CHRISTI, TEXAS

October 1978 to September 1981

Chief Naval Air Training Logo

Diann, Carla, and I arrived in Corpus Christi on 5 October 1978, back to our house at 906 Carmel Parkway. There were a few changes made from the time when we had left in May 1976, and the swimming pool was absolutely a mess. The water that was in it was as black as tar and the sides were all caked with algae. However, we couldn't be concerned with the pool at this time. The Preslars loaned us two air mattresses to sleep on until our furniture arrived. All the neighbors were glad to see us return to the area.

Early the next morning, the door bell rang. Being tired from the travel the day before, we were still in bed. I went to the door to find Perry Johnson, the neighbor from across the street. The first thing he said was, "Let me be the first to congratulate you, Commander." I told him that I was a Lieutenant Commander not a Commander. He said, "You are now, your name is on the Commander list." He had received a message from CDR Rogers, the Skipper of VP-4, stating that I was on the list for promotion to Commander. Although it was not an emergency, it was really great news first thing in the morning. The promotion list had been published on 1 October. I didn't even know I was in the zone for promotion.

Although I was happy about being promoted, I learned at a later date there were many men who were not happy for me and my classmates. I was in LDO Fiscal Year (FY) group 1965. There were so few men left in LDO FY group 1964, that the navy had included all the men in my LDO class in the promotion zone. All the men from my class were promoted, but none of the men in LDO FY group 1964 were selected. It just wasn't fair and it created some animosity among us.

Although I was not ready to check in for duty, I went to the base after breakfast to check on our household shipment and was told that it had arrived in Corpus Christi. I asked how soon it could be delivered and was told that there was a problem. That it had to be weighed again because it was overweight and that I would have to pay an overweight charge. I let them know that there had better not be any overweight charges because I had it weighed in Hawaii for fumigation and I knew exactly how much it weighed. I wish I had not made that statement because I could have possibly caught someone in a scam operation and prevented someone else from getting ripped off. However, the shipping company was called and our furniture was delivered the next day. When the movers packed the household goods in Hawaii, they packed everything. When the items were unpacked in Corpus Christi, one box contained the trash and garbage from the kitchen in Hawaii. But, it didn't have any bugs because we had had it fumigated.

Chief of Naval Air Training was headed by Rear Admiral Joseph J. Barth. The Chief of Staff was Captain Wynn, who was later relieved by Captain T. C. Wimberley.

I reported to Chief of Naval Air Training at 2000 hours on 6 October 1978, and was assigned to the Ground Support Equipment Division of the Aircraft Management and Accounting Department (N-5) under Captain John Roach. The Chief of Naval Air Training had jurisdiction over seven Naval Air Stations. The Ground Support Equipment Division was responsible for the management of all support and testing equipment at all seven bases. Commander Don Perkins was the Maintenance Department Head, later relieved by Commander Wally Laseur.

There was only one other sailor in the Division, AT2 Callahan; the other men were two civilians, Joe Priveto and Fred Burk. Joe was in charge until my assignment. Although the division usually had ten men assigned, it had just gone through a RIFF, commonly known as a reduction in force and pay, so eight of the personnel had resigned. When Captain Wynn was the Commodore of Wing Four, he had said that if he was in charge of CNATRA, he would fire all the high priced civilians. Well, he was now Chief of Staff and he initiated the RIFF and reduced the pay grades of the civilian personnel by one pay grade (GS-12 to GS-11, etc.) before I arrived.

Because of my experience as Ground Support Equipment Division Officer while stationed in Beeville, I could go to work immediately. The most pressing order of business was the hiring of Equipment Specialists with experience in aircraft ground support equipment management. After I had completed my indoctrination, I initiated procedures to hire someone to fill a vacancy of Equipment Specialist within the division. This turned out to be harder than expected.

Joe was not particularly happy with my assignment at first. It meant that I was his boss, but he knew more about the duties and responsibilities of the division. Joe had worked under Commanders before who didn't do any kind of work within the division. One of them was CDR G. G. Buc, who had been my boss in Beeville in 1969. He just knew that I would be like all the rest. He had told Fred that he would give me thirty days to prove myself, but if I was like the others, he would resign. I guess I proved myself to Joe because he remained in the command for the remainder of my stay. We even became good friends and fishing buddies.

I was still of the rank Lieutenant Commander. My promotion date was set for 1 July 1979. Since I was on the list for promotion, Joe Priveto asked Captain Roach to have me frocked to Commander, so I would have a stronger voice when speaking on behalf of the Command. I was frocked with authority to assume the title and wear the uniform of Commander United States Navy as of 23 October 1978, by Rear Admiral Joseph J. Barth, Chief of Naval Air Training. I received all the respect and privileges of a Commander, but not the pay and allowances of the pay grade. According to Captain Roach, it was necessary that I assume the rank of Commander so that I would have senior officer status at conferences in Washington, DC. On 1 July 1979, I was promoted to the rank of Commander United States Navy, at which time I did receive the pay and allowances.

Frocked to the Rank of Commander USN on 23 October 1979

As in all government organizations, there were two departments within CNATRA concerned with equal employment opportunities (EEO). One was concerned with discrimination, with racism and prejudice, but the other was particularly concerned with discrimination of women. The one concerned about women, the Federal Women's Liberation Coordinator, came to see me. She said, "Commander, you do not have any women working in your division. You must hire a woman to fill the position of the Equipment Specialist."

I told her that I had no problem with her request, provided they met the qualifications. I had already submitted a request to Civilian Personnel to hire an Equipment Specialist. Within a short time, Civilian Personnel called stating that they had five applicants for me to interview and requested that I set a date. Joe Priveto would be assisting me in the interviews. We started the interviews at 0900 with both the EEO Representative and the Federal Women's Coordinator present. I had to ask the same question of all applicants. Sure enough, all the applicants were women with no experience in support equipment maintenance or management. I did not accept any of them. Joe and I went through this procedure every week for three weeks. All people referred by Civilian Personnel were women with no knowledge about support equipment. At the end of the last interview, the Federal Women's Coordinator asked me why I did not hire one of those women. I told her that none met the qualifications of the job description and, therefore, I couldn't. She finally demanded that I hire one of them. This was my statement to her, "The position is for a GS-10 rating, not a TRAINEE position. You're telling me that I have to hire a TRAINEE and pay them journeyman's wages." She said, "You can't do that." I told her, "Thank you very much." From that time on, Civilian Personnel would refer only men with experience and those representatives did not attend the interviews. I had no more trouble with the offices of EEO and FWLC. I learned later the FWLC representative had conducted interviews with all the women who had been referred and told them if they had helped their husband work on autos or lawn mowers, then they were an equipment specialist.

Joe and I did hire two individuals with equipment maintenance experience, but I can't remember their names. There were vacancies in the equipment inventory area and we hired two people into those positions, one of which was a woman, the other one filled by Charlie Bridges, who had worked for me in Beeville.

It wasn't long before I knew most of the functions and requirements of the division and Joe thought I should learn how to conduct myself at conferences at Naval Air Headquarters in Washington, DC, and other facilities. The first conference I attended was a two-week conference at Naval Air Systems Command, Washington, DC, in late November 1978. By this time, my wife, Diann, and Joe's wife, Grace, had become acquainted. Joe asked me to plan a vacation for them in Washington, DC, during the time we were attending the conference. Of course, he and I would have to foot the bill for their airfare and hotel accommodations. That trip turned out to be fun, as well as educational.

During the day, Joe and I attended the conference while Diann and Grace toured the city. After work hours, we all did some sightseeing. We saw the Smithsonian, the Washington Memorial, the Lincoln Memorial, and the Iwo Jima War Memorial.

The Captain in Charge of N5, Captain Roach, was always stressing the point of saving government funds whenever we were on assignment at meetings and conferences. One of the conferences that I attended was in Lakehurst, New Jersey. The meeting was supposed to last two weeks. I arrived Sunday afternoon and checked into a hotel. My per-diem was fifty dollars.

On Monday morning, the conference monitor tried to set the schedule of the meeting. He stated that we would commence each day a 0900, break for lunch at 1100, reconvene at 1300, and close at 1500. I asked why and said that if we started at 0700, break at 1100 for lunch, reconvene at 1300, and go 'til 1700, we could accomplish all we came to do in one week instead of two weeks. The monitor was astonished by my remarks and asked what the others at the meeting thought of my idea. They all agreed with me. They didn't want to stay two weeks when it could be finished in one. So, the schedule was reset for the times that I had suggested. I saved the taxpayers several thousand dollars on that trip. Apparently, the Captain of the conference called my boss, Captain Roach, about what had transpired at the meeting. When I returned to work the next Monday, Captain Roach said, "I hear that you made yourself a reputation at the conference."

I tried the same tactic at another conference at NAS North Island, San Diego, California. I was told by that Captain that he set the schedule, not me. We stayed two weeks and accomplished very little, except working on our golf score, which we did every day after 1500. On Friday, the last day of the conference, I received a call from Charlie Bridges telling me to stop by the Duty Office when I got to Corpus to pick up my travel orders to depart Sunday to attend a conference in Washington, DC. I told him that I had just spent two weeks in San Diego, CA; I was ready to be home for a while. All he said was the briefing papers are in the folder for you to read on your flight to Washington. That conference was concerning funding of GSE maintenance. One of my LDO classmates, LCDR Jones, was there. He was also on the commander promotion list, but had not been frocked. He seemed astonished to see me in a Commander's uniform.

I attended several different conferences in Norfolk, Virginia. On one of those, I looked up Zeb Gray. He was working in the Electronics Test Lab. I walked in without him knowing I was in the area. We had not seen each other since Meridian, Mississippi, in 1964, when I had just been commissioned from Chief to Ensign. You should have seen the look on his face when he saw that I was now wearing a Commander's uniform. His first words were, "That must have taken a lot of hard work." We had a good visit and he took me to lunch at the Chiefs' Club.

Another one of those conferences was for one week. The conference was concerning aircraft tow tractor overhaul. I knew the Vanderhules, George and

Juanita, were in Norfolk. I asked Diann to go with me on this trip. It was funny, in a way. Diann and George were together all day and went sightseeing or shopping while Juanita and I had to go to work. No one got jealous and we all enjoyed the time together.

One Monday, Joe came in all excited and somewhat agitated. He had received a call from a Mr. John Jay in NAVAIR about the installation funding for an engine test cell that was supposed to have been installed at NAS Beeville. Mr. Jay wanted to know why the task had not been completed. The installation had to be completed within two months or the funding would be assigned elsewhere. Joe asked if I would go to Beeville to inquire about the situation. I called a Mr. Roger Behr in Beeville and told him I would be there to see him the next day, Tuesday. Commander Perkins went with me. Mr. Behr said the he had not received the drawing plans from the architect, so nothing had been accomplished. I asked how long ago the request had been sent to the architect and was told a year. Then I wanted to know why Mr. Behr had not demanded the plans be completed and delivered. Mr. Behr's reply was that he didn't think it was urgent. Commander Perkins told him about the funding deadline and that the installation had to be completed before that date. This was the same Mr. Behr whom I had dealt with when I was stationed in Beeville back in 1968 to 1971. He never considered anything urgent. He told us that as soon as the architect gave him the plans, he would initiate a bid to installation contractors. I asked him to call the architect and ask that the plans be delivered by Friday. Mr. Behr said that he would not do that, so I asked for the name and phone number of the architect.

When we arrived back to CNATRA, CDR Perkins told Captain Roach, "You should have seen Ed go into action in Beeville with Mr. Behr."

I called the architect and asked him about the plans. His answer was that he had not yet started drafting them. I told him to have them on my desk by Friday. He said that he could not and I said that if he couldn't, then we would give the contract to someone else that could. I let him know that there was a deadline and, if not met, the funding would be lost. He asked for a week. The engine test cell installation was completed on time.

Commander Ron Cramer was the Supply Department Head. Ruth Cramer, CDR Cramer's wife, became Captain Roach's secretary about the time I changed positions. I relieved Commander Glenn Gilmore as the Weapons Systems Manager, a division of N5. I really didn't want to leave the GSE Division, but the Captain thought I would better serve the command at this much needed position. There were several civilian specialists in the department. Chuck DeFries was the Airframes Specialist; Tony Ciochetto, the Reciprocating Engine Specialist; and Jack Leffingwell, the Jet Engine Specialist. This also put the Technical Library under my purview.

While in GSE, I would notice this woman passing my office about 0830 each morning. Joe told me that was Dorothy, the Tech Librarian. He said that she was supposed to come to work at 0730 when we did, but she was always tardy. I asked why her supervisor doesn't have her fired. Joe said that there was probably too much paperwork involved to get a civil service employee fired. I let it go at the time. Now that the library was my responsibility, I had to deal with her tardiness. Joe was right! There was a lot of paperwork and time involved in trying to fire a civilian employee. I checked with the Civilian Personnel Office concerning the procedure. Every incident had to be documented on the time card, a memo placed in a folder, and the employee counseled. After three days, the employee's pay would be docked. I also told the Department Head of my actions. Several of the secretaries came to me and said that it was about time someone took action. They were unhappy with her because she was getting away with tardiness without punishment, but if they tried being tardy they would be punished. The first month Dorothy received less pay, she came storming into my office and demanded an explanation. She had been counseled each time she was tardy, but that didn't mean anything to her. I explained that the tardiness was the reason for the pay cut. She cursed me out and left. I had her pay docked every month for a year, but I didn't have enough documentation to get her fired. I turned her over to my relief upon my retirement.

This is about the time I saved the government enough money to pay for my entire naval career, plus my retirement. It involved the T2-J aircraft and the J85 engine, mostly the engine. There were many engine failures occurring within a short time frame while in flight. Luckily, all the aircraft involved were able to land safely with the other engine. However, since the aircraft were primarily used for student pilot training, there was much concern about the safety in the abilities of student pilots making single engine landings. GE was the manufacturer of the J85 engine and their engineers, along with the Naval Air Engineers, were frantically trying to find the root of the failures, as well as a solution to the problems. It was determined that a forward rotor blade tang was the culprit. The tang would crack at its base, then break, allowing the blade to separate from the rotor, which would then do major damage to the other rotor blades as it went through the engine. Inspection of several other engines revealed the cracks in some blade tangs that were on the verge of breaking off. After much study, the team of engineers had devised a proposed plan of inspections that could detect the tang cracks and replace the blades before they broke and destroyed the engine. The planned inspections and repairs were necessary. However, the engineers had not performed a complete impact study to determine the feasibility or ramifications of the inspections they had laid out.

NavAir sent copies of the proposed inspection to CNATRA for information purposes only, with dates of meetings to finalize the implementation of the inspection. The inspection required the engine to be removed from the aircraft every 100 flight hours, turned in to AIMD, taken apart to physically inspect each blade tang, and then reassembled and reinstalled in the aircraft. The Captain told me that the Admiral wanted me to work up an impact statement and attend the planned meeting in Washington, DC. NavAir had not requested the attendance of a representative from

CNATRA. There were two civilians assigned to my division who were very knowledgeable on the workings and structure of the T2-J aircraft and the J85 engine, Jack Leffingwell and Chuck DeFries. They and I worked up the amount of man-hours required to perform an inspection of one engine as outlined in the proposed NavAir Instruction. In addition, there were several NavAir instructions in conflict with the new proposed instruction. I thought there should be an easier and less time consuming way to perform the inspection. I asked if a hole could be drilled in the engine at certain locations to allow a bore scope to be inserted to view the tangs. Both Jack Leffingwell and Chuck DeFries did a study of my suggestion and drafted a proposed inspection and stated the site to drill an inspection hole. After compiling all the information, I packed in my briefcase and hopped on a flight to DC.

The meeting was hosted by a Captain from NavAir. The attendees were engineers from NavAir, General Electric, Naval Air Rework Facility (NARF) Pensacola, and various maintenance representatives from NAVAIRLANT, NAVAIRPAC, and one from CNATRA.

The Captain opened with the usual welcoming remarks and then turned to me and asked what I had come to say. I told him that I had not come to say anything, but to listen to what the engineers had to say. They basically repeated what the message had stated—that an inspection would be performed every 100 flight hours, that the inspection would require the engine to be removed from the aircraft, and that AIMD would perform the inspection. I then told the Captain that I now had something to say.

My statement went something like this. "Your people did not perform an impact study in reaching their decision about how often or the manner in which the inspection would be performed. (1) How is the number of 100 flight hours determined? There already is in existence an instruction that requires that the aircraft airframe be inspected at 125 flight hours. Now, you want to issue an instruction to inspect the engine at 100 flight hours and then again 25 hours later, as per the existing instruction. (2) It requires two men four hours (eight man-hours) to remove the engine from the aircraft and take it to AIMD. Then, after AIMD has performed the inspection and returned the engine to the squadron, it requires two men four hours (eight man-hours) to reinstall it in the aircraft. (3) Each squadron has 60 aircraft with two engines each for a total of 120 engines. Each aircraft averages 50 flight hours per month. That means that each engine would require an inspection once every two months. That's two inspections per day, Monday through Sunday, requiring 16 man-hours each for a total of 960 man-hours per month. (4) For AIMD to perform the inspection requires two men two hours (four man-hours) to disassemble the engine to get to the rotor for the inspection. It takes about 30 minutes to inspect the rotor. Then it takes the two men about three hours (six man-hours) to reassemble the engine for a total of 11 man-hours. However, there is an existing NavAir instruction, which is not addressed here, that states, 'When an engine is disassembled to the point where the inspection can be performed, then the remainder of the engine will also be inspected.'

Commander is the highest rank an LDO could attain. Also by law, thirty years was the maximum time an LDO could remain in service. Diann and I decided to ask for a year extension at CNATRA. So, I called the detailer in Washington to discuss that possibility. He told me I was too late with my request. He had already prepared orders for my relief. Guess who! Al Treadway was to relieve me, again. He was my relief at VP-4 in Hawaii. He told me that he would like to send me aboard an aircraft carrier, but I lacked the experience in that field. He had decided to send me to the Washington, DC area. He just hadn't decided which billet. Man! I did not want to go to DC, period. I asked about retiring? Now that I had mentioned retirement, I had to submit a request within two weeks or I would have to accept the transfer orders.

In March, I submitted my request to be retired 1 October 1981. We had to start planning for that date. Man! I didn't know if we were or would be ready for retirement. I decided to buy some land through the Texas Veterans Land Board. The interest was a lot lower than a conventional loan. Also, I started drafting plans for the house I wanted to build. I could not buy a piece of property until I had the application from the Texas Veterans Land Board in hand. It was received in late March 1981. Not every realty company would sell land through that program. We ran an ad in the *Waco Tribune* stating that we were looking to buy some land through the TVLB. I received about twenty offers. So, I took a week's leave in April to go look at all the places offered. We settled on twenty acres just a mile outside of Eddy, Texas. After that, I would spend every spare moment drafting our new house plans. The finalization of the purchase was completed on 7 July 1981. After signing the purchase contract, we went to the property and opened a bottle of champagne in 90-degree weather.

Our New Property, 10 July 1981

Champagne Celebration

All the plans had been completed for retirement by mid-August. One day Diann awoke with a bad stomach problem. I convinced her to go to the doctor. We didn't need any medical problems so close to the retirement date. She had a large tumor the size of a football, which needed immediate attention. The doctor put her in the hospital where she underwent a full hysterectomy the first week of September 1981. She only had a short time to recover before the retirement.

I retired from the navy 30 September 1981. Vice Admiral Martin conducted my retirement ceremony and presented me with the retirement orders, lapel pin, and an American Flag that was flown over the White House on 25 September 1981. He also presented Diann with a Certificate of Appreciation for her courage and faithfulness during the time she was with me while in the navy, which was twenty-five years, six months. I had spent a total of twenty-eight years, ten months, and ten days in the navy. I considered that I had done well to attain the rank of Commander without a college education or having never been assigned duty aboard a ship. Although I had been on several ships, I was never been assigned as Ships Company. In navy terms, I was able to choose my own "Side Boys" to pipe me over the side.

Receiving My Navy Retirement Letter from Admiral Martin

Admiral Martin Pinning on My RETIRED NAVY Lapel Pin, 30 September 1981

Giving My Farewell Address at My Retirement Ceremony, 30 September 1981

Ed Hudson

Presented an American Flag Flown over the White House on 26 September 1981

Diann Being Read Her Letter of Appreciation by Admiral Martin 30 September 1981

Piped over the Side by Fellow Shipmates

Both Diann and I Being Piped over the Side

The Fellow Shipmates That Piped Me over the Side
Front Row: CWO2 Carpenter, AVCM Flores, Myself, Ensign (Unknown), and AKC (Unknown)
Second Row: AFCM Parkas, LCDR Treadway, AMC Holt, Ensign Smith

Carla   Ed   Diann
RETIRED!

AFTER RETIREMENT
1 October 1981

RETIREMENT! At times I had dreamed of this day during the past seven years. The reason I did not retire earlier, was that I had not made any plans for life after retirement. After the detailer had told me that I had to retire or accept orders to Washington, DC, in March 1981, I finally realized that I had to make plans. This writing is about the events during the first two years that affected my life after retirement.

Waking up on the day after my retirement ceremony did not, at first, seem any different than the past few days. But, sometime later in the morning, it dawned on me that I was now on my time and not navy time. I did not have to go to the base for work ever again. The next few days seemed strange that I was no longer responsible for anything having to do with naval affairs. Had I not made plans to build my own house and was looking forward to getting started, I might have had some form of anxiety or some other problem. I have heard of something like that happening to some retirees, such as heart attacks. It was amazing how suddenly I had lost all form of authority. I could not give a command to a single person. I had no authority over anyone.

Diann and I had our goals set and were ready to go to Eddy, Texas, and get our new home under construction. Our immediate plans were to move in with Mother-in law, while I amassed the materials and got the slab poured. Carla, our daughter, would remain in the house in Corpus Christi, along with our household items. We had one year in which the navy would move the furniture to a new location. Plus, we owned a rental house, for which we left Carla the responsibility of looking after. So, after getting all affairs settled in Corpus Christi, we headed for Waco, Texas.

The location of our new home would be about one mile outside of Eddy, Texas. I found a contractor to pour the slab, but I had to put in all the underground plumbing. Man! I was not a plumber. I had drawn the floor plans for our house, but had not given any thought to the inner workings of the house, such as plumbing and electrical wiring. Now, I was gonna do it all. My brother-in-law Howard came from Duncanville to help with laying the underground plumbing. He had a little experience in that field. The slab was poured the day before Thanksgiving 1981. I had learned during the construction of an aircraft high power hold back pad that it took twenty-seven days for concrete to reach full strength. So, I did not start to work on our new house until January 1982.

House Construction
My Ford Truck with Plumbing Materials   *House Slab*

During the waiting period, I went back to Corpus Christi and sold our rental house. This gave us a little extra money with which to buy materials for the house. At the time, we could only afford $1,000 per month to spend on the house. However, I physically could not build the house any faster than with materials, which $1,000 would purchase. I actually started in February 1982, building the garage first. The purpose of the garage first was to store the materials for the rest of the house. I would go by a lumber company and pick up a load on the way to work.

House Construction

Framing of Garage   *Garage (Almost Complete)*

By August of 1982, I was ready to start the decking of the roof, which turned into being a chore working by myself. By September, I had the house weathered-in, so I sheet-rocked three rooms and moved in. We had the furniture shipped from Corpus Christi and stored it in the garage.

House Construction

Decking the Roof   *Roof Decking Completed*

As you can see, I didn't have "time" to think about my past life in the navy. However, there were a few navy buddies that stopped by when passing through Eddy. I would take that time to reminisce and tell sea stories. Ha! Ha! Sea stories? I was never on a ship to know any stories.

The three rooms that we sheet-rocked were a bedroom, a living room, and a bathroom. The bathroom had only a commode. We had to use a water hose to take a shower after dark. A neighbor loaned us a small travel trailer to serve as the kitchen. Diann was a jewel during this time. Other women probably would not have endured these hardship living conditions.

My intentions were to build our house as fast as possible and then seek employment somewhere. But, the employment never materialized. On 3 September 1983, I suffered a massive heart attack. I was hospitalized for two weeks in the VA Hospital in Temple, Texas. I had lived up to the tradition of having major health problems within a short time after retirement. Luckily, I had gone to the VA Hospital because I was placed in the VA Health Care System.

After quadruple bypass surgery and with the help of relatives, friends, and neighbors, the house was completed during the next five years. Diann and I sold the place thirty years from the purchase date of 10 July 1981. I could never seek employment.

Completed Home Site
671 Hudson Lane, Eddy, Texas

ABOUT THE AUTHOR
Charles Edward Hudson

I was born on a Wednesday morning about 5:15 a.m. on 26 September 1932, to John Lloyd Hudson and Goldie Mae (Bowie) Hudson. My place of birth was at home in a house located in a small Texas village called New Hope. The village was located six miles northeast of McKinney, Texas.

House Where I Was Born

My father was a tenant farmer known in those days as a "sharecropper." He farmed the land owned by Mr. Harris. I don't know how many acres he worked, but he did it all with teams of mules. I had four siblings at this time, two brothers and two sisters. We moved from New Hope to Blue Ridge, Texas, when I was two years old in 1935.

We lived about three miles northeast of Blue Ridge on Mr. Zek Price's farm. Mr. Price bought me my first pair of tennis shoes for my fourth birthday. Daddy also farmed this place with teams of mules. My sister Elsie Marie was born at home on Mr. Price's farm. We moved from Blue Ridge in 1937 to Mr. Eck Brown's farm in the Rosamond Community about three miles northeast of Anna, Texas.

We actually lived in two houses on Mr. Brown's farm. The first, we always referred to as, "the house under the cedars." The room where I slept had a dirt floor. I was too young to let things like that bother me, even when we would see a scorpion crawling nearby. After a few months, Mr. Brown had the house remodeled. I now had a room with a wooden floor.

The next house was called, by the people in the neighborhood, "the Ol' Bell Place," but we called it "the House on the Hill." This house was considered to be very modern to us, even though it did not have electricity or indoor plumbing. The outhouse was about fifty yards behind the house. For light at night, we used kerosene lamps and Mom cooked our meals on a wood-burning stove. She was so happy when someone gave us a kerosene kitchen cook stove. It had an oven in it.

However, Daddy was still farming with mules. There were five separate fields with a combined acreage of about sixty acres for him to farm. I was too young and small to help in the farming, except the hoeing and picking of cotton. Dad made sure that I had a cotton sack each year.

The Anna area holds my fondest memories of my formative years as a youth and teenager. I started to school in the first grade at Anna Elementary School in September 1939. Due to the date of my birth, I was almost seven years old. That may be the reason for a successful year. I made the "Honor Roll" every month. I didn't fare so well in the second grade. I only made the "Honor Roll" six of the nine months of school. However, my third grade was a complete disaster. I failed and had to do the third grade over the next year. My youngest sister was born at home the year I started the first grade, 20 September 1939.

After living in the House on the Hill for seven years, Daddy became dissatisfied with farming for Eck and decided to move. We moved to Mr. Forman's farm about five miles south of McKinney, Texas. I was in the fifth grade and attended Fanny Finch South Ward School. I also completed the sixth grade at this school.

At least on this farm, Daddy didn't have to work with teams of mules. Mr. Forman had an F-20 Farmall Tractor and equipment. I was old enough now to help and learned to operate the tractor. I really enjoyed living on this farm. Daddy didn't plant cotton on this farm, but I still had to help with other chores. I was allowed to hunt with a 22 rifle and did a lot of trapping fur-bearing animals, mostly opossums. I would sell the hides in McKinney for my spending money.

In the fall of 1946, I started to school at L. A. Scott Junior High in the seventh grade, but after a month, Daddy decided to move back to Anna. We moved to Mr. John F. Hendricks' farm. I was now back in the Anna School. Here, again, I helped Dad with the hoeing and picking cotton. Sometimes we hired out to other farmers to hoe their field or pick their cotton. My wage was fifty cents per hour and we worked ten hour days, meaning I received five dollars per day. The wage for cotton picking was three dollars per hundred pounds. I was so slow that I could barely pick one hundred pounds in one day. I was too much of a daydreamer. I could think of all sorts of things I'd rather be doing.

We lived on the Hendricks' farm for two years, and then Daddy and Mr. Eck Brown reached an agreement for us to move back on his farm. However, the mules were put to pasture and the farming was done with an F-20 Farmall Tractor. I was now in the ninth grade of high school. Life for me was the same as far as farming, except now I had to milk five cows each morning before going to school. We kids had to ride the bus to school, so I had to get up early to get my chores completed in time to get ready and catch the bus. I also had to milk those cows at night, too.

Everything was going well for me until the last week of the school year. An event happened to me that turned my attitude toward school and I became rebellious during my tenth year. I did not get along with the superintendent. He was the one that caused the event to happen. He expelled me on three occasions because of my rebellion. However, before I could get my belongings and leave the building, he would stop me and tell me to go back to my class. I don't know, but I think he was afraid to tell Dad that he expelled me. I did stay in school in Anna High through the eleventh grade. During the summer, I went to Dallas and got a job with the City of Dallas Water Department working on water meters. In September 1951, Dad decided to move to Plainview, Texas, where I went to Plainview High during my senior year from September 1951 through February 1952.

After we were settled and I had started school, Dad told me to go to the cotton fields each day after school to pull cotton. He said that he didn't want me hanging around with those "Drugstore Cowboys" and getting into trouble. I told him that I didn't have a cotton sack or money to buy one. My cousin, who lived next door, said she had one I could have. The first day when I came home from the field, Dad asked how much I had picked. I said about 90 pounds. He wasn't happy with that answer. The next day, same question, I said about 125 pounds. The next day when he asked I told him zero. I went to Furr's Grocery Store and got a job as a stock clerk.

In February 1952, we moved back to Eck Brown's farm, but this time in the house we called the "Rock House." We were living on Mr. Brown's farm when I completed high school.

After graduation, I finally received my driver's license and got a job at the Murray Gin Co., making city deliveries and working in a warehouse. After a few months, the Water Department called and wanted me to return to work for them.

On my twentieth birthday, I decided to join the navy to prevent being drafted into the army. The navy didn't need me immediately, so I went to work for the Austin Brothers Steel Co., working in the warehouse and making city deliveries. In November 1952, I received my draft notice. I called the navy recruiter about the notice and was inducted on 20 November 1952.

This book has been the story of my naval career from this point.